Protestant Christian Evidences

Protestant Christian Evidences

A Textbook of the Evidences of the Truthfulness of the Christian Faith for Conservative Protestants

by

BERNARD RAMM, B.D., Ph.D.

Professor of Systematic Theology
California Baptist Theological Seminary
Covina, California

MOODY PRESS

CHICAGO

Seventeenth Printing, 1977
ISBN: 0-8024-6910-8

Printed in the United States of America

DEDICATED TO

Dr. R. L. POWELL

Pastor of the Temple Baptist Church of Tacoma, Washington, in gratitude for his profound theological and spiritual influence on the writer and his family.

PREFACE

THIS BOOK is addressed to Christians whose faith needs stabilization, or whose critical spirit has been aroused and needs evidence adequate to the issues involved. It is also addressed to those few who are yet willing to hear evidence. Religious liberalism has become so entrenched in its presuppositions and has become so bitter toward orthodoxy that we expect not an iota of appreciative evaluation from that quarter. So-called modern mentality has become so antitranscendental that any appeal to the supernatural is contemptuously labeled as *medieval*. This book is not written for illiberal liberals or for dogmatic scientists, but for those spirits who still have enough flexibility in their mentality to hear a case on its own merit.

Devout Christians will wonder why so much philosophy, science, and criticism is delved into. The obvious answer is that we must fight the battle where it is. It would be far easier for the writer to quietly condemn all philosophy, criticism, and science out of court, leaving himself as the sole authority to be heard; or to brand all opposition as open or disguised unbelief; or to preëmpt the name of God and truth to himself and reject all opposition as being "mere human opinion." As nice and comfortable as such a procedure might be, it ceases to challenge unbelief and to fight the fight where it needs to be fought. A pious, sentimental apologetic might be less disconcerting to many, but if it is to be a serious, meaningful, and telling defense we have no other recourse than to delve into science, criticism, and philosophy. In no other way can telling blows be made.

Some might ask, Why the title, *Protestant Christian Evidences?* A reviewer of a previous work of mine, *Protestant Biblical Interpretation,* criticized my position on the grounds that hermeneutics is hermeneutics no matter what one's theology is. This is hardly the case. There is a distinct Catholic system of Biblical interpretation, and even though it overlaps many of the Protestant principles, it is distinctive enough to be specifically Catholic. We have examined dozens of Catholic works on apologetics and evidences, and a major section of each such treatise is a treatment on the divine origin and authority of the Roman Catholic Church. The Protestant belief in the *sole* authority of Scripture cannot include such a section in a treatise on Christian Evidences. For these reasons the title *Christian Evidences* is ambiguous and so we add *Protestant.*

We send forth this book in the spirit of Paul when he wrote that he was "set for the defense (*apologian*) of the gospel" (Phil. 1:17). May God use it to strengthen and help and encourage Christians everywhere who believe in historic, Biblical Christianity.

BERNARD RAMM
St. Paul, Minnesota

TABLE OF CONTENTS

Preface

Protestant Christian Evidences

CHAPTER I

GENERAL INTRODUCTION TO CHRISTIAN EVIDENCES

I. DEFINITIONS

CHRISTIAN EVIDENCES is a discipline within the boundaries of the Christian religion. Christian theology is the Christian religion adequately stated, systematically interrelated, and appropriately defended. It works with the data provided by exegetical theology on the one hand and philosophy on the other. Christian theology assumes the truthfulness of the Christian religion. It is the function of Christian apologetics to show that this assumption is defensible. If it is the function of Christian theology to construct the Christian system, it is the function of Christian apologetics to verify it. Apologetics is not always so named. Sometimes it is called Christian theism or philosophical theology or philosophy of religion. However apologetics be labeled its function is still clear, namely, to show that Christianity is the true religion of God.

Christian evidences is a subdivision of Christian apologetics. Christian apologetics is the comprehensive philosophical, theological, and factual demonstration of the truthfulness of our Christian religion. Christian evidences, as we conceive of it, is especially concerned with the demonstration of the *factuality* of the Christian religion. That there have been wider definitions than this is evident from a study of the contents of books on Christian evidences. Van Til, for example, defines evidences as "the defense of Christian theism against any attack that may be made upon it by science."[1]

[1] C. Van Til, *Christian-Theistic Evidences*, p. 1.

Other authors fuse together philosophy of religion, apologetics, and Biblical introduction, e.g., F. Hamilton, *The Basis of the Christian Faith*. We shall not be able to isolate Christian evidences from these disciplines but a division of labor now obtains. Theism is turned over to the Christian philosopher, and matters of introduction to the Old and New Testament scholars. However, it must be admitted that it is still a matter of taste as to what material a scholar will include under such captions as theism, apologetics, and Christian evidences.

If it can be demonstrated that Christianity is a religion that actually obtains in the universe by showing its *factuality*, we have also proved its truthfulness. This is not the total evidence of Christianity, but that it is indispensable cannot be controverted. Religious liberalism has no real doctrine of Christian evidences. The reason is not far to seek. In that it makes religion essentially the function of man's religious nature—after Schleiermacher, Ritschl, Troeltsch, and Harnack —it has no need for the supernatural nor for the relevance of religion to concrete fact. But religious liberalism, though fond of ridiculing Christian evidences, has failed to see that in the measure that religion is isolated from fact, it by the same measure is removed from reality. Thus, religious liberalism tends to be a system of religious beliefs based essentially upon a philosophy or psychology or history of religion, but not on concrete data. But orthodox Christianity by demonstrating the *factuality* of the Christian religion by means of Christian evidences has gone a long way toward proving the truthfulness of the Christian religion, and in a manner and method religious liberalism can offer no valid parallel.

II. PURPOSES OF CHRISTIAN EVIDENCES

At this point the *purposes of Christian evidences* for the Christian should be made evident:

A. The Christian is established in his faith not only experientially but intellectually and factually. He sees the Christian religion not only as that which gives him a blessed experience of salvation and assurance within his heart, but also as a system *universal and factual* in its scope. He sees it in its cosmic, historic, and factual breadth. His personal experience is thus related to a universal and valid system of religion. The snipings of psychologists at his religious conversion are emptied of much of their pertinence, for although his religious convictions commenced with his conversion they now no longer rest solely on such a narrow base, but are part of a comprehensive world view.

B. Further, the Christian well versed in Christian evidences understands the nature of many of the attacks on the Christian faith, and knows their invalidity. His knowledge of textual criticism enables him to silence the argument that the text of the Bible has been appreciably tampered with during the course of its transmission; his knowledge of literary criticism enables him to defend the trustworthiness of his documents; his knowledge of all the other items in the arsenal of Christian evidences is a powerful weapon for not only the silencing of attacks upon the faith, but for the positive evangelistic presentation of the gospel of Christ.

C. Apologetics and Christian evidences are not the gospel, but if a man has a prejudice against the gospel it is the function of apologetics and evidences to remove that prejudice. The value of apologetics and evidences for evangelistic purposes (public, personal conversation, literature) is too frequently underrated usually on the grounds that people are won by preaching of the Word alone. Two observations are pertinent to this assertion. First, no well-grounded apologist will state that the philosophic demonstration of Christianity saves a man, but it is, to the contrary, quite evident that no man will give the necessary credence to the Word if he has certain mistaken notions and biased opinions about the facts and nature of the Christian religion. Apologetics and Chris-

tian evidences cut down these objections to enable the gospel
once again to directly confront the consciousness of a man.
Spurgeon's oft-quoted remark that the Bible is a lion that
defends itself is very pious of sound, but very fallacious of
fact.[2] The huge slashes of radical criticism into the Christian Church reveals the Bible is defenseless unless defended
by its believers. Is every cavil, every slander, every false accusation, every gross misrepresentation, to go unnoticed, unanswered, unchallenged? Can the stabs into the vitals of theology be answered by quoting a verse or two of Scripture?
We think not. Christian evidences and Christian apologetics
are indispensable to the health, welfare, and progress of the
gospel.

Second, the opponents of Christianity figure that it is
worthwhile to argue and debate their case. It is the basic theory of all propaganda that successful efforts are possible by
argumentation, specious or genuine. Lunn correctly observes
that "'Nobody is ever converted by argument' is a formula
as popular with Christians as it is unknown among politi-
cians and political canvassers."[3] The Nazis and the Communists were not slow to see the power of argumentation on human belief and conduct, and sought to influence it by enormous propaganda efforts. Human opinion is not always
formed from argumentation, but a good measure of it is, and
therefore Christian evidences is the Christian arsenal of data
and facts for any Christian who wishes to defend and debate
his faith.

III. Scope of Christian Evidences

We interpret the scope of Christian evidences to be that
of *demonstrating that Christianity is the religion which pertains to reality by reason of its factuality.* What is objective,

2 *Sermons*, (1896), p. 256.
3 A. Lunn, *The Third Day*, p. xviii. See L. M. Sweet, *The Verification of
Christianity*, p. 22 ff. For examples in Church history wherein a great Christian
apology performed a remarkable service for the gospel and Church.

demonstrable, and credible pertains in some measure and in some sense to reality. In Christian evidences the focus is upon the *factuality* of the Christian religion and so makes its contribution to Christian apologetics whose duty it is to show that the Christian religion in the most comprehensive sense is true. Christian evidences, for this reason, tends to be more concrete and more specific than Christian apologetics. By *fact* we mean either some objective *thing* (as an archaeological dig or artifact), or some *event* (as a historical battle), or some *phenomenon* which may be personal (as in the case of Paul's conversion), or *social* (as in the spread of the Christian Church). These *facts* may be classified three ways and so form the basic outline of the subject of *Christian evidences*. First, there is *material fact*. By *material fact* we refer to anything of a very concrete, specific nature, e.g., things, historical events, meteorological phenomena, documents, or monuments. Secondly, there is *supernatural fact*, which involves *events* or *phenomena* which can only be satisfactorily accounted for by invoking the category of the supernatural. Thirdly, there is *experiential fact* which refers to the experiences of people, and social phenomena which are traceable back to the impact of the Christian religion.

A. *Material fact*. By showing the tangency of the Bible to material fact we show its factuality and relevancy to this actually existing world, as well as showing that no objection can be made to it on the grounds of being contradictory to fact. Our knowledge of the Christian religion is derived from, first, a sustained historical testimony from antiquity until now that two groups of people, the Jews and the Church, held to certain beliefs and practices in reference to God and religion; and, second, from the sacred documents of these peoples preserved in what is called the Holy Bible.

1. *History*. By the usual avenues of historical knowledge a considerable body of information has reached us as to our knowledge of the Hebrew-Christian religion. The Jews in

their Talmud and other national writings have preserved much of their history in addition to what we know from the record in the Bible itself. For example, an entire survey of Biblical and Jewish history is contained in the writings of Josephus. Although the references are not as full as we could wish, the Jewish historical documents even bear some witness to the Christian religion. The Christian Church also has extra-Biblical records of its origin that are somewhat independent of its sacred writings. Of greatest importance are the writings of the Apostolic Fathers, but the other Fathers are not to be neglected for their historical worth.[4] Eusebius' *Ecclesiastical History* though not written according to the highest standards of historiography yet has a valued place in our knowledge of the Christian religion. Nor are we to neglect the information about our Christian religion from early Christian architecture, art, and burial places.

Besides the information which the Jews and Christians carried along with them as a relative independent witness to their sacred Scriptures, we possess non-Jewish and non-Christian information. Directly and indirectly the archaeological remains of Egypt, Palestine, Asia Minor, Babylonia, the Grecian peninsula and Italy have contributed to our knowledge of the Hebrew-Christian religion. Monuments, coins, murals, tombs, memorials, and the all-important written materials as tablets, papyri, ostraca, inscriptions, and parchments contribute to our extra-Biblical knowledge of the Hebrew-Christian religion. Besides this is the data gained from ancient historians, directly and indirectly, of our knowledge of the Jews and Christians, their origin, their beliefs, and their practices.

By the sources of information available to us outside the pages of the Bible itself, we are able to ascertain the truthfulness of many of the facts claimed within the Bible itself. This

---

[4] Reference must be made to N. Lardner's famous *Credibility of the Gospel History*, 10 volumes, in which all the references to the gospel are dealt with from the Fathers and from all non-Christian sources.

contributes to the demonstration of the historical *factuality* of the Hebrew-Christian religion.[5]

2. *The Hebrew-Christian documents.* The Hebrew Old Testament and the Greek New Testament constitute the sacred documents of the Hebrew-Christian religion, and our chief source of our knowledge of it. It is the province of Christian evidences to show the *factuality* of these documents, i. e., showing that as documents they have (1) a reliable history, and (2) a factually trustworthy content.

a) *The Bible as a document.* It is the ideal goal of Biblical criticism to trace back the text of our Hebrew and Greek Testaments to the times of their composition and to the penmen that wrote them. This task varies in its degree of success with each book of the Bible. It is the goal of Christian evidences to show that what evidence we do have, whether it be little, e.g., as in reference to Job, or much, e.g., as in reference to Romans, we nonetheless can show that such evidence confirms our belief in the Bible as a trustworthy document.

(1) The first task is that of Biblical criticism, or Biblical introduction. The Biblical critic in the good sense of the term has as his task the determination of the *canon of the Bible, the text of the Bible,* and *the genuineness and authenticity of the Bible;* i.e., what is called higher or literary or historical criticism.

It is the conviction of the believer of the Bible that when all the data are studied the canon of the Hebrew Bible and the canon of the Greek New Testament are seen to include only those books which met the required tests of canonicity. We firmly believe that in the historical processes the providence of God was at work protecting the canon so that only the inspired books were included in the canons of the

[5] Cf. G. Rawlinson, *The Historical Evidences of the Truth of the Scripture Records.* Modern scholarship is strangely indifferent to the type of argument found in such works as William Paley, *Horae Paulinae or, The Truth of the Scripture History of St. Paul Evinced,* and, J. J. Blunt, *Undesigned Coincidences in the Writings of the Old and New Testament, An Argument for their Veracity,* yet has this type of argument been refuted?

Old and New Testaments, and no inspired books were lost. The Christian points to two thousand years of Church history to indicate that in spite of every type of effort, nobody has been able to convince the Jews or Christians that another book ought to be added to the canon, nor that any book now in should be excluded. The story of the *Apocrypha* is such that an impartial investigation of the facts will show that it constitutes no problem at all to the Protestant conception of the Old Testament canon. Out of a multitude of facts we mention two: (1) The Jews had as their province to settle their canon, and the Jewish canon agrees with the Protestant Old Testament canon. The Church had no right passing any decision on the Old Testament canon even though the inclusion of the Apocryphal books was done in Alexandria under Jewish supervision, however, not under conditions too clearly known. (2) The story as to how the *Apocrypha* achieved status of inspired Scripture at the *Council of Trent* is one of the saddest commentaries on improper scholarship in the history of western culture.[6]

In reference to the lower criticism of the text of the Bible it can be safely said that the text of the Bible is the most reliably transmitted text of all antiquity. The important variations of the Old Testament text are approximately one to a page. So carefully has the Old Testament been transmitted that Green claims that "it may be safely said that no other work of antiquity has been so accurately transmitted."[7] In comparing the text of the New Testament with the texts of classical antiquity J. Finegan judges that the certainty "with which the text of the New Testament is established exceeds that of any other ancient book."[8]

---

[6] Cf. Bernard Ramm, "The Apocrypha," *King's Business*, 38:15–17, July, 1947.

[7] W. H. Green, *General Introduction to the Old Testament: Text*, p. 181. Cf. Bernard Ramm, "Can I Trust My Old Testament?" *King's Business*, 40: 8–9, February, 1949, where we have surveyed the evidence for the integrity of the Masoretic Text up to the discovery of the Dead Sea scrolls.

[8] J. Finegan, *Light From the Ancient Past*, p. 352. For similar commendatory statements see F. Grant, *An Introduction to the Revised Standard Version*

The problems of canon and text are difficult but nothing compared to what conservatives have to face in reference to higher or literary criticism. Practically every book of the Bible has been subject to severe critical analysis and doubt by some critic of note in the past one hundred and fifty years. However, it is the conviction of the conservative Christian that large measures of such critical activity is inspired by and guided by presuppositions that invalidate much if not most of radical criticism. To the contrary, he affirms that the patient, reverent, and careful study of the problem will reassure one of the genuineness, authenticity, and credibility of the Bible as a literary document. By so doing he shows the *factuality* of the Bible as a document.

This task in its many details must be turned over to the conservative Old Testament and New Testament scholar, and no longer can be handled adequately apart from specialists in these studies. We, therefore, refer the reader to conservative works in Bible matters: H. S. Miller, *General Biblical Introduction;* Angus and Green, *Cyclopedic Handbook to the Bible;* Edward Young, *An Introduction to the Old Testament;* Merril Unger, *An Introductory Guide to the Study of the Old Testament;* H. C. Thiessen, *Introduction to the New Testament;* T. Zahn, *New Testament Introduction,* and the various articles in *The International Standard Bible Encyclopedia.* These works in turn have adequate bibliographical guides for much further detailed study in the matters of canon, text, and literary criticism of the Bible from the conservative standpoint. Nor are we to forget that there are outstanding Jewish scholars who defend the conservative position in Old Testament studies, and outstanding Catholic scholars who defend conservative views in both Old and New Testament studies.

(2) The Christian defender next indicates how the Bible

---

of the New Testament, p. 42; F. Kenyon, *Our Bible and the Ancient Manuscripts,* p. 23; A. Hort, *The New Testament in the Original Greek,* p. 2.

has been miraculously preserved as a document. He indicates
what a long journey it has had from days of composition until now; how it has been persecuted by violence and by ridi-
cule, and yet survived. He delineates the wonderful ways in
which its transmission has been vindicated from time to time,
e.g., the discovery of the Nash papyrus, the Scheide papyrus,
the Dead Sea Scrolls, the Codex Sinaiticus, or the John Rylands fragment of the Gospel of John as well as the Chester
Beatty papyri. By his justification of the claims of the Bible
to be a trustworthy document, and by its miracle of preservation, the Christian defender is showing the integration of the
Hebrew-Christian religion with fact.[9]

b) *The Bible as a record.* We now pass from considerations
of the Bible as a document to the Bible as containing a record. As a record the Bible mentions many things that are
factual in nature. It is the endeavor of Christian evidences
to show the coincidence of Biblical content with such fact,
hence showing the *factuality* of the Hebrew-Christian religion.

(1) First is geography. The Bible mentions such things as
rivers, mountains, lakes, and plains, etc. It is the work of Biblical geography to show the conformity of the Bible to fact
in geographic matters. It is not necessary that every single
geographic reference be verified. We do not always know
the precise nature of the Biblical reference and we do not
always have full geographic information. But the correlation
of Biblical geographical references with known information
is very great. We refer the reader to articles in Bible dictionaries, Bible encyclopedias, and to Bible atlases and geographies. J. M. Adams, *Biblical Backgrounds* is an acceptable
text for conservatives in the study of Biblical geography.

(2) The Bible also makes many references to the culture of
people. By material culture we mean the tools, implements,
clothes, houses, animals, birds, weapons, and variety of gadg-

[9] Cf. F. F. Bruce, *The Books and the Parchments.*

ets with which people carry on their livelihood. By social culture we mean the manners, customs, and practices of people in social intercourse from cradle to grave. This includes such a diversity of things as birth rites, puberty rites, economic systems, political systems, legal systems, marriage customs, and burial customs. It is the purpose of the Biblical anthropologist to show the tangency of the Bible to fact in cultural matters, and so adding to the accumulative evidence of the factuality of the Bible. Here again there is a vast amount of information to substantiate the factuality of the Bible at this score, information that can be dug out of commentaries, out of Bible dictionaries, out of lexicons, out of monographs, and out of specialized studies. Archaeological studies are greatly increasing our knowledge of cultural data and affording many remarkable parallels of Biblical customs. The tangency of Bible to fact is here constantly increasing.

(3) The Bible mentions many matters of historical nature, e.g., kings, rulers, peoples, nations, confederacies, military campaigns, political customs, and great battles. It is the obligation of the study of Bible history to show that where we have evidence it substantiates the historical references of the Bible. It would be foolhardy to say that every solitary historical reference in the Bible has had extra-Biblical confirmation, as it would be also to say that there are no problems in Bible history. But researches in these fields are constantly confirming the historicity of the Bible, and a rather lengthy chapter could be inserted at this point to show how such researches have made such amazing confirmations of Biblical historical references. We have, for example, the amazing evidence presented by Robert Dick Wilson in his *A Scientific Investigation of the Old Testament*. In 184 cases where the names of kings are transliterated into the Hebrew, the task has been done accurately. This means that for 3900 years the names of these kings have been faithfully transmitted. There are about forty of these kings living from 2,000 B.C. to 400

B.C. Each appears in chronological order "with reference to the kings of the same country and with respect to the kings of other countries . . . . No stronger evidence for the substantial accuracy of the Old Testament records could possibly be imagined, than this collection of kings."[10] Mathematically it is one chance in 750,000,000,000,000,000,000,000 that this data would be correctly recorded.

The best works dealing with the history of the Bible are the works in Biblical archaeology. Out of a great number of works we suggest for the average student Caiger, *Bible and Spade;* J. M. Adams, *Ancient Records and the Bible;* G. Barton, *The Bible and Archaeology;* and J. Free, *Archaeology and Bible History.* However, such books give great attention to Old Testament archaeology, and though not neglecting, do not always pay sufficient attention to the New Testament. For such studies we suggest the works of A. Deissmann and W. Ramsay in general, and specifically, S. Caiger, *Archaeology of the New Testament,* and C. Cobern, *Archaeology and the New Discoveries.* Many articles on New Testament archaeology will be found in *The International Standard Bible Encyclopedia* and in *The Biblical Archaeologist.* Biblical chronology has also been seriously studied recently and the latest results will be found in the specialized scholarly journals.

(4) Sacred Scripture mentions things that refer to nature, i.e., references to astronomical bodies and their movements, references to flora and fauna, references to chemicals, and to meteorology. It is the function of the student of Bible and science to show that when the Bible deals with nature it does so chastely, i.e., not necessarily in accord with modern terminology, but in such a reserved way as not to contradict scientific fact; or to show that in some measure the Bible is anticipatory of modern science. It is almost a miracle to behold when one considers that although all peoples have fantastic,

[10] R. D. Wilson, *A Scientific Investigation of the Old Testament,* p. 86.

nonscientific notions about plants and animals, the Old and New Testament references are free from fantasy and folklore. There are two special problems to be faced here: First, the doctrine of evolution that is so widely accepted today and held to be contradictory to the Genesis account, and second, the antagonism of science to Biblical miracles. Here again we can do no better than to refer the reader to acceptable conservative treatises on the subject, e.g., R. Short, *The Bible and Modern Discovery;* A. Everest, editor, *Modern Science and Christian Faith,* and the relevant articles in *The International Standard Bible Encyclopedia.* Many good articles will also be found in *The Transactions of the Victoria Institute, The Journal of the American Scientific Affiliation,* and in *Religion and Science.*

How does all of this make a case for Christianity? Obviously, the fact of conformity to fact does not *prove* inspiration. Conformity to fact does provide us with two things. First, it shows that no objection to inspiration of the Bible can be made from the Bible's conflict with fact or lack of substantial factual relevancy. Second, it shows that Christianity, as a true religion, does have tangency to fact, and if the factuality of the Christian religion can be demonstrated all along the line its tangency to reality is also greatly assured.

B. *Supernatural fact.* It is possible for a book on history to be completely faithful to all matters of fact and yet not be inspired. It is possible to show that the Bible is remarkably free from errors of fact, yet we would not have *necessarily* demonstrated its divine origin. However, as we previously argued, if of divine origin it must be in accord with fact, and that is the necessity of showing the concord of Bible with fact. However, certain evidences are necessary to show that the Bible and the religion it teaches are from God, and these evidences are of such a nature as to show the divinity of our religion *necessarily.* They are evidences that reveal the presence of *supernatural activity* in human affairs.

A reaction more than a century ago set in against such a form of Christian evidences. Schleiermacher told his readers that the days of fairy tales are over and we need not worry our heads about the supernatural in Christianity.[11] Religion, to Schleiermacher and a great host of theologians since his day, is native to the human soul. The spiritual world hovers around eagerly seeking our fellowship. No rude doctrine of original sin prevents the soul from taking her flight to God. If Christianity be so interpreted, obviously the supernatural is a problem to Christianity, not a help. It has been very popular with many writers on such matters to affirm that the miraculous and supernatural is a *hindrance* to faith, not a help.

Two things may be said about this: (1) If one does assert such profound and metaphysically far-reaching doctrines as the Deity of Christ, eternal hell, eternal heaven, and personal salvation, then such tremendous doctrines need a method of verification in keeping with their seriousness. Pure philosophical theism is not enough. Something compelling, trenchant, incontrovertible is necessary and such demands are only met in the Christian teaching of the *supernatural verification* of Christian religion. (2) However, if the Christian religion be diluted down to Schleiermacher's or Ritschl's or Fosdick's interpretation, then obviously all that is needed in reference to Christian apologetics is a mixture of philosophical theism (something from Royce or Berkeley or Bowne), of philosophy of religion, of psychology of religion, and of comparative religions. But when such an interpretation of Christianity is taken Christianity loses its unique status and becomes just another metaphysical system among several. The gain in rejecting the supernatural is slight and the loss is enormous.

But God has set His seal upon Biblical religion with indelible stamps of a supernatural nature. It is the function of Christian evidences to indicate these indelible stamps and describe their nature and their evidential value.

[11] In his *Addresses on Religion to Its Cultured Despisers.*

1. *Biblical religion is supernaturally verified by the supernatural origin of Israel.* Abraham was called into his faith by a manifestation of the God of glory (Acts 7:2); he was maintained in it by further revelations and by the providence of God. His progeny was assured when in his body and in that of his wife a supernatural work was done (Romans 4:19), and they had a son, Isaac. His family when the size of a nation was supernaturally and miraculously delivered from Egypt, and throughout the history of the Jewish nation there were supernatural revelations, supernatural preservations, and miracles. The supernatural especially attended and blessed the ministry of the prophets.

Israel's religion and theology were given by divine revelation. This does not mean that there were no reinterpretations of some religious elements already in Israel's culture, but the religion of Israel was of divine origin.[12] Israel's preservation as a nation is also due to the activity of God. Biblical religion is therefore verified by the supernatural origin of Israel as a people, and as a nation; by the supernatural origin of the religion of Israel; and by the supernatural preservation of this people over centuries of time and through multitudes of adversities.

2. *Biblical religion is supernaturally verified by supernatural miracles.* For practical considerations in view of the general lack of education of the masses of humanity, no method of impressing the human intellect with the presence of the supernatural surpasses the clearly miraculous. From the supernatural miracles of Genesis to the last miracle of the book of Acts is one great tradition of the miraculous. The constant, varied supernatural deeds in both Old and New Testament are supernatural seals of the message taught.

[12] G. Wright, *The Old Testament Against Its Environment,* is a breath of fresh air in Old Testament studies. He takes issue with the trend in Old Testament studies which finds nothing in Israel's religion not imported from outside, and defends the thesis that the major elements of Israel's religion come from within, i.e. by revelation. The companion volume is F. Filson, *The New Testament Against Its Environment.*

3. *Biblical religion is supernaturally verified by supernaturally fufilled prophecies.* If miracles prove the immediate presence of the supernatural, prophecies prove the extended and constant presence of God in human history. The numerous predictions and fufillments that are found in the pages of both Testaments, are a wonderful and unmistakable evidence of the supernatural activity of God in human history and of the divinity of Biblical religion.

4. *Biblical religion is supernaturally verified by reason of a supernaturally inspired Book, the Holy Bible.*[13] It comes to us with a distinct claim found on page after page that God is speaking by the written word. Imbedded in its pages are not only the records of fulfilled prophecies and credible miracles, but other marks of its divinity. Its doctrine of God, its wonderful system of theology, its theocentric-Christocentric-soteriocentric unity, its purity and nobility of ethics, and its philosophy of history are watermarks of its supernatural origin.

5. *Biblical religion is supernaturally verified by the presence of supernatural visitors, the angels.* Although to contemporary consciousness the world of spirit, angelic and demonic, is very remote, this is not so in the Biblical account. The Biblical universe is one that is centered around spiritual personalities—God, good angels, evil spirits, and man. Hence, the presence of good angels and demons is *natural* in Biblical accounts. In both the Old and New Testaments, messengers from Heaven and emissaries from Satan take active part in human affairs and so reveal the presence of a transcendent, supernatural realm. The angelic activity is found deeply imbedded in New Testament religion. Angels announce the birth of John and Jesus; an angel is sent to Jesus in His temptation and in His Garden of Gethsemane experience. Angels gather round the tomb of the risen Christ. Angels come to the

---

[13] The writer has never read anything that compares to Dyson Hague, *The Wonder of the Book,* for showing the supernatural origin of the Bible on considerations as to what kind of Book it is as a literary production.

aid of the Apostles in Book of the Acts. Without the angelic hosts of Heaven the great scenes of the book of Revelation would be impossible.[14]

6. *The Christian Religion is supernaturally verified by the supernatural person of Christ.* He was supernaturally born; He received supernatural witness from the Father and the Holy Spirit at His baptism and His transfiguration; He lived a life of supernatural purity; He conducted a life with supernatural composure, majesty, grace, wisdom, and self-control; He taught supernatural doctrines; and He had a supernatural influence on human personality. He died a death surrounded by supernatural events, rose supernaturally from the grave, lived a remarkable supernatural life on earth for forty days, and supernaturally ascended into Heaven.

7. *Christianity is supernaturally verified by the supernatural resurrection of Christ.* Because of the tremendous theological importance of the resurrection both as to our Christology and soteriology it demands special attention in addition to considerations of miracles and the supernatural Person of Christ. It is *the* Biblical miracle, and sets the seal of divinity as nothing else does on the brow of Christ, and upon the contents of Christian theology.

8. *Christianity is supernaturally verified by the supernatural activity of the Holy Spirit.* The Holy Spirit brought to pass the virgin birth; He empowered Christ supernaturally in His teaching and healing ministries; He co-operated in His resurrection; He descended on the day of Pentecost with a great show of the miraculous; and continued to work miraculously in the life of the early Church.

9. *Christianity is supernaturally verified by the supernatural conversion of Paul.* The leading foe of the Christian faith

---

[14] Apologetic references to angels are scarce but see S. Zwemer, *The Glory of the Empty Tomb*, Chapter V, "A Vision of Angels," and D. E. Harding, "Are Angels Superfluous?" *Theology* 55: 97–100, March, 1952. For example he remarks that "Plainly the medieval universe was top-heavy [with angelic activity], just as ours is bottom-heavy, and plainly hierarchical symmetry is what we need," p. 100.

who called himself a blasphemer, persecutor, and insulter (I Tim. 1:13), is miraculously converted to Christianity by the personal manifestation of Christ to him. He then becomes Christianity's greatest apostle, missionary, and theologian. All efforts to account for Paul by explaining his conversion medically (epilepsy, sunstroke), or psychologically are inadequate. Further, all efforts to account for the Pauline theology other than by revelation as Paul claimed (Galatians 1:11, 12), e.g., by reference to mystery cultus, or liberal diaspora Judaism, or his independent Messianic theology, also are inadequate.[15] The conversion of the great apostle is a singular and remarkable proof both of the supernatural in the New Testament, and of the reality of Christ's resurrection.

C. *Experiential fact.* The Hebrew-Christian religion is not only declared factual by its concord with mundane routine fact, e.g., history, geography, or archaeology, and by its supernatural *imprimatur*, but also in its power to find lodgment in human experience. If Christianity is the true religion of God, no religion should be able to compare with the experiential and beneficial features of the Christian religion. This we believe to be the case, and therefore declare the *factuality* of the Christian religion on the grounds of its unsurpassed experiential and beneficial characteristics.

1. *Christianity is verified experientially by reason of the religious experience it provides.*

a) The Bible records remarkable religious experiences of men from Enoch who walked with God, Noah who found grace in God's sight, Abraham the friend of God, David the man after God's own heart, to the profound religious experiences of Peter, Paul, and John. The only adequate explana-

---

[15] Speaking of Bossuet's famous theory as to the origin of Paul's religion in his *Kyrios Christos,* C. H. Dodd says, "Seldom, I think, has a theory been so widely accepted on more flimsy grounds." *The Apostolic Preaching and Its Development,* p. 15. A. H. Hunter, *Interpreting the New Testament* indicates that the scholarly trend is away from interpreting Paul as a Hellenistic Jew and back to considering him an orthodox Jew. Pp. 70-71. Note also the return to substantially the position of J. Machen, *The Origin of Paul's Religion* in W. D. Davies, *Paul and Rabbinic Judaism.*

tion of such an unbroken tradition of powerful, transforming, glorious religious experiences is that there was an adequate, objective source of them, namely, the self-revealing God.

b) The Bible accentuates one remarkable experience in particular, regeneration, and thousands of Christians will testify to its reality in their own lives. From Paul to Evangelist Billy Graham is one huge swollen river of human testimony to the transforming power of the grace of God as it regenerates the soul.

c) Men of the Bible and men of Church history will vouch for the reality of daily religious experience—the nearness of God in meditation; answers to prayer beyond all human explanations in terms of chance or coincidence; inspiration and courage in hours of deepest gloom or tragedy; a precious sense of the nearness and dearness of Jesus Christ; new-found moral strength and ethical courage; wonderful releases from sins, habits, and evil customs.

2. *Christianity is verified experientially by reason of its remarkable propagation.* The Early Church, few in numbers, limited in resources, humble of constituency, spread with breathless rapidity and amazing success throughout Palestine, Egypt, Asia Minor, Greece, Rome, and then to the rest of western Europe. Whenever the Church experiences revival, the gospel spreads in a most remarkable way, as witnessed by the great revival of the Reformation and the great revivals of Great Britain and America. Not to be neglected are the great missionary triumphs of the gospel in planting the Church in all the world. No other religion has this evangelistic momentum, this missionary fire, as the Christian religion.

3. *Christianity is verified experientially by reason of its beneficial influence.*[16]

a) There are hundreds of thousands of Christians, living and dead, who will admit that because they believed in

[16] Richard S. Storr, *The Divine Origin of Christianity Indicated by Its Historical Effects.*

Christ their lives have been cleaner, sweeter, nobler, more worthwhile. They will testify to the blessedness of a Christian family, of the Christian Church, and of Christian fellowship.

b) Christianity has fostered institutions of mercy such as hospitals, orphanages, and homes for the aged.

c) Christianity has fostered education in a remarkable way. Our great universities of today are rooted in the medieval universities of Christian origin. Our great American universities and hundreds of smaller colleges have been founded by Christian ministers or denominations.

d) Christianity has fostered better social conditions, e.g., the ennoblement of womankind, the emancipation of slaves, the censoring of cruelty to criminals, and in general, has engendered a high moral and ethical standard for society.

IV. Methodology in Christian Evidences

A. *Our fundamental thesis*

Christian evidences is a subdivision of Christian apologetics. No well-meaning effort at evidences can be really telling without working with a well-formulated system of Christian apologetics. Systematic and Biblical theology provide Christian evidences with its Biblical data and perspective; Christian apologetics supplies Christian evidences with its basic theory of verification. Most approaches to Christian evidences have been eclectic or philosophically noncommittal. The eclectic approach uses what comes to hand as the argument progresses. The philosophically noncommittal approach usually employs the philosophy of common sense realism, e.g., that of Joseph Reid or Noah Porter. Although the approach is professed to be nonphilosophical, it is philosophical, and by analysis usually resolves down to common sense realism, i.e., that objects of perception exist "out there," that God would not deceive us as to either the use of our minds or senses, that we have a common internal sense that associates for purposes of combination our sensory information, and that the mind has certain primitive rules given to it by God for correct thinking.

It is certainly a task bordering on the impossible to expect to prove the resurrection of Christ to a man owning a materialistic metaphysics, or to prove miracles to a logical empiricist. Christian evidences cannot be indifferent to philosophical positions, and that discipline of Christianity which deals with the Christian faith and philosophy is Christian theism or Christian apologetics. We do not think it possible to controvert the position of James Orr in *The Christian View of God and the World* that whoever utters the words, "Jesus is my Saviour," has thereby willingly or unwillingly, knowingly or unknowingly, espoused a definite distinct philosophy with certain necessary metaphysical implications.

We assert as our fundamental apologetic thesis the following: *There is an infinite, all-wise, all-powerful, all-loving God who has revealed Himself by means natural and supernatural in creation, in the nature of man, in the history of Israel and the Church, in the pages of Holy Scripture, in the incarnation of God in Christ, and in the heart of the believer by the gospel.* The hypothesis is directly supplied from the supreme norm of Christian knowledge and theology, the Holy Bible, but it is helped and guided by philosophical considerations. Our personal experience of the gospel is the psychological motivation to seek such a hypothesis; it is the Bible which supplies us with it, and it is Christian apologetics that formulates it, explains it, and defends it. We accept this thesis on the following grounds:

1. The Christian religion supplies our hearts with an adequate answer to the basic needs of the human heart, e.g., the thirst for the supreme good is found in God Himself; the quest for peace of heart due to irritations of a guilty conscience is found in the forgiveness and justification of God made possible by the death and resurrection of our Lord

Jesus Christ; and the hope for a future life is answered in the victory of Christ over death. We are Christians because our hearts find their fullest satisfaction in the Christian religion. This is the thesis defended in E. J. Carnell's *A Philosophy of the Christian Religion.*

2. The Christian Religion has a fundamental set of theological propositions which form an interrelated noncontradictory system of religious truth. Certainly, the acceptance of any system of belief (scientific, philosophic, religious) demands that that system be free from contradiction. We find in the Christian system a set of theological affirmations which do form a genuine noncontradictory system. This does not mean we know all and understand all. We always must caution ourselves about first our own infirmity and ignorance, and then the greatness and incomprehensibility of God. But this does not relieve us of the necessity of seeing if our propositions agree, nor from, as in neo-orthodoxy, literally glorying in the paradoxical.

3. The Christian religion is tangent with fact. This is the domain of Biblical introduction, Biblical archaeology, Bible and science, and Biblical geography. This is part of the great strength of the Christian religion, namely, its great conformity to so many kinds of facts.

4. The Christian religion is supernaturally verified by the witness of God through the miraculous, e.g., prophecy, miracles, and the resurrection of Christ.

5. The Christian religion renders the universe metaphysically intelligible. Something is rendered scientifically intelligible when the phenomenon to be explained is shown its necessary place in a web of circumstances or causal chain. Metaphysical intelligibility is this same process on a much wider scale, i.e., the hypothesis espoused compasses a vast stretch of data and systematizes it, correlates it, and renders it meaningful. It is for this reason that broad scientific laws and metaphysical assumptions are very similar in both form

and method of verification. "The rational task of the apologist for Christianity is just the natural task of the advocate and exponent of any great generalization of science," writes Sweet, "to vindicate it, on the basis of evidence, as *the most reasonable hypothesis to explain undoubted facts. . . .* Christian apologetics is the explication of the fact that the Christian religion explains the world, man, and human history more comprehensively and more satisfactorily than any other explanation which can be devised."[17] Of all the philosophies the human mind has entertained, none can compare with the Christian religion for making the best sense out of the universe (its origin and destiny); out of man (his origin, nature, and purpose); and out of human history.

Our fundamental thesis is then accepted on this fivefold ground: Its ability to satisfy the heart, to satisfy logic, to satisfy our scientific sense, to satisfy our demand for the transcendental, and to satisfy our philosophic reason. It is a combined argument. Each part contributes to each other, yet each has a strength of its own. It is an argument that drives forward on all five fronts and must be met in its full force, not settled by some small skirmish among patrols. No finer statement has been made as to the *culminative* impact of Christian evidences than that made by Cardinal Wiseman when he wrote: "Were it given unto us to contemplate God's works in the visible and the moral world, not as we now see them, in shreds and little fragments, but as woven together into the great web of universal harmony; could our minds take in each part thereof, with its general and particular connections, relations, and appliances,—there can be no doubt but religion as established by Him, would appear to enter, and fit so com-

[17] L. M. Sweet, *The Verification of Christianity*, p. 17. Italics are his. This is a healthy intellectualism and reminds us of the remark of Russell: "In our day, only the fundamentalists and a few more learned Catholic theologians maintain the old respectable intellectual tradition. All other religious apologists are engaged in blunting the edge of logic, appealing to the heart instead of the head, maintaining that our feelings can demonstrate the falsity of a conclusion to which our reason has been driven." Bertrand Russell, *The Scientific Outlook*, p. 102.

pletely and so necessarily into the general plan, as that all
would be unraveled and destroyed, if by any means it would
be withdrawn. And such a view of its interweaving with the
whole economy and fabric of nature, would doubtless be the
highest order of evidence which could be given us of its truth.
But this is the great difference between nature's and man's
operation, that she fashioneth and moulds all the parts of her
works at once, while he can apply himself only to the elaboration of single parts at a time, and hence it comes, that in all
our researches, the successive and partial attention which we
are obliged to give to separate evidences or proofs, doth
greatly weaken their collective force."[18]

B. *Essential features of the Christian religion*

We have already indicated that Christian theology, Christian apologetics, and Christian evidences is a co-operative effort each re-enforcing the other. Apologetics must work in full
recognition of the content and nature of Biblical theology,
and evidences is in turn indebted to apologetics. It is very
germain to evidences that the essential elements of the Christian system be delineated. If the evidence is to be seen fairly
and in its correct light, these considerations from theology
must be set forth.

Christianity like any broad scientific hypothesis or metaphysical assertion is accepted as a network or pattern of
hypotheses. It can be likened to the interweaving of evidence
by a skillful lawyer to show that the hypothesis suggested
cannot be denied with prudence. Hence, to argue miracles or
prophecy in complete detachment from all the other essential
elements in Christianity is like trying to prove a theory in
which science has been artificially separated from all basic
scientific theory.

1. Christianity first asserts that God is omniscient, omnipotent, sovereign and free. The materialist or naturalist looks

[18] Cardinal Wiseman, *The Connection Between Science and Revealed
Religion*, I, 1–2.

upon nature as inviolate territory. But within the Christian system God is both able and free to do what He wills. *This is basic metaphysics.* If this is a universe governed by a free, sovereign, omnipotent Spirit, then miracles and the supernatural are certainly credible; only if nature is considered inviolate is the supernatural considered intolerable.

2. Christianity insists on the divine initiative in the knowledge of God, i.e., revelation. We do not so much construct a world view as we verify one given by divine revelation. Hence, the scientist and the revelational theist are working at different ends of the rope. Of course, the revelation theists expect all sorts of opposition from those working from the bottom of the rope up. Both ends of the rope are necessary and revelation theists need to show respect to the findings of empirical science. But in the matters of the existence, nature, and purposes of God as well as redemption and salvation, the Christian approach is through revelation, and not through empirical generalization nor idealistic philosophical speculation.

3. Christianity rests great weight on the experience of grace. The Christian religion is not pure spiritual metaphysics arrived at either mystically, empirically or philosophically. Nor is it solely a body of theological propositions. It does contain both a metaphysics and a theology, but it is essentially a *religion*, and thereby demands from men spiritual responses such as faith, trust, love, and devotion. It was the essential apologetic of Calvin to integrate the witness of the Spirit within to the rational verification of Christianity from objective considerations.[19] It is the measured judgment of Mullins that Christian assurance is established by the "union and combination of the objective source and the subjective experience" of the Christian religion.[20]

This consideration means that Christianity can never be a

[19] Cf. John Calvin, *Institutes of the Christian Religion*, Book I, Chapter VIII, "Rational Proofs to establish Belief of the Scripture."
[20] E. Y. Mullins, *The Christian Religion in Its Doctrinal Expressions*, p. 11.

matter of simple intellectual or factual demonstration. It must make its peace with logic and fact, but upon such a rational superstructure it does erect a doctrine of experience that may not be dispensed with in intellectual deliberations.

4. In the Christian theistic system sin is considered an indispensable category for interpretation of man and religion. If man is not alienated from God then certainly the supernatural is extraneous to the divine relationship between God and man. But if man is estranged from God the supernatural is essential to redemption. The Christian theist dogmatically insists that miracles cannot be discussed apart from anthropology and its doctrine of sin. Even neo-orthodoxy has re-awakened to the necessity of considering sin in the construction of a Christian theology and philosophy.[21] To argue against miracles on the assumption that man is in harmonious fellowship with God is not to set the miracle in its proper setting.

5. Certainly the love of God for man cannot be held as secondary in Christian evidences. Both the providence and redemption of God are tokens of His love, and the supernatural activity of God must not be likened to the unnecessary and unwelcomed intrusion of some amateur in a machine shop, but like unto the self-sacrificing activity of a parent who will do anything his power and resources will permit to spare the life of his child from sickness or danger. A Puritan knew this well when he wrote: "That Providence must be included in the true notion of a Deity, is evident from this consideration, that to own only such a deity as we are not oblig'd to worship; and from whom we can expect no benefit by any service we perform unto him, as to all purposes of religion, or any interest we can serve by such a useless God, is, in effect, to own no God at all. A God without a providence being to us an

---

[21] Cf. Reinhold Neibuhr, *The Nature and Destiny of Man* (2 *vols.*); Mary Thelen, *Man as Sinner in Contemporary American Realistic Theology;* and C. Henry, *The Protestant Dilemma,* Chapter III, "The Mid-Twentieth Century View of Sin."

empty name, and a thing insignificant, which we as freely and securely may deny as own; for to what purpose should we pray to a God who regards none of our addresses? or hope in a God who is not concerned to help us? to fear a God who will inflict no evil upon us? to obey a God who regards not our actions? . . . Why should we thank Him, if we receive nothing from Him? or praise Him, if He be no ways beneficial to mankind?"[22]

It has been frequently argued that the size of the universe as reported by modern astronomers as well as the number of astral bodies shrinks our earth to practically a nothing, and man upon it to even less than that. Of course, it is never boldly stated in this form: *size governs importance.* Certainly human affairs are not so conducted. Jewels of minute size are worth many slabs of concrete or tons of sand. When a tiny tot of three years of age, of San Marino, California, fell down a shaft, over ninety feet into the earth, five hundred thousand dollars was spent (in twenty-four hours) in rescue efforts.

However, the Bible itself asks and answers this question. When viewing the immensity of the starry space the Psalmist wondered why God ever notices such an infinitesimal speck as man. The answer given is: "Thou hast made him" (Psalm 8:3–6), and one man in the image of God is worth more than countless tons of astral bodies; and the earth, though a very minute astronomical body and not the center of the universe, is certainly its stage.

6. It is the uniform witness of the Old Testament that the uniformity of nature, i.e., the regularity of the movements of the stars, and the dependability of the cycles of the seasons, and the constant routine of the meteorological phenomena, are due to the constant watch of God over His creation. Philosophers of science admit that the actual historical origin of the modern conception of the uniformity of nature—abnormally used to uproot Christian metaphysics—was in scholas-

[22] Daniel Whitby, *Sermons on the Attributes of God* (1710), I, 3.

tic theology in which it was asserted that an orderly God kept an orderly universe. It is either deliberate falsification or willful negligence to facts to affirm that one believes in either (i) an orderly universe as described exhaustively by science, or (ii) in a universe of utter spontaneity and irregularity in which everything and anything can happen.

It is essential to the theistic doctrine of miracles that nature be uniform in her daily routine. If nature were utterly spontaneous, miracles would be as impossible of detection as it would be to establish a natural law. To insist that the doctrine of the supernatural would wreck all science and jeopardize all natural law is a gross and unfair misrepresentation of Christian theism. But as Machen reasons "the existence of a real order of nature" is necessary to supernaturalism, otherwise "there would be no distinction between natural events and those that are above nature—all events would be supernatural, or rather the word 'supernatural' would have no meaning at all."[23]

C. *The Christian Doctrine of Fact*

The import of the section on our fundamental thesis, and essential considerations, is that they supply us with the material for our Christian theory of knowledge and theory of fact. In Christian evidences we talk about *facts*. But any discussion of fact involves a doctrine of knowledge and theory of fact. As a guide for our discussion we suggest the following:

1. The Christian must reject all epistemologies which have atheistic, materialistic, or agnostic tendencies. He is suspicious of the epistemologies held by positivists, naturalists, and agnostics. Generally speaking, these are metaphysical systems which grant far too much authority to either the scientific method (always defined too narrowly), or empirical data (always too strictly conceived).

2. The Christian rejects all epistemologies that deny room

[23] J. G. Machen, *Christianity and Liberalism*, p. 99. Cf. also C. Van Til, "Nature and Scripture," *The Infallible Word*, pp. 255–293, in which the same thesis is elaborated.

for the authority of God as stated in Scripture. He is therefore suspicious of pantheisms, idealisms, personalisms, or religious modernisms (considered philosophically) because in so many instances the authority of God is not admitted.

3. The Christian accepts that epistemology which grants God ultimate definitive powers and right, and which truly acknowledges that man is in the image of God. The writer thus conceives Christian epistemology to be an authoritarian rationalism. It is *authoritarian* because it recognizes that there can be no truth without the TRUTH, Almighty God. God has disclosed His will in Holy Scripture, and therefore we recognize the authority of Scripture as the authority of God. It is *rationalism* because it is an admission that if man is in the image of God, he bears in his nature the impress of the divine reason which John 1:9 seems to teach. This authoritarian rationalism was first propounded by the great Augustine, and today his philosophy of religion is gaining a new following.[24]

It is this philosophy and epistemology which gives the Christian defender his theory of fact in dealing with Christian evidences. Truth is determined metaphysically by the authority of God; it is determined individually by the impress of the divine reason on human mentality; and it is determined objectively by the combined appeal to the inward contribution of reason and the outward contribution of sensory experience.

4. We see a fact to be true in Christian evidences because

a) We commence with the authority of God in the realm of metaphysics and fact

b) We see the fact in the Christian doctrinal setting

[24] E.g., E. Casserley, *The Christian in Philosophy;* E. Carnell, *Introduction to Christian Apologetics;* A. Richardson, *Christian Apologetics.* Van Til's *philosophy* of theism is far more Augustinian than he will admit on paper. His doctrine of "God-interpreted fact" is just another method of stating Augustine's doctrine of illuminationism. The author has dealt with Christian apologetics and epistemology in his work, *Types of Apologetic Systems* which may be consulted for Christian epistemologies which are empirical or existential.

c) We are able to "handle" the fact because we are in the image of God and possess a gift of His rationality

d) We are able to apply the canons of logic and experience to divide particular truth from particular error.

Our procedure in this book shall be to take certain leading elements in Christian evidences and develop them, rather than attempting to extend our lines over the entire range of Christian evidences. We shall discuss in order: A criticism of antisupernaturalism, prophecy, miracles, the resurrection of Christ, the person of Christ, Christian experience, and the divine origin of the Bible. The author was confronted with the decision of writing several short chapters and covering all of the topics, or writing more comprehensively on fewer topics. He has chosen the latter on the grounds that a few points well-made are better than a superficial defense of many points.

5. Previous efforts in field of Christian evidences.

A word may be said here about previous efforts. The finest treatise as far as the author is concerned both for cogency of argument and beauty of literary expression is M'Ilvaine's *Evidences of Christianity*. His chief criticisms of previous efforts are:

a) Far too much space was given to Biblical introduction. Perhaps in other times such chapters were necessary, but at the present status of theological studies, matters of detailed investigation of Biblical introduction are more the province of Old and New Testament scholars. These matters cannot be ignored by the modern writer on Christian evidences as will be witnessed by the following pages, but we feel that such studies are no longer part of the principal material of evidences.

b) Too many of these previous efforts worked with little philosophical guidance, which most contemporary theologians would say is indispensable. If logical positivism has done no other service than this, it has done a good service, *viz.*, to point out that any sentence or proposition that claims to be true, can only be verified or falsified within a given system to which it belongs. That five and five makes ten is true in arithmetic, but not necessarily true about raindrops or rabbits. Therefore, any *fact* involves a *theory of fact*, and any theory of fact is essentially metaphysical of nature. It is not possible to discuss fact without a philosophical theory of fact. Hence, the writer in Christian evidences must work with a theory of fact developed by Christian apologetics. As an example of a work needing better philosophic guidance we mention Hamilton's *The Basis of Christian Faith*. In the first chapter Hamilton defends a Kantian epistemology. It is weird philosophical reading as he calls Kantian categories innate ideas.[25] How Hamilton picked upon Kantian epistemology to defend Christian theism is a mystery to this writer. The epistemology of Kant is the foundation of much of contemporary metaphysical agnosticism, not to mention that Kantian epistemology is the philosophical parent of modernism and of Barthianism. Hamilton does reject positivism, pragmatism, Ritschlianism, and Barthianism.[26] But positivism looks to Kant as one who showed that many metaphysical problems were insoluble because meaningless; one of the very roots of pragmatism is to be found in Kant's concept of the practical reason; Ritschl's distinction between judgments of value and judgments of fact is directly of Kantian origin; and Brunner in *The Christian Philosophy of Religion*[27] defends Kant's critical idealism. This is given by way of example to show that evidences cannot be adequately developed apart from philosophical considerations of a competent nature.

c) Many of the previous writers in evidences confused theism, apologetics, and evidences. Proofs for the existence of

---

[25] Cf. pp. 19–27, especially p. 27 where he calls space, time, and cause "innate ideas," whereas in reality they are Kantian categories or forms of pure intuition.
[26] *Ibid.*, p. 21.
[27] See Chapter V, "The Element of Truth in Rationalism." Does not Van Til in *The New Modernism* argue that liberalism and Barthianism are brothers under the skin because both are built on Kant's philosophy which grants self-legislative powers to man?

God are the domain of theism not evidences, as is the refutation of antitheistic theories. Further, the problem of Christian ethical theory is really part of apologetics and theism
rather than Christian evidences.

d) Finally, the renunciation or the minimizing of the supernatural element in Christianity by some apologists is a stra-
tegical blunder. Row in his *A Manual of Christian Evidences*
beats a retreat from evidences as traditionally conceived for
what he calls "the moral evidence" (in contrast to former
treatises which emphasized the supernatural element in
Christianity). The foes of Christianity have said that a non-
supernatural Christianity is far more digestible than a supernatural Christianity. Many apologists acceded, thinking it was
a movement to gain leverage.

If in apologetics and evidences we let such moral considerations lag too far to the rear, the correct strategy is hardly
to retreat the supernatural so as to advance the moral argument. The strategy is to bring the moral argument up into line
with the supernatural. Further, the essential consideration
for evidences is the nature of Christianity itself not contemporary moods, not that they should be ignored. Christianity is
supernatural to the core, and to retreat at that point is to
silence one's biggest artillery. Granted many of the scholars
or thinkers toying with Christianity will say that they might
become Christians if the supernatural were eliminated from
the Christian faith, but such toying goes on for centuries.
When a man does convert to Christianity he wishes something
real, and this thirst for reality can only be supplied by the
supernatural. Let the converts to Christianity tell us what
really appeals and what really holds, not those playing the
game of "weddings" and "funerals" with the Christian theologians (Matthew 11:17).

CHAPTER II

ANTISUPERNATURALISM

(For students deficient in philosophical background this chapter may be skipped without detracting from the main course of argumentation.)

IN ORDER TO PROCEED with a positive argument it will be necessary to indicate the antisupernatural mood of contemporary thinking, and something must be said in refutation. The root of the current antisupernaturalism can be readily traced back to the birth of modern science (Galileo) and modern philosophy (Bacon, Hobbes, Descartes). The development of the modern scientific mentality has been traced by such scholars as J. H. Randall, Jr., in his *The Making of the Modern Mind,* and E. A. Burtt in his *The Metaphysical Foundations of Modern Physical Science.* A new secularistic mentality has emerged. There is now endemic upon the masses of civilized people today such plagues as atheism, dialectical materialism, and secularism. In such schemes there is no room for the supernatural and transcendental.[1]

After science was well under way it was able to increase the number of well-founded empirical laws, and to bring more and more phenomena within the scope of the explanatory powers of these laws. With the maturation of the sciences and the increase of the scope of the sciences went increased veneration for law itself and for the scientific method. Eventually such veneration gave birth to twentieth century scien-

---

[1] Cf. E. Brunner, *Revelation and Reason,* p. 5.

tisms, e.g., materialism, positivism, naturalism, pragmatism, and new realism.

Bringing up another flank against the lines of the supernaturalists were the philosophers. Hume laid down a terrible mortar fire on miracles and the attributes of God, whereas Kant thundered out like a Big Bertha against all speculative metaphysics. He sent his huge projectiles crashing and exploding with dreadful effect into such time-honored items as proofs for the existence of God, proofs for the existence of the soul (paralogisms), and proofs for a natural theology (antinomies). As if to say that the ranks of supernaturalism must not only be beaten back but decimated, came the Cossacks of radical criticism riding hard and roughshod with glistening swords over every single book of Sacred Canon. Moses, Isaiah, Paul, and Jesus were not spared the thundering hoofs or the cut of the sword. Prophecy was reduced to ethical preaching; miracles were declared hindrances rather than helps; the divine authenticity and authority of the Bible was cut asunder to joints and marrow; traditional theological formulations were laughed out of court for, as Schleiermacher said, we are no longer children that we should believe in fairy tales. In less than a hundred years great and honored universities, hundreds of important theological seminaries, and thousands of ministers capitulated to the "modern mentality." It seems as if there were a willfully plotted effort for every conceivable department of human knowledge to rise up and denounce Biblical supernaturalism. Has there ever been in the history of humanity such a revolution of such measure and such success in such a short span of time?

"Modern mentality" means that man is no longer central to the interpretation of the universe, but is accidental. Moral, ethical, spiritual, and aesthetic maxims are judged as personal preferences due in the main to social conditioning. High ideals are of purely human origin. Everything that cannot be stamped with the purple ink of scientific approval is either spurious, or not to be trusted, or of inferior grade. God, our heavenly Father, is replaced by Nature, our earthly Mother. However, men may believe in God but with the reservation that fervent religious activity and belief is undesirable, and "evangelism" is really proselyting and is, therefore, unethical.

I. Objections from Science

The scientist opposes the supernatural on two counts:

A. He opposes the supernatural on the basis that the supernatural is contradictory to natural law.

B. On the grounds that miracles do not fit into the universe the scientist works in.

A. However, the concept of natural law is not as simple as appears on the surface. Although the scientist may handle the law as a simple axiomatic notion, it does not admit of such simplicity upon analysis. The first premise of every natural law is the principle of the uniformity of nature.[2] If the uniformity of nature is not predicated the law is meaningless, i.e., it becomes provincially true of one experiment or a cluster of experiments at one point of time in one section of space. It is the principle of the uniformity of nature that universalizes laws so that what is discovered at one place and time may be predicated of many spaces and times.

Not only is natural law dependent on the principle of uniformity, but all prediction is dependent on it. There is no demonstrable method of proving that the future shall be like the past. It can only be assumed in terms of the principle of uniformity.

It is recognized that the principle of the uniformity of nature is a dictum that comes from the medieval period. It was a theological tenet which stated that in that God was an

[2] Studied historically and somewhat definitively by F. H. Seares, *The Concept of Uniformity.* Involved in this discussion too is the problem of induction and probability, two more very knotty and difficult problems in the philosophy of science over which there are very sharp divisions. There are three or four leading theories of the justification of the process of induction, and as many more over the nature of probability.

orderly Person the universe must reflect His orderliness. The original source of the principle is to be found in the theistic undergirding of Nature. Now by the strange concourse of events the uniformity of nature is used to controvert theism. In the theistic system the principle of the uniformity of nature finds its rational justification and its metaphysical undergirding in the character of Almighty God.

Further, although the Christian may locate the source of the principle in his theistic metaphysics, the scientist has no method of proving the principle. There is no single experiment that proves it for it is the first premise of all experimentation. To extend the principle from one experiment to all is to use the principle to prove itself. There are two ways out. The scientist may give the principle full metaphysical status as a pervasive feature of reality, but in so doing he has become a metaphysician. Or, he may with the positivists state that the principle is one of the assumed principles of scientific investigation which one takes as true but does not bother to prove.[3] In this case the question is begged or dodged. Another variety of the positivistic position is to assume the truthfulness of the principle on pragmatic grounds. But if grounded pragmatically it cannot be used viciously to exclude the miracle in Biblical history. Pragmatic verification leaves it possible that other situations may occur in which the principle does not hold.

Finally, the Christian theist insists that the uniformity of nature is not the point of the argument at all. For the daily routine of life, for the regular procedures of science, and for the practical needs of the commercial world, the principle of uniformity holds true. As will be noted in the discussion of miracles, the Christian insists on a regular order in nature for the very detection of the "irregular." That is to say, the Chris-

---

[3] This is precisely what logical positivism does. Cf. H. Feigl, "The Logical Character of the Principle of Induction," *Philosophy of Science*, 1: 20–29, January, 1934.

tian theist is not arguing for a chaotic or a spontaneous or a haphazard universe when he argues for the supernatural. At this point he only insists that science does not mercilessly and blindly extend the uniformity to all of human history without full appreciation of *the nature of scientific knowledge itself,* and *the worthy contentions of Biblical theism.*

The Christian attitude toward the principle of uniformity is this: For the general routine of life and existence the principle is granted its validity. Its ultimate grounding is in the consistency of God's nature. But the principle is not to be used to mercilessly rule out all conceivable supernatural events if for other *sound and rational arguments* such events can be shown to fit into the entire system of the universe.

B. The second objection of science is that miracles do not fit into the universe scientists work in. The bodies of the astronomers do not imitate the events of the long day of Joshua; there is no parthenogenesis in the higher forms of life; and sick people are not instantaneously cured of major illnesses, such as leprosy. The question at issue is whether the scientific method is valid enough to pass on all *possible* occurrences in the universe, and the Christian theistic answer must be in the negative. To begin with, such an extension of the scientific method to pass on all conceivable occurrences is far from being made within the boundaries of strict science. It is a metaphysical dictum, clear and certain. To state: "We scientists have not discovered parthenogenesis among *homo sapiensus*" is one thing; but to state: "No virgin birth is ever possible" is bald metaphysics. It may be correct metaphysics, but the point we make is that it is not science.

If the conflict between theologians and scientists in bygone ages was over matters of geology and biology, today it is over the panapplicability of the scientific method in which science is converted in metaphysics, as in logical empiricism, naturalism, new realism, and modern materialism.

II. Analysis of the Scientific Method

This contention of the theologian with scientism involves at least a passing analysis of the scientific method. There are at least five leading notions to the scientific method.

A. *Science endeavors to state qualities in terms of quantities.* Colors are reduced to wave lengths; masses to pounds or tons; motion must be stated in terms of time and distance; planetary motion in terms of the law of gravitation. Science *tends* as much as possible to deal with nature quantitatively which means it emphasizes the measurable. Further, the emphasis on the quantitative is *mutatis mutandis* an emphasis on the mathematical. An emphasis on the mathematical is *mutatis mutandis* an emphasis on the abstract. Thus, the more science advances the more it become abstract and quantitative.

B. *As much as possible, science endeavors to predict.* Some have been so bold as to state that prediction is the chief test of a hypothesis. But prediction is in turn based on sequence, and sequence only has meaning if the word "causal" is smuggled into it. Causality is the root notion of prediction.[4]

However, although the principle of prediction may not be the sole test of a scientific hypothesis, and although causality might be difficult of formulation, nevertheless prediction is one of the central notions of science.

C. *Science deals as much as it can with the stable,* and what is "unstable" is treated by some means to give it a *quasi* stability. This is another way of stating that science deals with the repeatable. Science does not deal entirely with the repeatable, as some have insisted, as this is not strictly possible in astronomy and geology. But science does seek the stable elements of Nature.

---

[4] We are not defining causality here in any other form than the most general assertion that the future will be like the past. If the logician defines it as a function of an if-then relationship, the argument in the text remains the same.

If something is apparently "unstable" science endeavors to bring stability in by statistics. In the atomic physics where specific prediction of the pathways of single particles is impossible, statistical formulations bring in a form of order. Although the date of the death of any particular person is of difficult determination, yet mortality tables impose sufficient order to permit the solvent operation of huge insurance companies.

D. *Science deals with observables as much as possible.* True, there are some things scientists never see directly, e.g., force, gravity, electrons, and fields. But as much as he is able the scientist endeavors to describe observables in connection with what is observable. Because no observable data could be obtained on the ether drift, the concept itself was rejected. If a drift would have been detected—and there was the claim that later experiments did detect it—then ether, though invisible, would have been accepted as existing.

E. *Science endeavors to unify as much data as it can under general principles.* The goal of a universal law of gravitation is to explain all phenomena of motion from atoms to stars. Einstein's newly proposed unified field theory is perhaps—in its paper form—the most generalized theory ever to be propounded in the history of science. But in all such procedures there lurks the danger of reductionism. In the effort to unify as much territory as possible under a general principle, that which is actually dissimilar is cut to fit the Procrustean bed. This is exemplified in the current passion of some philosophers to reduce all science to physics.

When these goals of the scientific method are examined, the limitations of the scientific method to explain *all* of reality or experience becomes apparent. *Wherever the universe or reality or our experience moves in an opposite direction of the goals of science, then science cannot assimilate that factor in its system.*

III. Limitations of Scientific Method

A. Qualities are not quantities. Qualities can be stated in terms of quantities, but the quantity is not the quality. A deaf man can learn the physics of sound, and may photograph the pattern of a given note of the scale and see it. Perhaps psychophysicists can tell us the number of impulses traveling along the auditory nerve. But motions and impulses are not qualities. Until further mysteries of consciousness are fathomed, qualities are not comprehended within the scope of the scientific method.

B. Whatever is genuinely novel or unpredictable is not capable of genuine scientific treatment. One of the features of the universe that Bergson has made apparent is its novelty. Evolutionary theory faces a most serious problem at this point. If there is no genuine novelty, there is no real epigenesis. If there is real epigenesis there is genuine novelty, and genuine novelty science cannot comprehend. Human activity is, at the present stage of actual comprehension, laden with novelty. The continuous stream of advertising schemes is eloquent testimony to this. As soon as one notion wears out or is exposed a new one must be presented to the public.

C. Science cannot handle what is transtemporal or transspatial, i.e., a genuine inobservable. For this reason science may talk of the empirical soul, but not of the transcendental soul; science may talk of empirical mind, but not pure mind; science may talk of empirical energy, but not of creative energy; science may talk of empirical teleology, but not metaphysical teleology.

D. Finally, science cannot comprehend genuine individuality. Personalities may be typed; factors causing various personality features may be examined; but there can be no comprehension of individual, unique personality in the scientific scheme.

The most general conclusion is that the categories of science are adequate within the goals of science (the quantitative, the stable, the predictable, the observable, the general), but not for the comprehension of the sum of all experience, or reality, or the universe. Therefore, it is still for metaphysics to decide what these categories are, and the criterion of verification of such metaphysical assertions will be *rational intelligibility*.

E. A further investigation of the scientific method reveals that for its very operation it is dependent on certain other items. It is these dependencies that form the logical and rational framework in which the scientific method works and that without it, it could not. But the problems connected with the framework have a metaphysical character to them.

1. To begin with, the *orderliness* of nature is assumed. The future will be like the past. Oxygen will behave today like it did yesterday. Geological processes are similar today to what they were millions of years ago, and will be the same in time to come. But *why* elements and processes remain constant is not explained, nor is it explicable in strict scientific terms. Science may not even ask the question. But on the other hand, if a scientist did not assume it he would never experiment again, or if he did, he could not extrapolate his findings beyond the given experiment. The *why* of constancy is left over to metaphysics.

2. The integrity of the powers of the human personality must be assumed. If the scientist thought his mind were continuously playing tricks on him he could not experiment. He could not reason. Even though he knows that he makes mistakes, he feels that he or somebody else will have the rationality to detect them. He assumes that if careful enough he will add up his figures accurately. He must trust his memory with unabashed confidence. He must pledge himself and his fellows to *absolute* honesty, i.e., he must not "fudge" in his experiments or in his deductions. Yet *why* he is rational, and *why* he may depend on human rationality, and

why memory is both possible and dependable within limits, and *why* honesty is the best policy are not within his province to answer. These he must assume. Every effort to prove them involves them. Rationality is a necessary assumption to prove rationality, or to even investigate it. Memory must be predicated to prove memory or investigate it. Honesty is necessary to investigate why honesty is the only scientific policy. Therefore, it is left over to metaphysics and epistemology to endeavor to propound the answers to these and to be guided by the categories of adequacy and rational intelligibility.

3. Science must work with a theory of truth but there is no experiment that verifies a theory of truth. Truth-theory is dependent upon either epistemological or metaphysical analysis and the membrane dividing epistemology and metaphysics is often a mere film.

In concluding this excursus on the scientific method, two statements have been the goal: The statement that the supernatural does not fit into the universe science talks about is an invalid objection to miracles. Any pronouncements about the total nature of the universe must come from metaphysics and not from science. The battle must be fought with the same weapons common to all and the assumption of a privileged position is begging the question, a case of the *petitio principii*. Science as science may rightfully say that miracles do not occur in science. But science as science cannot make pronouncements as to the universality of the possible or the impossible. If any pronouncement is made, it is made by a metaphysician, not by a scientist. This leads to the second observation, namely, that the power, or utility of the scientific method is not the point at all. In science, for the problems of science, for the mysteries of science, the Christian theist has no substitute for the scientific method. He pledges himself to it as firmly and sincerely as the positivist or naturalist.

The real question is this: Is there a metaphysical view of the universe that will grant full rights to the scientific method within its own defined sphere yet permit at certain specified junctures the operation of the supernatural? The Christian theist affirms that there is such. If he is controverted it cannot be by a naïve or a dogmatic extrapolation of the scientific method into methodology and as a definitive authority in metaphysics. He can only be controverted by a metaphysician.

The theist is not trying to argue for too much. He is not arguing for a Nature that operates sporadically, nor for the superstitions of the nonscientific cultures. He is as adverse to the fanciful, mythological, and absurd as the scientist. What he insists upon is that the concepts, first, that Nature operates regularly, and, second, that the scientific method is the best method yet devised to investigate Nature, are true for the general, usual, customary, normal routine of the acquisition of knowledge. But neither the concept of the uniformity of nature nor the panapplicability of the scientific method are of such philosophical nature that they can pass on all conceivable events in the universe. A Christian theist believes that there are just and defensible reasons for believing in certain supernatural activity at specified junctures. In so doing he believes that he is just as scientific, just as tough-minded, just as academically thorough, as the devotee of scientism.

We do not consider at this point that we have either proved the supernatural or the miraculous. We assert only that science cannot be so used to even deny the conceivability of such occurrences. Having obtained breathing space we have leverage to adduce substantial reasons for the Christian theistic position.

IV. Objections from Naturalism

A. To say that the supernatural is conceivable does not *prove* that it exists.

In the section just concluded it was argued that the scientific method, or science itself, may not legitimately say the supernatural is inconceivable. This does not, as indicated, constitute a proof that the supernatural exists.

B. All that there is, is Nature: Naturalism's Creed.

However, there is a movement in philosophy that does profess to be metaphysical and to declare that miracles cannot happen and that they are inconceivable. This is a philosophical system which endeavors to interpret Nature in terms of Nature, i.e., it does not have recourse to any idealistic or supernatural categories such as God, spirit, design, or providence.[5] Nature is *self-operative* in the absolute sense of the term. In a narrower sense naturalism is the philosophy that says that all there is, is Nature. Nature is defined as that which *all* the sciences report as existing including the modes of existence. It differs from modern dynamic materialism in that the latter takes the category of *substance* seriously, whereas agnosticism about the ultimate nature of the Weltstoff characterizes naturalism.[6]

S. Lamprecht defines naturalism as:

> A philosophical position, empirical in method, that regards everything that exists or occurs to be conditioned in its existence or occurrence by causal factors within one all-encompassing system of nature.[7]

A. Edel writes that "Reliance on scientific method, together with an appreciation of the primacy of matter and the pervasiveness of change, I take to be the central points of

[5] Sidney Hood's statement that "Naturalism is opposed to all known forms of supernaturalism, not because it rules out *a priori* what may or may not exist, but because no plausible evidence has been found to warrant belief in the entities and powers to which supernatural status has been attributed," does not seem in keeping with other definitions of Naturalism which do state *a priori* what may not exist. Sidney Hood, "Naturalism and Democracy," *Naturalism and the Human Spirit*, p. 45. Cf. B. A. G. Fuller's definition: "Naturalism . . . holds that the universe requires no supernatural cause and government, but is *self-existent, self-explanatory, self-operating, and self-directing*." *Dictionary of Philosophy* (D. D. Runes, editor), p. 205. Italics are ours.

[6] The omnibus of recent naturalism is Y. Krikorian, editor, *Naturalism and the Human Spirit*; of recent logical empiricism, H. Feigl and W. Sellars, editors, *Readings in Philosophy*; and of recent materialism, R. Sellars, McGill and Farber, editors, *Philosophy for the Future.*

[7] *Naturalism and the Human Spirit*, p. 18.

naturalism as a philosophic outlook."[8] Y. Krikorian says that "for naturalism as a philosophy the universal applicability of the experimental method is a basic belief . . . still another basic belief that is characteristic of naturalism [is] that nature is the whole of reality."[9]

Summing up the essays on naturalism, J. Randall, Jr., observes that:

> For the present-day naturalists "Nature" serves rather as the all-inclusive category, corresponding to the role played by "Being" in Greek thought, or by "Reality" for the idealists . . . Thus naturalism finds itself in thoroughgoing opposition to all forms of thought which assert the existence of a supernatural or transcendental Realm of Being and make knowledge of that realm of fundamental importance to human living. There is no "realm" to which the methods for dealing with Nature cannot be extended. This insistence on the universal and unrestricted application of "scientific method is a theme pervading every one of these essays.[10]

An analysis of these comments by naturalists clearly reveals that all there is, is Nature as defined by a philosopher critically systematizing the data provided by the scientists. Nature is one vast chain of events, one immense rug with woof and warp causally connected. If the naturalist is right, supernaturalism is impossible. But if the naturalistic metaphysics can be shown to be necessarily impossible, then once again the supernaturalist has both standing room and breathing space. Ripping up the rug of Nature as defined by naturalists does not *mutatis mutandis* prove the existence of supernatural events. It would, however, show the existence of a supernature.[11]

If this supernature (not as yet supernatural) can be demonstrated to exist, then the miraculous is at least conceivable, or

[8] *Ibid.*, p. 65
[9] *Ibid.*, p. 242.
[10] *Ibid.*, pp. 357–358.
[11] Cf. C. S. Lewis, *Miracles*, Chapters II through V.

negatively, the supernatural proper cannot be legislated against *a priori* from the premises of naturalism.

V. DEFENSE AGAINST NATURALISM

The following arguments are presented to show that the naturalist's formulation of reality is erroneous:

A. All that has been said about the objections from science apply at this point as the naturalists are avowed believers in the universal applicability of the scientific method. If what has been said about the uniformity of nature and dependencies of the scientific method are true, then naturalism cannot deny the supernatural by merely invoking the name of science.

B. Both Nevius[12] and Hocking[13] believe that the current shift in physics from the older Newtonian physics to the new relativity and atomic physics is seriously damaging to the naturalistic program. Of course, naturalists are aware of this change in scientific theory and have done their best to accommodate to it.

However, if the contentions of such men as H. Weyl, A. Compton, J. Jeans, W. Carr, A. Eddington, and F. Northrop are correct, then it is conceivable that fifty more years of science will see an abandonment of the naturalistic program itself by the scientists. Hocking makes it clear that metaphysical statements based on recent changes in physical theory are premature, and with this we agree.[14] But nevertheless the slight breeze in the direction of idealism may turn to prevailing winds. Even the slight breeze is sufficient indication that the case for naturalism is not a set and established affair.[15]

---

[12] W. Nevius, *Religion as Experience and Truth*, p. 197 ff.
[13] W. Hocking, *Types of Philosophy* (revised edition), p. 88 ff.
[14] *Op. cit.*, p. 88.
[15] Cf. Bernard Lawrence Ramm, "The Idealism of Jeans and Eddington in Modern Physical Theory" (unpublished master's thesis; The University of Southern California, 1947); and, "An Investigation of Recent Efforts to Derive Metaphysical Statements from Science with Special Reference to Physics" (unpublished doctoral dissertation; The University of Southern California, 1950).

There is a strong probability that Bouwsma's judgment about naturalism is correct, namely, that naturalism is not a profoundly demonstrated metaphysics but a pragmatic solution to the vexing problems of metaphysics. He writes:

> I think the naturalists' defense is this. Metaphysics and science aim at the same thing. Metaphysics fails. Science succeeds. Accordingly, naturalism is nothing but the adoption of a successful policy.[16]

C. The categories of naturalism are inadequate to explain the totality of experience. Hocking states the objection at this point when he writes:

> If I am right in thinking that the strong side of naturalism is the completeness of its explanations, it becomes vulnerable at once if at any point its explanations are incomplete and *necessarily* so.[17]

Dennes[18] lists the three basic categories of metaphysics: event, quality, and relation. *Event* is the old concept of matter brought into alignment with recent developments in physics. *Quality* is limited to what is observable or otherwise sensible. *Relation* is actually the category of space. To attempt to derive all the vastness of the experience of the human race recorded, contemporary and personal, from these three categories *is not metaphysics but magic*. Naturalism, to be truly comprehensive, must either add materially to its list of categories, or else it must—contrary to its announced platform—engage in a most crippling reductionism.

Naturalism finds itself in the same predicament as Kant. Kant set forth his philosophy of science in his *Critique of Pure Reason*. He realized fully the place of moral experience in human life and made room for it in his *Critique of Practical*

---

[16] O. K. Bouwsma, "Naturalism," *Journal of Philosophy*, 45: 12:21, January 1, 1948.
[17] *Op. cit.*, p. 94. Italics are his.
[18] *Naturalism and the Human Spirit*, p. 271.

Reason. Even yet his keen mind realized that he had not reached comprehensiveness so he had to add on to these two *Critiques,* a third, the *Critique of Judgment* dealing with beauty and teleology. If the first *Critique* is the only one invested with genuine scientific validity, then the other two appear as needless appendages. But the full range of experience is such as to show Kant—and many others too—that a truly *valid* and *comprehensive* philosophy must also reckon with morality, religion, beauty, and teleology. Kant wrote three mighty *Critiques* but they do not form one comprehensive, *integrated* philosophy.

Naturalism following the categories of event, quality, and relation, leaves much of the totality of human experience completely inexplicable. Some of these matters will appear in the subsequent discussion. Hocking asks at this juncture: granted Naturalism can explain the universe by law, the question is then to be asked why are laws existing at all? and why are they like they are?[19] This carries the problem over to the matter of final causes. If we have to resort to final causes, to purpose, to explain why there is law in the first place and why they are what they are, then the logic of naturalism is broken.

D. However, perhaps the most serious refutation of naturalism is the self-transcendence of man.[20] Another way of stating this is to assert that the mind is more than the brain. In naturalism the brain and the mind must be equivalent. In fact, the mind is nothing more than a functioning brain. If the self-transcendence of man can be demonstrated then naturalism stands completely refuted and a new metaphysics

---

[19] *Op. cit.,* p. 105 ff.
[20] Cf. C. S. Lewis, *Miracles,* Chapters I–V; Hocking, op. cit., p. 96 ff. in which he gives five points in which the mind transcends the brain; D. Allan, *The Realm of Personality,* Chapter I, "The Rival Views of Personality," especially Section 3, "Transcendental Views of Man," and, Chapter VII, "Brain and Personality." C. E. M. Joad, *Mind and Matter,* p. 58 ff. in which he shows the difficulty of equating the mind with the brain.

is in order that has a greater comprehensiveness and adequacy of interpretation than naturalism. This we believe to be the case.

1. *Reason transcends neurology.* In the naturalistic scheme the mind is the brain functioning. Krikorian, a naturalist, writes that "In relation to the study of mind the belief that nature is the whole of reality implies that mind should be examined *as a natural phenomenon among other natural phenomena. It has its origin, growth, and decay within the physical, biological, and social setting.*"[21]

For a philosophy to be true it must not only be able to explain the universe in general, but itself in particular. If the mind is the brain, the brain must in some sense "secrete" naturalism. But in natural processes there are no rights or wrongs. There are no erroneous *effects* that proceed from the correct *causes.* If naturalism is true, naturalism provides no means of proving such to be the case. It can only prove itself to be true by assuming the transcendence of *mind over neurology.* If it does this it has ruptured the fabric of naturalism. If it does not do this then naturalism can never prove itself to be the true philosophy. Just as the brains of men "secreted" materialism in one century, and rationalism in another, they have secreted naturalism in this generation and might secrete pantheism in the next. A neural circuit, no matter how complex, is still physically determined. You cannot have determinism and truth value. But man's ability to use his reason shows that he does have truth value. If he has truth value he

---

[21] *Op. cit.,* p. 243. Italics are ours. The views of outspoken behaviorists and logical positivists on the matter of mind are far more extreme than this. The neo-positivists consider the mind-body problem as a pseudo-problem, i.e., really a confusion of two different vocabularies of speech. Cf. Herbert Feigl, "Logical Analysis of the Psychophysical Problem. A contribution of the New Positivism," *Philosophy of Science,* 1:420–445, October, 1934. This position is literally ripped to shreds by Stephen C. Pepper, "A Criticism of a Positivistic Theory of Mind," *The Nature of Mind* (University of California publications in Philosophy, 1936), pp. 211–232.

transcends neurology. If he transcends neurology the metaphysics of naturalism is punctured.[22]

2. *Morality transcends stimulus.*[23] The fact that tensions
arise within human personality is a most strange situation to
naturalism. Nature is supposed to get along with itself. If a
bit of acid contacts an amoeba we could surmise that the
physical contact of the acid with protoplasm causes a shrink-
ing of tissue resulting in what appears to be a withdrawing
action. We can further surmise that in reflexes a closed nervous circuit is at work. In neither case is there any tension in
the organism. Nature is at peace with itself. Response corresponds harmoniously to stimulus.

But if the situation is changed, something new enters. Think
for a moment of plunging a knife into the heart of a child. Is
there an inward revulsion against the act? Contemplate how
you may cheat to win some money. Is there a struggle set up
within your mind? *Here is a direct opposition of mind to
stimulus.*

Readily the psychologist springs to his feet and shouts
"conditioning." Obviously, a host of anthropological data can
be suggested that shows how X approved in society A, is immoral in society B. This sort of argument goes back in modern
philosophy to Locke.[24] Granted, a woman in America would
go through the most terrible pangs of conscience if she killed

[22] This is argued with great cleverness by Lewis, *op. cit.*, Chapter IV; by
Hocking, *op cit.*, pp. 102–104; and by A. S. Eddington, *Science and the Un-
seen World*, p. 58. Eddington shows how naturalism cannot tackle the multi-
plication table. The answers are right or wrong irrespective of the events in
our "brains" and we are held accountable for the right answers because our
minds transcend natural law. "Therefore dismiss the idea that natural law
[mechanical explanation of the brain] may swallow up religion," is his conclusion.

[23] This is the gist of the second objection Lewis brings against naturalism.
Further splendid philosophical analysis on the self-transcendence of man will
be found in R. Niebuhr, *The Nature and Destiny of Man*, I, Chapters I–IV.
For a critique of empirical epistemology from the standpoint of Christian
Augustinian rationalism cf. E. Carnell, *An Introduction to Christian Apolo-
getics*, p. 34 ff.

[24] The first "relativity of culture" argument is that of Xenophanes in his
remark that each people make their gods after their own racial characteristics.

her twin babies, whereas a woman in some heathenish country would have a guilty conscience if she did not kill them.[25]

But the argument that *morality transcends stimulus* is not based on any specific demand of any specific culture. It is not an argument based on innate specific concepts of morality. It is an argument that states that there must be an *inner structure* to condition.[26] The peculiar nature of this inner structure is that it can fight a stimulus; it can undergo the strongest of stimulation (theologically speaking, temptation), yet refuse to respond. Or, the person may turn to the stimulus and respond in a measure far beyond the strength of the stimulus. In either case, mind transcends stimulus, be it even the will to evil.

According to the naturalist's definition of Nature, Nature cannot war with itself. A relatively isolated system cannot set up tensions within itself. Once the circuit is entered, determinism reigns. To think that a moral tension could be set up within a determined system is incredible, yet these moral tensions are the daily fare of all of us. Hitler may have exterminated the Hebrews by the millions but anybody that tried to take his own life was something unspeakable. It is routine in ethic books to point out that thieves are moral parasites, for they insist upon honor among themselves. Gangsters will kill innocent people upon occasion, but have been known to submit to capital punishment rather than "squeal" and "be sprung."

We set it down then as a phenomenon that punctures the naturalist's metaphysics, that human beings transcend stimulus in their moral judgments.

3. *Memory transcends time.* The miracle of living in the past, present, and future does not seem to have even raised a

[25] A primitive woman reproached by an Occidental for throwing her child into the river to pacify the gods replied, "Doesn't your god demand your best?" She would have felt guilty to sacrifice the poorest child in the family.
[26] The word "condition" is used here in reference to the larger conditioning effects of culture, not in reference to something like conditioning a reflex by use of an electric shock.

flicker of an eyelid from the naturalists. If it turns out that the various data suggested by Bergson[27] and Allan[28] is verified, science itself must thoroughly repudiate naturalistic premises. In a word, men with large portions of their brains removed or destroyed have been able to regain much or most of their former knowledge. Post-mortem investigations confirm the extent of tissue destruction. At least there is such a body of evidence at the present time that it cannot be considered idle speculation to propose that memory is more than matter. The naturalist's rebuttal is far more a matter of refuge in ignorance than positive demonstration. In fact, there is an increasing body of evidence to show that the brain works as a whole in many reactions rather than as a collection of parts such as the way a radio set works. But if the brain works as a whole, then the most acute problem faces the naturalists as to how a collection of physical parts can have a holistic functioning.[29]

However, the argument at this point is not dependent on examinations of people with brain injuries. It is a patent, experienced *fact* of the consciousness of every man that he lives in three times. True, his body moves with the current of time. However, our minds can set up a reverse eddy. They can also leap ahead of stream. In the naturalist's conception of Nature this is incredible.

Memory is not just a peculiar type of effervescent poppings in our complicated nervous system or a sort of by-product of complex neural organization. *Truth judgments may be applied to memory.* Supercalculating machines are so constructed as to store up electrical impulses for a fraction of a second and then discharge them. But how do we tell a good

[27] H. Bergson, *Matter and Memory.*
[28] Allan, *op. cit.*, Chapter VII, "Brain and Personality." For a naturalist's refutation, cf. Krikorian, *op. cit.*, p. 256 ff.
[29] Two articles defending very ably this position in psychology are Dayton Phillips, "The Foundations of Experience," *Philosophy of Science*, 13:15–65, and, George Yeisley Rusk, "Salvaging Physiological Psychology," *Philosophy of Science*, 13:123–30.

machine from a bad one? We apply a truth judgment to the result. We get the answer by some other method and then test the machine. But a machine cannot be made to test any and all such machines. If memory were purely mechanical, purely chemical or electrical, truth judgments could not be applied—but the application of truth judgments to memory is daily courtroom routine.

Equally as phenomenal is the ability of the mind to anticipate the future. For a process to be conscious of process is absurd. Only that which transcends process can be conscious of process. The statement "meet me tomorrow at noon" can only be made by a mind that is aware of the process, yet is transcendent above it.

Here again in the anticipations of time it is possible to apply truth judgments. Tremendous sums of money and hundreds of lives are involved in predictions about markets, stocks, possible wars, weather, and gambling. Shrewd, intelligent decisions of men are justified by the future course of events. Pragmatic verification follows many other of our daily assumptions about the future.

The argument is not based on perfect prediction, nor is it destroyed by the fact that the very fact of causal systems makes predictions intelligible. The argument is that mind can transcend time and look forward or backward, a phenomenon that destroys with acidic burning the fabric of naturalism.

Returning to memory, it is an amazing thing that we can toy with memory. We can decide that which we wish to remember. We can think of periods in our lives; of types of people we have known; of certain kinds of incidents—our loves, our sicknesses, or graduations; of different sensory experiences, e.g., sound, taste, motion, or vision. Further, the content of memory is enormous. We can go on and on and on almost endlessly remembering places, people, conversations, events. We can remember the emotional associations of the events—pleasure, disgust, fear, or revulsion. Dennes' categories of event, quality, and relation are helpless to cope with memory.

We conclude, then, that the ability of the human mind to transcend time is a refutation of the premises of naturalism.

4. *Psychological freedom transcends causality.* If immediacy, vividness, testability, and repeated confirmation be tests for truth, then human freedom is one of the most assured facts of human knowledge. It is asserted that the sense of freedom is a delusion. First, if anything so vivid and fruitful as the experience of choice is a delusion, then the entire rationality of man and all his powers is under suspect. Second, if the sense of freedom is a delusion then both the assertions that there is no freedom and that there is freedom are delusions, for both involve selection of data which is only possible if man is free. *If selection of data is determined with everything else, then the complete rationality of man expressed in science and knowledge stands condemned.* Yet the very success of science and human knowledge is proof that *selection of evidence is not determined.*[30] And if that is not determined then man is free, and if free, Nature is transcended and naturalism is hopelessly punctured.

Krikorian, writing on "A Naturalistic View of Mind," climaxes his essay with the remark that "At higher levels of integration mind attains not only unity but also its supreme achievement, freedom."[31] For recognizing freedom he is to be congratulated. However, this is in complete disaccord with his previous statement that "life must be interpreted and defined within the medium of mechanism, whether strict or mild."[32] You cannot have freedom and mechanism.

[30] It is granted that *selection* is integral to the scientific method and that without selection science would be impossible. For example, this is admitted by Sidney Hood himself. Cf. Sidney Hood, "Bertrand Russell's Philosophy of History," *The Philosophy of Bertrand Russell* (Paul Schlipp, editor), p. 651. If the selection of the "brain" is determined, then science is impossible. If selection is a combined process of rationality and psychological freedom then naturalism is an impossibility.

[31] *Op. cit.*, p. 269.

[32] *Ibid.*, p. 245.

Krikorian admits that there is no precise mechanical definition of life, and that life is more than *mere* mechanism. But will he really face the issue? Will he dare assert that there is a factor in life that is more than nature? If he does he must part company with his friends the naturalists. If he does not is he not guilty of gross inconsistency? In truth, there is a most palpable inconsistency throughout the entire essay, for the effort to be naturalistic in metaphysics and to talk about mind as we experience it will always be grotesque. For example, he states that "Provisionally, mind may be defined as response to the *meanings* of stimuli."[33] But let a thoroughgoing naturalist endeavor to trace a stimulus through the brain. If the brain is *completely* natural, as it must be in the naturalistic definition, then when does a neural impulse, an electrical current with a measurable speed, change to an image, then a meaning? Bare perception cannot be the same as meaning or else dogs would be as intelligent as men; and in that in some senses they have more acute sensitivity, they actually would be more intelligent. Do naturalists profess to have solved these tremendous mysteries, namely, what makes an electrical impulse an image and what gives an impulse meaning? Electrical currents either cause chemical changes, or heat reactions, or set up electrical fields. But which of these is an image or a meaning? If the brain is the mind, the obvious transcendence of the human intellect over mere matter and spatiality is an unutterable enigma.

Even more may be urged at this point. "Mind must be analyzed as behavior, since behavior is the only aspect of mind which is open to experimental examination," Krikorian writes.[34] If this means I cannot peer into the brain of a rat to see what is transpiring, I concur. If this means that scientific standards should replace old wives' tales in psychology, I concur again. But if I take this assertion seriously it means this:

[33] *Ibid.*, p. 252.
[34] *Loc cit.*

My behavior observes the behavior of the rat. But in behavioristic terms my behavior has to be something as objective and scientific as the rat's behavior. *But behavior is not
meaning.* A rat running around in a problem box is exhibiting
motion. But if there is any meaning for the rat, it is in his brain
not his legs; and if there is any meaning to the experimenter
it is in his mind, not in the behavior of the rat or in his own
muscles. *To say that behavior observes behavior is meaningless. Only a conscious mind with powers of memory, rationality, and meaning* can observe behavior and give it scientific
interpretation.

The effort of logical empiricism to reduce psychology to
physics is even a more extreme position in psychology. All
psychological statements must be converted into physicalistic
statements. But, first, who can even use sentences, let alone
be critically analytic of them, but a minded organism? Second, who can even interpret another scientist's statement but
a minded organism? Third, what neurological or electrical
mechanism could detect an error in one of the elaborate
proofs of a book on symbolic logic? The presence and transcendence of mind is patent at every point.

Another equally abject presentation of the panobjectivist
point of view is that of Arthur Bentley.[35] To him the terms
subjective and objective, knower and known, are divisions
marked by the human skin. "Bluntly the separation is the
skin; no other appears" in his dictum. The author is not familiar with any subjectivist or idealist in the history of philosophy that would subscribe to that dictum. Bentley rhetori-
cally adds that "Skin, in its way even operates as that which
demarcates those bits of the universe destined to sing in the
hereafter, and those destined to singe." To Bentley, *knowing*
is a form of *behaving* and is biological of nature. The knowledge process is part of the natural course of events. But how

[35] Arthur Bentley, "The Human Skin: Philosophy's Last Line of Defense,"
Philosophy of Science, 8:1–19, Jan., 1941.

Bentley can extricate himself from the natural course of events to discuss the significance of skin and to point out the falsity of the mentalistic philosophy is nowhere treated in his essay. How does one *biologically* verify a philosophy? What is the *biological* criterion that verifies philosophy A, and falsifies philosophy B?

We conclude, therefore, that the very ability to conduct the affairs of life, the experiments of science, the proofs of logic, and the pursuit of philosophy involves man's freedom, i.e., his transcendence of causality.

Summary. If our surmises in this section are correct, naturalism fails as a metaphysics. The evidence that establishes the failure of naturalism *mutatis mutandis* establishes a *supernature*. The basic insights of naturalism that are of worth are not lost or depreciated but are oriented to a new center. This new center admits the conceivability and the possibility of the supernatural. The puncturing of naturalistic metaphysics does not establish the supernatural; it simply makes it conceivable.

For fear of misunderstanding we assert that Christian theism is not antagonistic to science as science. It is at swords points with scientisms. Theism accepts: (i) the legitimacy of the scientific pursuit. The scientific endeavor is as much an honored task as that of farming or carpentering. Theism does not believe that experimenting with Nature is unnatural tampering; rather, controlling Nature was one of the first commands of God to humanity. (ii) Theism accepts the validity of the scientific method for the tasks of science. Theism offers no substitute for the scientific method in chemistry or physics. It further concurs that the scientific method is a good model to follow in all academic work. It puts no premium on ignorance, mysticism, carelessness, hunches, or any other substandard method of trying to secure truth. (iii) Theism accepts the validity of large tracts of scientific truth. The vast number of empirical laws of all the sciences are accepted for what any such scientific law is worth. Theism is not at heart antiscientific and protradition. It is the genuine conviction of theists that a man can be a thorough scientist, exact and competent, and be a Christian of the highest order. However, Christian theism does indicate that Nature is not fully or adequately known apart from theistic hypotheses; and that the scientific method used without reference to Christian theism tends to become an epistemology and metaphysic in itself. In this latter sense the scientific method is not as innocent and impartial as sometimes it is paraded to be.

VI. Objections from Religious Modernism

Religious modernism concurs with theists that man transcends nature, and that the realm of supernature exists, but liberals join with the scientists and naturalists in discrediting the supernatural elements in Holy Scripture. Burrows, for example, says that the argument from miracles "is of no use to us. To the modern mind the miraculous element in the Bible constitutes a difficulty rather than evidence of inspiration."[36]

A. *Liberals are inconsistent in joining in with the scientists and naturalists in asserting the inconceivability of miracles.* A dragonfly will eat its own tail and kill itself. By joining with the naturalists in accepting the inconceivability of miracles, liberalism follows the folly of the dragonfly. James Orr in *The Christian View of God and the World* clearly demonstrates that whoever believes in a monotheistic religion *already* has accepted a large measure of supernaturalism. Liberals may "deny supernatural actions in the sense of miracles, but they have affirmed supernatural Being on a scale and in a degree which casts supernatural action quite into the shade. If God is a reality, the whole universe rests on a supernatural

---

[36] M. Burrows, *An Outline of Biblical Theology*, p. 17. In this chapter we are taking as a general guide for liberal thought the September, 1948 issue of *The Modern Churchman* (vol. 38). The entire issue is given over to "The Necessity for a Christian Modernism."

basis."[37] Machen also criticizes liberalism and says the liberals' method of retreating from science is poor, inefficacious strategy "for after the liberal apologist has abandoned his outer defences to the enemy and withdrawn into some inner citadel, he will probably discover that the enemy pursues him even there."[38]

It is characteristic for liberals to state that although there is actually no resurrection, or pentecostal miracle, or no virgin birth, yet these supernatural stories contain truths worthy of belief, e.g., Christ does have supreme importance to religion, the Spirit is at work in the world, or we may hope for immortality. The literal interpretation of the record is abandoned because it conflicts with science, and so the liberal spiritualizes which means, *he beats a retreat from history.* He thereby thinks he has tilted gloriously on the field. He has unseated the Fundamentalist and he has not crossed the scientist. But this he can only do by a fatal retreat from history and fact. Whatever may be said against the supernatural, this can be said for it: *It endeavors to put truth squarely and unmistakably in history.* As the liberal retreats from history he thins out his religion into some form of speculative metaphysics, e.g., personalism or Berkeleian idealism or neo-Hegelianism or Kantian critical idealism. Certainly the liberal has his books on God in history, but the God of religious liberalism is far more difficult to detect in history than the God of theistic supernaturalism.[39]

If science and naturalism are opposed to the supernatural they are also opposed to the entire spiritualistic program. If the liberal accepts the word of the scientist in reference to the inconceivability of the supernatural what will he do to prevent science from denying immortality, e.g., as C. Lamont does in his *The Illusion of Immortality?* The same science that

[37] P. 76.
[38] J. G. Machen, *Christianity and Liberalism,* p. 6.
[39] Cf. how C. H. Dodd shows how Christianity is essentially historical in *History and the Gospel,* Chapter I, "Christianity as a Historical Religion."

liberals use to rout the virgin birth, Lamont uses to rout immortality. Where is the essential point of difference in arguing for immortality, or for the virgin birth? And if there is one in favor of immortality, how big is it? Is it big enough to let the liberal accept immortality within scientific respectability and condemn the virgin birth as disrespectable?

But the liberal wants his immortality, and if faced with refutation he will have to argue against science on similar lines in defending his immortality as the conservative does when he argues for the virgin birth. The situation is the same with the resurrection. How much material difference is there in debating (1) science versus the resurrection, or, (2) science versus immortality? The conservative has a far better chance of establishing the resurrection of Christ than a liberal has of immortality if scientific procedure is closely followed. Immortality is a concept argued for on extenuated inferential grounds, e.g., the simple nature of the soul, the thirst for perfection, or the goodness of God. The physical resurrection of Christ is *potentially* capable of historical demonstration. The liberal has solved nothing by rejecting the inconceivability of miracles. If he grants the same, then the subsequent chapters will be his reply. But if he doesn't, what has he gained? He may gain a measure of commendation from the scientist and naturalist for his "good sense," but let him try to lead his bedpartners into a full-fledged religious commitment and he finds himself arguing for his religious metaphysics much the same way the conservative argues for his supernaturalism. *Religious liberalism is inconsistent in representing the supernatural as inconceivable.*

Liberals are fond of mentioning that they are scientific with the implication that orthodox theologians are either non- or antiscientific, e.g., Moehlman writes that "Liberalism is that kind of theological science which refuses to work with any other means and methods of research and interpretation than the scientific."[40] But what is the scientific method in this regard? Many scientists think that only physics has attained the status of a science. Others will let biology and chemistry squeak by but anything from psychology and beyond cannot be considered science. Where does this put theology? or better, liberal philosophy of religion? On the other hand, if by scientific the liberal means "good scholarship," then he cannot draw any such line to divide liberal from conservative; for if the doctor's degree from an accredited seminary or university be taken as a rule-of-thumb guide—and who would be bold enough not to?—for deciding scholarship there happen to be several hundred conservatives in the United States alone to warrant the title of scholar. This is, of course, not to mention the great host of conservative Biblical scholars, Protestant, Catholic, Eastern Orthodox, and Jewish.

Supposing for the moment that the liberal means by *scientific,* "rigidly scientific." If he means that, then all he can accept as scientific is what *rigid science* proposes. But narrow, or rigid science is *solely* preoccupied with matter and its properties (physics, chemistry, biology). Strict science has no room for spirit, value, God, or immortality. Obviously, if the liberal means *rigid science,* his whole metaphysics is *kaput.* Therefore, he must show why he believes in propositions which science has no verification for. He must become a metaphysician. Now he may be an empirical theist but nonetheless he is metaphysician and not pure scientist. Now when he becomes a metaphysician he can make no strict claim to be scientific in the sense that an orthodox theist is not. The best he can say is that he is an "empirical theistic metaphysician," to which the orthodox replies that he is a "revelational theistic metaphysician."

Thus, there is a basic inconsistency in the entire liberal program. The virgin birth is unscientific because scientists

[40] C. H. Moehlman, "Liberal Protestantism," *Religion in the Twentieth Century* (Ferm, editor), p. 259.

say it is; but immortality is a precious religious truth even though as yet there is no *scientific* evidence. Creation by fiat is declared counter to scientific notions of gradual development by the liberals; yet the depositing of a soul in some human-beast, or beast-human between 1,000,000 B.C. and 5,000 B.C. is utterly bereft of scientific demonstration. Wherever liberals can get together with the scientists against the Fundamentalists they apparently do so; but when their metaphysical system calls for it they part company with the scientist just as readily as does the conservative.

This is further illustrated in R. G. Griffith's *The Necessity of Modernism.* He rejects the guiding star of Bethlehem, the herald angels, the ascension of the body of Christ and the miracle of Pentecost as "physical impossibilities" (p. 25). If he had said "physical improbabilities" our objection would not be so pointed. What he means, if I interpret him correctly, is that Nature, *as interpreted by science,* offers a world scheme that has no place for angels, stars, resurrections, or miraculous gifts. But if that picture of Nature is taken seriously it also has no place for religious modernism or God or spirit or value or immortality. What kind of legerdemain of logic does a modernist follow who can render the orthodox theistic system as *impossible* in the name of science, and yet in the name of the same science let his theistic system go unscathed?

B. *Liberals have adopted an erroneous philosophy of religion.*[41]

1. Their doctrine of immanence is erroneous. Liberalism borders closely on pantheism.[42] The continuity between God and man is made so close in their doctrine of immanence it is with extreme difficulty that liberals keep it from becoming pantheistic. In a pantheistic system miracles appear as much out of place as in a naturalistic system. In pantheism

---

[41] We can only speak in generalities. There are liberals of so many shades, opinions, and schools.

[42] "And modern liberalism, even when it is not consistently pantheistic, is at any rate pantheizing." J. Machen, *Christianity and Liberalism,* p. 63.

there is logical determinism and in naturalism, causal determinism; but in either case, determinism. Further, a God of pantheism is so integral to the process that the miracle is extraneous.

The pantheism of liberalism is subject to all the philosophical difficulties that accompany such a position, e.g., the problem of preserving the individuality of man, or of accounting for the existence of evil.

Even if liberals avoid pantheism their doctrine of immanence is an exaggeration of the truth. The difference between pantheism and liberalism must be that in liberalism God is in some sense transcendent. *If that is true the supernatural is then conceivable.* The conceivability of miracles is all we urge at this point.

If God cannot interact with human history transcendently (miracles, prophecy, virgin birth, etc.), He can only do so immanently. The liberal's acceptance of scientific naturalism prevents him from accepting transcendent activity of God. With the scientist he rules out all that is "irregular." But he must have his God and his religion. He can only get them back into the universe from "underneath," i.e., immanently. Religion must be "natural" to man, and God must be merged or welded to the processes of Nature. But all of this is religious, philosophical speculation. Christianity has become *another* school of philosophy. It has no uniqueness nor any authority nor special position. Is Hitler or Stalin or Lenin to be *greatly* blamed if they have rejected simply *another* philosophical system? If the liberal be driven to the wall and if his ultimate foundations be tortured out of him he must say "these are the best metaphysical speculations I can give." If he says this, he admits Christianity is just another school in the perpetual emergence of philosophical schools. If he states, "God has revealed Himself in history" (whatever he may mean by that), he has admitted the transcendent and the conceivability of miracles.

What we are trying to say, in part, is that the liberal wishes liberalism to be treated as if infallibly established when he deals with race prejudice, minority groups, and ownership of property; but when faced with the stiff philosophical problem of the verification of his religion, he must admit that it is a matter of probability of the best interpretation he can make and culpable of all the weaknesses and errors that characterize any philosophical system. How then can he consistently proclaim the brotherhood of man and racial tolerance or pacifism with such intensity of conviction, and yet admit that his religious metaphysics rests on the same tenuous line of reasoning which any philosophy rests on?

His only escape is to retreat to transcendence to thus gain the necessary authority he needs to propound his dogmas—for that is what they are. But if he does this then he will find out what Newman found out, namely, that just as Anglo-Catholicism was inconsistent Romanism, so liberal transcendentalism is inconsistent orthodoxy.

2. The liberal's doctrine of the nature of religion is wrong. There is such a diversity of opinion at this score that is is hard to shoot at liberalism with anything less than a double-barreled shotgun to get the appropriate spread. In essence they all partake of the same fundamental structure. Whereas Catholicism is ground in the authority of the Church, and orthodoxy in an infallible Bible, liberalism grounds itself autonomously in *something psychological.* It may be in morality (Kant), or feeling of dependence (Schleiermacher), or filial piety (Sabatier), or valuation (Höffding), but it is a grounding in something other than revelation.

In order to do this a Christian philosophy must (i) directly break with the historic Christian position as found in the New Testament records, and (ii) face all the infirmities of any religion grounded purely in philosophy or psychology.

Granted that religious activity, subjectively considered, is a type of psychological response. But liberalism practically turns the response into object, i.e., confuses the psychological nature of religion with the objective nature of religion. There still remain the profound theological problems of (1) morality in reference to what? (2) feeling toward what God? (3) valuation of what enduring entities? or filial piety with which God?

As soon as the objective element of religion is considered, i.e., *that toward which religious act is directed,* the purely subjective considerations of liberalism are ended. Many liberals do engage in consideration of the objective referents of religious act. *As soon as they do, the supernatural becomes at least a problem* for religion. Religion must now be related to the world of fact and history, i.e., has God ever been manifest in Nature or history?

3. Liberal theories of the Bible are wrong. It was conceivable that the radical theories of the nineteenth century were too restrained. The twentieth century might have seen a movement in criticism that would make the radicalism of Wellhausen seem rather tame. Certainly, the trend of much of Old and New Testament scholarship is away from the more radical development and towards a more conservative development. The present conservative tendency in Old Testament scholarship is a most remarkable phenomenon.

It would be claiming too much to say critics were becoming thoroughly conservative as it would be claiming too much to say that archaeology has verified everything in the Old Testament or solved all our problems. But it is not too much to say that as the evidence increases it increases for the more conservative viewpoint of the Old Testament rather than the more radical. It is of some moment when outstanding archaeologists admit that the radical critics of the past century were far too extreme and that the trend of criticism is in a conservative direction. Furthermore, it has not only been the conservatives and fundamentalists that have retained traditional view of the Bible, but many competent Jewish and Catholic scholars have done so too.[43]

The conservative insists that (1) the antisupernatural bias of the liberal; (2) his evolutionary view of the religion of Israel; (3) his *unchecked* methodology of radical criticism; (4) his intrenched antipathy to conservative theology; and (5) his arbitrary exegesis prevent him from adequately seeing the true nature of the Bible. If the sins of radical critics be listed we would suggest the following:

a) They became so intent on the critical study of the Bible they neglected the theological study of it. The sympathetic and spiritual understanding of a document which comes through its theological study was sacrificed in the too eager search for documents, emendations, and redactions. As a result the genuine spiritual and theological magnitude of the Bible became lost. The noble ox was buried neath a heap of winnowing straw.

b) They became so enamored with such categories as "continuity," "borrowing," "development," and "progress" that the uniqueness, the originality, and the peculiarity of Biblical religion became obscured. It has been only the last few years that works on the Old Testament have appeared stressing the *uniqueness* of Old Testament religion rather than its continuity with ancient religions.

c) They became so enmeshed in the modernistic theology that all they could see in the Bible of any merit were examples of the beliefs of religious modernism. This is quite a contrast to contemporary *realistic exegesis* that can scarcely find anything in the Bible of the older religious liberalism.

d) They became so engrossed in their own theory of religious epistemology and in their harmless conception of revelation that they could not detect anything in the Bible

[43] Cf. Felix A. Levy, "Contemporary Trends in Jewish Bible Study," pp. 98–115, and, James Harrel Cobb, "Current Trends in Catholic Bible Study," pp. 116–128, both in Willoughby, editor, *The Study of the Bible Today and Tomorrow.*

that hinted at, shall we say, as "existential" experience, or any concept of revelation as found in contemporary neo-orthodox exegesis.

The result is that liberalism had become so entrapped in its own presuppositions it could no longer understand the nature of the Bible. It is of importance to note that the best and most serious exegesis in both Testaments is done today either by men of conservative or realistic convictions, or of neo-orthodox persuasion, i.e., by men freed to a large degree from the crippling assumptions of older biblical rationalism.

The author by no means denies the place and function of literary criticism. Unless we engage in literary criticism we are too credulous. Literary criticism alone can tell us if the documents we revere so highly are authentic and genuine. We want a faith grounded in a Bible with a respectable pedigree. The author has no sympathy with Fundamentalists of the narrow pietistic school who consider all Biblical introduction as unnecessary, and who think that the certainty of religious experience gives them a high hand to be dogmatic in literary criticism. He is aware of the inconsistency of many of the brethren who only too eagerly apply critical canons to false cult literature, yet object to any such treatment of the Bible—a clear case of special pleading. His quarrel is with the radical critic who rules out any considerations of inspiration or providence or the supernatural. He also objects to the identification of scholarship or science with radical views of the Bible. He believes firmly that the highest scholarship and soundest learning may go with a reverend and devout approach to literary criticism. He also resists the disjunctive type of reasoning which states that we either believe in inspiration and some magical theory of the origin of the Bible, or in radical criticism and no theory of inspiration. We believe in the conjunctive relationship of *inspiration and criticism.*

Summary: In view of our analyses we feel justified in stating that religious modernism cannot rule out the conceivability of miracles. Religious liberalism may believe that religion is in a stronger position without them, but the point being made is simply this: Is the supernatural conceivable or inconceivable?

Neither science, nor naturalism, nor modernism can rule out the supernatural on *a priori* grounds. *If the supernatural is conceivable,*[44] *then there is conceivable evidence for its presence in Biblical religion.* It is the purpose of the rest of this volume to demonstrate that the possibility of the supernatural is in Christianity an actuality, and that the evidence is sufficient to justify a genuine and responsible act of faith.

[44] One of the finest analyses of what is credible and incredible, possible and impossible, will be found in H. Bett, *The Reality of the Religious Life.* Bett argues very ably, and to us conclusively, that science by no means has proved the impossibility or incredibility of miracle, providence, and prayer.

CHAPTER III

SUPERNATURAL VERIFICATION THROUGH FULFILLED PROPHECY

IT IS GENERALLY ACCEPTED among Old Testament scholars that the fundamental notion of the word *prophecy* is not that of prediction, but of declaring God's will and Word. But some have assumed that in having said that, they have eliminated the predictive element from prophecy. However, although the prophet is primarily a *forth-teller*, he is also a *fore-teller*. Forth-telling often involved fore-telling, for knowledge of the *future* dispositions of God was necessary to influence *present* conduct.

Prophecy is not mere mantic display but is a profoundly religious and ethical activity. The ethical and spiritual ministries of the prophet are co-mingled with the predictive as is evident in page after page of Old Testament books. If it was a mistake to emphasize the apologetic element out of all proportion and in neglect of the religious and spiritual ministries of the prophet, it is as much a mistake to ignore the predictive elements to heighten the ethical and spiritual elements. Both elements are there and it is purely for our present apologetic purposes that we are treating solely the predictive element of prophecy.

The argument from prophecy is essentially the argument from omniscience. Limited human beings know the future only if it is told them by an omniscient Being. Thus, in predictive prophecy God informs the prophet of the future. The nature of that prophetic inspiration need not detain us here, but we do indicate that the constant objection of the liberal to the conservative notion of inspiration and prophecy is frequently misrepresentation rather than representation. If the conservative is in the danger of violating the sacredness of human personality by an amoral thrust of knowledge upon the prophet, the liberal is in a far greater danger of hedging and circumscribing the sovereignty and freedom of Almighty God. Whatever the means of inspiration might have been, certainly we have before our eyes the concrete phenomena and manifestation of it in prophetic Scripture, and for our argument all we need is the concrete manifestation.

I. Prophecy Defined

In a remarkably clear definition M'Ilvaine defines prophecy as "a declaration of future events, such as no human wisdom or forecast is sufficient to make—depending on a knowledge of the innumerable contingencies of human affairs, which belongs exclusively to the omniscience of God; so that from its very nature prophecy must be divine revelation."[1]

First of all, the prophecy must be more than a good guess or a conjecture. It must possess sufficient precision so as to be capable of verification by means of the fulfillment. Furthermore, prophecy deals with contingencies, i.e., those events that "just happen" not with events in a causal order. That is, prophecy deals with human affairs which are to human mentality contingent and therefore unpredictable. Predictions in science deal with a causal order and are therefore not genuine prophetic predictions. Prophecy is thus by its nature a manifestation of the supernatural light of God. The reason for this is derived from an inspection of the powers of the human mind. We can probe into the past by the means of the science of historiography. We can probe into space by virtue of the

[1] E. P. M'Ilvaine, *The Evidences of Christianity*, p. 238.

telescope and the ancilliary sciences developed around astronomy, e.g., photography and spectroscopy But we have no mental faculty of prescience. We may occasionally predict a trend in business or a movement in politics, but there is no knowledge of the future that compares in certainty and accuracy with our knowledge of past time and outer space.

Scientific predictions are not of the same order as prophecy. Predictions of eclipses or the appearances of comets are judgments with a causal, not a contingent, system. The prediction is in reality a judgment of confidence in the continued orderly routine of nature. Predictions within a causal nexus as in chemistry, physics, or biology are therefore not prophecies. Nor are vague generalizations prophecy, such as "it will rain next year," or "airplanes will fly faster," or "politics will move more toward paternalism." These are either statements about a causal state of affairs, e.g., weather predictions, or are assumptions from an already known and detectable trend, such as predictions about political conditions. Further, they are characterized by great generality. Therefore, these general assumptions are not of the prophetic order.

II. BIBLICAL REFERENCES TO PROPHECY

There is a wealth of material on prophecy in the Bible, but there are two very significant passages which deal with the *evidential value* of prophecy which illustrate the contention that fulfilled prophecy is not the invention of the apologist, but in itself is a Biblical claim. First, in Deuteronomy 18 God warns Israel not to contaminate himself with the religious rites and theologies of the peoples in the Promised Land. Rather, Israel was to await the Great Prophet which God Himself shall raise up (vv. 9–19). But there is the danger that someone shall claim to be a prophet when he is not. "But the prophet, that shall speak a word presumptuously in my name, which I have not commanded him to speak, or that shall speak in the name of other gods, that same prophet shall die"

(v. 20, A.R.V.). "And if thou say in thy heart, How shall we know the word which Jehovah hath not spoken? when a prophet speaketh in the name of Jehovah, *if the thing follow not, nor come to pass,* that is the thing which Jehovah hath not spoken: the prophet hath spoken it presumptuously, thou shalt not be afraid of him" (vv. 21, 22, A.R.V.). This passage is unmistakably clear in showing that *fulfilled prediction* was the means of determining what God said. Fulfilled prophecy is thus denoted by God Himself as His means of indicating to us that He is speaking.

The same truth is contained in Isaiah 41:22, 23 in which God challenges the pagan gods. How is the true God distinguished from the false gods? Let these pagan gods "bring forth, and show us *what shall happen:* let them show the former things, what they be, that we may consider them, and know the latter end of them; or declare us *things to come.* Show the things that are to come hereafter, *that we may know that ye are gods.*" It is by the principle of omniscience manifested by a knowledge of the contingent future which proves Jehovah to be true, and other gods to be false. Liberal scholarship with a distaste for evidences may rule such an argument out, but that it has a Biblical basis may not be ruled out. We do not see how the force of these two passages can be either abated or eliminated.

III. The Characteristics of Biblical Prophecy

In order to fully understand the argument from fulfilled prophecy, a more comprehensive understanding of its nature is essential.

A. Real prophecy is peculiar to the Bible. This does not mean that other religions do not have prophetic elements. But whereas prophecy is an occasional phenomenon of non-Christian religions, it is part and parcel of Biblical religion. Prophecy is not part of the very fiber of non-Christian religions, and is believed because the system is already believed.

But Biblical prophecy is not only deeply buried in the very tissues of the Old Testament religion; *it was a means of establishing it.* Israel constantly declined from the original revelation of the law and covenant through Moses, and was recalled by the prophetic ministry. It was the prophetic ministry that called people out of idolatry and sin, back to the true God. And, part of the prophetic word was the predictive word, for it was by the predictive word that people could differentiate between the false prophet and the true prophet. *Fulfilled prophecy then was part of the means of establishing Old Testament religion.*

B. Prophecy pervades the entire Bible. It is not an isolated phenomenon, but prophetic material is found in the historical books, in the poetical and wisdom books, and in the prophets. It is found in the Gospels and Epistles, and the Bible concludes with a rather large prophetic volume. Here again it is to be noted that prophecy has deeply and vitally penetrated into the very heart of Biblical religion.

C. Prophecy in many cases is very minute in its specifications. It is not, as shall be dealt with later, a matter of vague generalization or happy guesses. People are named before birth; kingdoms are outlined before their historical existence; battles are described before occurring, and personal destinies are delineated before the persons themselves are born.

D. Prophecy frequently deals with the very remote in time and with people or kingdoms that do not as yet exist. Certainly, if the traditional date of Daniel be accepted, and if Rome is the fourth kingdom of Daniel, the prescience of the Book is incontrovertible. It is again true if Isaiah be given its traditional dating that specific detailed predictions have amazing fulfillments. However, the actual examples of fulfilled prophecy that we shall give below will supply many cases in which even the latest dating of the books do not damage the argument from fulfilled prediction.

E. The fulfillment of the prophecy is clear; in other words, fulfillment is not equivocal or ambiguous. This does not mean that this is so in every case. That would be certainly overstating the argument; but it is true that in many cases the fulfillment is unequivocal and unambiguous. Prediction itself is not proof of supernaturally known information. It is the fulfillment that indicates the presence of the supernatural, and the fulfillment of prophecy is *"evidence before our eyes addressed to our senses."*[2]

F. One real case of fulfilled prophecy would establish a supernatural act. But if our interpretation of the prophetic passages be correct, there are great numbers of them. One unequivocal miracle, one indubitable fulfilled prophecy would show the fallacy of naturalism, for the causal web of the universe would be ruptured at that point through which the supernatural is intruded. Therefore, radical doubt must be certain it has silenced the testimony of all prophecies, whereas the Christian asserts that rather than resting the case on one prophecy, we have dozens at our beck and call.

G. Prophecy is occasionally of a nature as to be in exact opposition as to what unguided human intelligence would predict. This is especially true of great cities or civilizations whose doom is predicted while the power of the city or state had no signs of waning. Relevant to this are the predictions about the destruction of Jerusalem, the downfall of Nineveh, the capture of Babylon, and the rout of the Assyrians.

Now the success of the Bible in reference to prophecy is an amazing thing because man has not been lacking in a desire to know the future. In fact, he has exerted a great deal of energy in that very direction. A knowledge of the future is of unmeasured value to most of us, e.g., our financial ventures, our physical welfare in occasion of possible war, or the outcome of a marriage for weal or woe. Yet for all mankind's efforts the future still hangs as a heavy, black impenetrable curtain. In

[2] M'Ilvaine, *op. cit.*, p. 242. Italics are his.

the pages of Holy Scripture alone is there a shaft of light that can dart ahead of the human race and illuminate the future so that we may know things that shall come to pass.

IV. Arguments Against Prophecy

A. *The language is vague.* The first objection affirms that prophetic utterances are vague of nature so that fulfillment is not difficult to find. If the greens of a golf course were funnel-shaped, the holes-in-one and par scores would be greatly increased. A shot with a general measure of accuracy by reason of the shape of the greens takes on the appearance of a highly accurate shot. So, it is argued, vague predictions appear to be very sharp when we locate their fulfillment; but because of the vagueness of the prophecy any number of possible fulfillments could be latched onto. For example, if one were to utter in the year 1900 A.D. that "a great power shall rise up and do much harm," the prophet could simply wait for the next great war and say, "This is it," and he would certainly have a great selection to choose from in the twentieth century.

Now it is to be granted that not all prophecy is *sharp*. Some predictions do partake of a generality of language, e.g., Genesis 3:15 does not in itself indicate the precise nature of the details of its fulfillment. Students of the Old Testament are not amiss when they affirm that history is the best interpreter of prophecy. However, two observations are in order.

1. Predictions are sharpened by fulfillments. There is a measure of detail in a prophecy that is not apparent at the time of its utterance which is sharpened by fulfillment. Further, several such examples would indicate that more than human factors are at work. The calculus of probability starts to pile up in advantage for the Christian.

2. If the critic is to make his case he must show that all fulfilled prophecies are vague of nature. Showing that three or four or ten or twenty are vague is not sufficient. As long as

there is the possibility of one or more cases unresolved by this method the antisupernatural position stands in jeopardy. However, when we give specific examples we hope to indicate how many cases there are that are far too specific to be explained away as being vague predictions.

B. *The prophecies are artificially fulfilled.* No doubt some of the statements of the prophets could be fulfilled by the might and will of some man. A man could go to Bethlehem for the birth of his child and claim fulfillment of Micah 5:2. In reply to this it must again be stated that it cannot be considered adequate to show that some or many prophecies were or could be artificially fulfilled. *The enemy of Christianity must silence all of our guns: we need to fire only one of them.* Therefore, all the potentially fulfilled prophecies must be explained away on this basis or the objection is futile.

Many prophecies are beyond the contrivance of man to artificially fulfill.

1. How could one man arrange the events for the Babylonian captivity?

2. How could one man artificially fulfill the prophecies of the return from Babylon?

3. How could the predictions of the great nations and their destinies be controlled by one man?

The concrete evidence of fulfilled prophecy veritably crushes the life out of this objection.

C. *The prophecies were written after the events.* This is a very frequent device used to break the back of lucidly clear predictions and fulfillments, e.g., those about the return from the captivities in Isaiah 40–66, those of the book of Daniel, and those of the destruction of Jerusalem (Matthew 24, 25). As a result, critics date these prophecies after the events.

1. It must be observed that a reversal in higher criticism at this point would rupture the entire antisupernatural fabric of the critic's philosophy. Just when most radical criticism had rested its oars, archaeologists started turning up disturb-

ing evidence. First came the John Rylands fragment of the Gospel of John pushing the date of John back to the close of the first century A.D. Sir Frederic Kenyon in his Presidential Address to the Victoria Institute expressed extreme displeasure with critics of the Gospel who went their way completely ignoring this manuscriptal evidence.[3] Now has come the discovery of the Dead Sea Scrolls with manuscripts of Isaiah and Daniel, and as we write we hear that another cave with more manuscripts has been discovered. It would certainly be arrogant scholarship and not scientific empiricism to assert today that no evidence shall ever be found that goes contrary to radical Old Testament or New Testament criticism. On the other hand, the hope of the conservative cannot be considered idle that someday a real bit of evidence will turn up that will indubitably establish the conservative opinion. Thus, if a fragment of Daniel or Isaiah should turn up which itself antedates its fulfillment, the radical critic's position will be annihilated. As yet no such evidence is in, but the evidence is getting warmer.

2. We shall endeavor to show that even if the prophecies are dated by the critics they still fall outside the possibility of being explained as prophecies after the event. In fact, that shall be the weight of our examples we shall give at the conclusion of this discussion.

3. Here again it must be demonstrated that such a hypothesis must account for all the prophecies. Every gun must be spiked. This we do not think the evidence will permit.

D. *It is a matter of misinterpretation.* It is argued on the one hand that some prophecies are a mere coincidence of language such as "out of Egypt I have called my son" (Hosea 11:1 with Matthew 2:15); and on the other hand, that it is a case of misinterpretation, e.g., interpreting Isaiah 53 as Messianic.

1. It is freely admitted that not all of the Old Testament

---

[3] *Journal of the Transactions of the Victoria Institute,* LXXXII, 223–231.

verses quoted in the New Testament are quoted as fulfilled predictions. Sometimes the Old Testament is quoted because of coincidence of language or thought, and students of this problem usually refer to Romans 10:5–8 as an example.

2. It cannot be questioned that both radical Protestant scholars and Jewish exegetes resort to every conceivable type of exegetical maneuvering to break the back of Messianic passages. Very evidently, if Isaiah 53 is taken in the way the New Testament takes it, it is Messianic and it is fulfilled in Christ. The antisupernatural bias of the liberal is so great that absolutely every predictive prophecy must be leveled to the ground. We directly claim that this is not fair and honest exegesis, giving due and impartial respect to the facts, but a spirit of exegesis that knows its conclusions before it commences its inductions.

3. It must be demonstrated that *all* so-called fulfilled Scriptures are matters of misinterpretation. This we do not think possible. The case for divine verification through fulfilled prophecy remains even when some most amazing concessions (for sake of argument) are granted the radical critic.

E. *The same phenomenon occurs in other religions.* To answer this objection we summon to court R. S. Foster and M'Ilvaine. Foster writes: "No well-accredited prophecy is found in any other book or even oral tradition now extant, or that has ever been extant in the world. The oracles of heathenism are not to be classed as exceptions. There is not a single one of them that meets the tests required to prove supernatural agency, which every Scripture prophecy evinces. So far as we have been able to find there is not exception to this sweeping remark."[4] M'Ilvaine observes that "The history of pagan nations indeed abounds with stories of auguries and oracles and detached predictions . . . . But an immeasurable distance separates all the pretended oracles of paganism from the dignity of the prophecies of the Bible. The avowed end

[4] R. S. Foster, *The Supernatural Book*, p. 111.

of the former was to satisfy some tribal curiosity, or aid the designs of some military or political leader. . . . Who could think of comparing such pitiful mockeries of divine omniscience with the dignified and sublime and holy prophecies which are spread out so openly and widely in the Scriptures?"[5]

V. The Concrete Data of Fulfilled Prophecy

A. *General considerations.*

1. We shall limit our concrete examples to the Minor Prophets. Since the prophetic material is so great some limitation of material is necessary. However, by so limiting our scope to the Minor Prophets we would not give the impression that that is all the data available. There are great and important prophecies all the way through the Old Testament. Entire treatises have been devoted to the examination of this material. There are prophecies of the destinies of the Jews both in terms of individual tribal predictions and of the people as a whole; prophecies about individuals both Jew and Gentile; prophecies about the course of nations—their successes and their defeats; and Messianic prophecies mentioned in the New Testament. There is a great wealth of material which by special limitation of subject matter is obscured.

2. There is a prophetic element in the typology of Holy Scripture. Typology is not in good repute with radical scholars for they consider the whole matter a case of artificial tampering with the Old Testament record. However, it is a judgment based upon their antisupernatural view of the Bible and the Christian religion. According to the New Testament the older economy had many typical anticipations of the New, and this is not a matter of forced exegesis but is the nature of the case. The Old Testament period was a period of theological education by special use, in part, of the material and concrete. The Tabernacle was given as a means of teaching

[5] *Op. cit.,* pp. 246–247.

theology in terms of a ritual, of furniture, of persons, of actions. The Book of Hebrews asserts this and proceeds to give examples of the theological significance of these Old Testament material elements. To break with typology one must break with the authority of the New Testament. It is our assertion that (1) by the very nature of the relationship of the Old and New Testaments, namely, that the former is predictive, anticipatory, and instructive of the New, and (2) by the natural, sensible, and chaste typology of Hebrews, that typology is a genuine form of predictive prophecy, and although symbolic of nature, forms part of the chain of evidence for the argument from fulfilled prophecy. To our mind the typology of the brazen altar, the laver, the mercy-seat, etc., are not artificial contrivances, but are wonderful and marvelous anticipations of our great salvation in Christ. A radical antisupernatural approach to the Bible can obviously *a priori* leave no room for the typical interpretation of the Tabernacle and so typological studies are objects of deep scorn to radical critics. We rebut that the beautiful harmony of Hebrews and Leviticus is natural, not strained.

3. The general anticipation of Christ in the Old Testament.

Whereas most nations look to the past to some Golden Age, the Jews looked to the future for their day of glory. Central to their anticipations was the figure of the Messiah. The strength of a given proposition is its relatedness and connectedness to a system, and so the individual prophecies of Christ gain evidential value and added depth as they are related to the general portrait of an expected Messiah. It is difficult to controvert the fact that, first, such a Messiah is both recorded in the Old Testament and expected among the Jews, and that, second, a most credible case can be made for Jesus of Nazareth as the Messiah. There is value in examining each individual Scripture anticipating the Messiah, and there is value in seeing the entire picture painted. Critics too minutely questioning each individual text are accustomed to confuse the chemistry of paints with art. Such a passage as Micah 5:2 which predicts the birthplace of the Messiah has much more evidential strength when viewed as part of the entire scheme of Messianic prophecy, than when isolated from the same and analyzed with the chemistry of radical criticism.

Furthermore, evidence appears in a vastly different light when the actual state of affairs is known than when it is not known. Imagine a long, complicated, debated murder trial in which the lawyer for the defense uses every device known to the legal profession to save his client. Every bit of evidence suggested by the prosecution is challenged, or made equivocal or ambiguous. The evidence suggested by the prosecution pales under each counterattack. However, by sheer dint of the evidence the criminal appears to be more probably guilty than innocent. The jury brings in the decision of *guilty*. Forthwith the criminal breaks down and confesses all. What a difference is now made in the nature of the evidence! The devices of the defendant's attorney are now apparent. No longer is it possible to take the evidence and make it equivocal or ambiguous. Knowing the true state of affairs the evidence now appears in its true light. As individual facts they remain the same after the confession as before; but as part of a comprehensive story they now loom as incontrovertible evidence. So the radical critics can attack every single Messianic Scripture and try to blunt its force or make its testimony equivocal or ambiguous. But if Jesus of Nazareth really is the Messiah, then Old Testament Christology stands out in an entirely new light. The individual passages are now seen in terms of the true plot, or the real facts of the case. What can be made uncertain *if the plot is not known* now is incontrovertible because *the plot is now known*.

The conservative looks at a Messianic passage far differently from a radical critic. The radical critic admits no supernatural element, tries to see the prophecy completely within the local situation, and denies the reference to Christ. The conservative approaches the Messianic passages with a supernatural philosophy of religion, sees the passages as links in the drama of Messianic revelation, and finds fulfillment in Christ. This divergence of approach can readily be seen by a comparison of the radical critics' commentary, *The International Critical Commentary,* and any good conservative Old Testament commentary. In the former there is a steady, cool, critical, skeptical treatment of every single predictive passage. It is made a case of "prediction after the event," or denied any predictive quality. If the predictive element is unequivocal, the prophecy is placed after the fulfillment; if the prophecy can in some way be interpreted as nonpredictive, then that is done. In the latter is a spiritual warmth, insight, and sympathy with the Biblical writer. When the critic is through with an Old Testament prophet he has a jumble of verses, notions, and concepts, artfully or artlessly strung together bereft of all genuine spiritual vitality and strength.

There is no small wonder, therefore, that the critic never finds Christ in the Old Testament. His philosophy of religion, his notions of theology, and his methodology of Biblical criticism are all such as to prevent him from seeing anything genuinely spiritual, predictive, or Christological even if it is there. But the conservative, coming with a very different set of guiding principles, finds the prophets a wealth of spiritual treasures, and the vehicle of much Christological truth.

4. There is not only a general anticipation of Christ in the Old Testament; there is also the general anticipation of Christianity. Let us get the matter correctly before us. There is *specific* anticipation of both. Consider the number of verses quoted in the New Testament in reference to Christ. The New Testament appeals to the Old in reference to His place of birth, His trip to Egypt, His residence at Nazareth, His Messianic call, His healing ministry, His death and resurrection. Bible dictionaries and study editions of the Bible con-

tain all this information in codified form. The New Testament also quotes the Old in reference to many things about Christianity. For example Paul makes over seventy direct quotes from the Old Testament and makes over one hundred allusions. The New Testament as a whole contains well over six hundred quotations or allusions to the Old Testament. There is, therefore, a good deal of specific anticipation of Christ and Christianity.

But we have more in mind at this juncture the anticipatory spirit of the Old Testament, namely, that a great Person was coming, and a higher, more dynamic type of religion would be ushered in. This is the thesis of Alan Richardson in his chapter on prophecy in his *Christian Apologetics.* (We do certainly disagree with Richardson's position that the case for literal interpretation and literal fulfillment of prophecy must be given up. We believe in the "Lord of truth" as much as he does, and therefore we are very much interested in the facts of the case. We feel after reading his chapter that he is not fair to the concrete phenomena of predictive prophecy. He has simply capitulated to the radical view of Old Testament prophecy. Perhaps he has taken his Bible in hand and studied prediction after prediction and come to the conclusion that all is a matter of forced exegesis or coincidence of language. Perhaps he is scared by the invectives that one must expect if a stand for predictive prophecy be taken in a generation of radical criticism and intense antisupernaturalism.) However, in his chapter there is a genuine contribution to the argument from prophecy, namely, that the entire Old Testament economy in its broad outlines and outlook is anticipatory of, and finds its realization in, Christianity. The argument from specific prophecies and the argument from general anticipation, both in reference to Christ and Christianity, are mutually supporting, and are evidences that intersect and so determine a definite fact. Fischer in stating the argument from general anticipation of Christianity writes: "Follow back the course of prophecy, and you find traces of this expectation . . . in the earliest records of Hebrew history. Concede all that, with any show of reason, can be said about the variety in the ideals and anticipations of the Hebrew prophets, there remains enough of correspondence to them in the origin, character, and progress of Christianity to suggest a problem not easy to be solved on any naturalistic hypothesis."[5a]

B. *Specific predictions and their fulfillments.* We now come to the concrete data of fulfilled prophecy. First, we have limited ourselves to various passages in the Minor Prophets for reasons of economy of space. Those students interested in greater details than here contained may consult the classic on this matter, Keith, *On Prophecy*, or Edghill, *The Evidential Value of Prophecy*, although the latter tends to make too many concessions to the radical view of the Old Testament. For our authorities we have used: R. Pheiffer, *An Introduction to the Old Testament*; E. A. Edghill, *An Inquiry into the Evidential Value of Prophecy*; Henderson, *Commentary on the Minor Prophets*; Lange, editor, *Commentary on the Minor Prophets*; *The International Critical Commentary* (hereafter designated as ICC); *The Cambridge Bible* (hereafter designated by CB); Feinberg, *The Major Messages of the Minor Prophets*; Pearson, *The Prophecy of Joel*; Keil and Delitzsch, *Minor Prophets* (hereafter designated by KD); Jamieson, Fausset, and Brown, *Commentary* (Vol. IV, Jeremiah through Malachi, and hereafter designated by JFB). Furthermore, in practically every case we have given the radical the benefit of the doubt in dating the prophecies, so that the examples of fulfilled predictions *lie outside the dates of the passages set by the radical critic.* These dates have been determined from Pheiffer and the ICC. We have thereby tried to silence every rebuttal on the grounds of *vaticinium post even-*

[5a] G. P. Fischer, *The Grounds of Theistic and Christian Belief*, p. 323. This reminds us of J. Orr: "Date your books when you will, this religion is not explicable save on the hypothesis of Revelation!" *The Christian View of God and the World*, p. 15.

tum. If our exegesis and treatment of these passages in the Minor Prophets is fair and accurate to the facts, then the case for divine verification of the Christian religion is thereby made.

1. *Hosea*

Hosea 1; 4, 5, "And the Lord said unto him, Call his name Jezreel; for yet a little while, and I will avenge the blood of Jezreel upon the house of Jehu, and will cause to cease the kingdom of the house of Israel. And it shall come to pass at that day, that I will break the bow of Israel in the valley of Jezreel." These two verses state that Israel, as a military force and as a national commonwealth, was to pass out of existence. There is no mention here of momentary defeat or temporary submergence. To the contrary, permanent destruction as a kingdom is predicted. Most commentators see the fulfillment of this progressively, first in the corruption of the kings of Israel, and secondly in the Assyrian captivity. For example, Feinberg writes:

> Though the northern kingdom was prospering at the time and all seemed well, Hosea forewarned of the end of Jehu's dynasty and the destruction of the northern kingdom with its military power in the valley of Jezreel . . . . These events took place, though at least forty years apart, just as foretold . . . . Hosea lived to see this prophecy realized in Shalmaneser's victory at Betharbel.[6]

Thus, by the slaughter of Zechariah by Shallum, the fourth and last of Jehu's line, the prophecy of verse 4 receives its first fulfillment, and in the successive miserable histories of the

---

[6] C. L. Feinberg, *Hosea: God's Love for Israel* (in the series, *The Major Messages of the Minor Prophets*), pp. 15, 16. T. K. Cheyne in *Cambridge Bible* writes: "Hosea represents . . . the destruction of the northern kingdom as synchronizing with the overthrow of Jehu's dynasty. This was a remarkable proof of the insight into God's purposes. [He] saw the beginning of the end, though the final catastrophe (722) took place about nineteen years later than the death of Jeroboam II (741)." Keil writes: "Of the five kings who followed Zechariah, only one, viz., Menahem, died a natural death and was succeeded by his son. The rest were all dethroned and murdered by conspirators, so that the overthrow of the house of Jehu may well be called 'the beginning of the end, the commencement of the process of decomposition.'"

kings of Israel, its complete fulfillment. The defeat and captivity of Israel by the Assyrians fulfills verse 5. Never again has Israel been a military power or a kingdom. The return from the captivities was primarily a movement of Judah proper.

Hosea 1:7, "But I will have mercy upon the house of Judah, and will save them by the Lord their God, and will not save them by bow, nor by sword, nor by battle, by horses, nor by horsemen." Here is a prophecy for Judah just the opposite of that of Israel. Could a more reliable test of prophecy be set forth? Israel was to perish militarily and as a nation. Judah is to be preserved by neither sword nor by power.

The tribe of Judah was attacked and threatened by Sennacherib (II Kings 19:35). Yet Judah was delivered by a marvelous intervention of God. *"And though they were afterwards carried away to Babylon, their civil polity was restored, which was not the case with the Israelites,"* writes Henderson.[7]

The opposite predictions of the histories of Israel and Judah, and their remarkable fulfillment speak of divine inspiration of Hosea.

Hosea 1:11, "Then shall the children of Judah and the children of Israel be gathered together, and appoint themselves one head, and they shall come up out of the land: for great shall be the day of Jezreel." It is not possible to put too much strength in any interpretation of this verse due to the great variety of opinions by the interpreters. However, if one interpretation is followed, we have here a pointed prediction that Judah and Israel would return from captivity under the lead-

---

[7] Henderson *op. cit.* Italics are ours. Cf. also, "The miraculous deliverance of Jerusalem from Sennacherib . . . and the restoration from Babylon as here predicted, Judah governed by kings of David's line, and having the true worship of God, the temple, and the sacrifices, was to experience a mercy which was denied to Israel, as being founded and governed in apostasy from God. Not one of their kings that did not follow the sin of Jeroboam, the worship of the symbol of God, the calves, and some of them had fallen into the grossest idolatry, Baal worship, etc." JFB.

ership of one man. This then would be fulfilled in the return from the captivities under the leadership of Zerubbabel.

Hosea 3:4, "For the children of Israel shall abide many days without a king, and without a prince, and without a sacrifice, and without an image, and without an ephod, and without teraphim." Here is an amazing prediction. Israel shall be without a king or prince; he shall be without a priestly ministry; *and he shall be without idolatry.* The national life of Israel was smashed beyond repair for almost two thousand years by the captivities. There was a token reign by Zerubbabel and by the Hasmoneans, but with the coming of the Romans even token kings were ended. With the destruction of the temple in Jerusalem at 70 A.D. no regular Levitical sacrifice has been offered to this day. But then to add to this the prediction that they would be free from idolatry is phenomenal, especially when critics date the prophecy *circa* 750–44 (Pheiffer).

"It is a very remarkable peculiarity of the prediction in this verse that while it describes Israel as having neither sacrifice nor oracle, it describes her also as abstaining from image-worship, and even from those forms of heretical or heathenish divination which are known to have been in use among them for a thousand years . . . . *This was a future of her condition, which no one could have forecast from anything found in her previous history.* It is, therefore, not without point that the Prophetic Spirit lays reiterated stress upon this hitherto unknown peculiarity: 'no sacrifice and no statue; no ephod and no teraphim.' "[8]

[8] HBC, italics are ours. Cf. also Feinberg, *op. cit.,* pp. 33–34. Other prophetic material that could be appealed to in Hosea are Hosea 9:3, a prediction of the Assyrian captivity; and 9:17, the dispersion of the ten tribes as contrasted to the recovery of Judah and Benjamin.

Henderson has some very splendid remarks on 3:4 showing how remarkably this verse is fulfilled in the past history of Jews—belonging to no church, yet firmly professing belief in Jehovah; cut off from the land and submitted to a thousand trials, yet free from the idolatry of the pagans she has been scattered among.

2. Joel

Joel 2:28–32. This passage contains a promise with the following items: (a) That the Spirit of Jehovah would be poured out in an unprecedented measure; (b) that all flesh would be the recipients of it; (c) that unusual manifestations would accompany it (dreams, visions, prophecy); (d) that there would be no differentiations of sex; (e) that accompanied with it would be a gracious call to salvation; (f) that the call would extend to whomever God wished to extend it to, and (g) that this was to be before a great and notable catastrophe would fall upon the Jewish people.

Could a one-to-one correspondence of prophecy and prediction be closer than this as this prophecy is fulfilled on the day of Pentecost? (a) The New Testament promise of the coming of the Spirit was one of the great truths that Jesus Christ emphasized repeatedly. The Church-age would be also the Spirit-age. The Holy Spirit was given in the book of Acts in a measure unprecedented in divine history. (b) The Spirit was not restricted to priests, prophets, or kings but was given to all the Church, and eventually to Samaritans and Gentiles. (c) Unusual manifestations accompanied the immediate giving of the Spirit (sound from heaven, great wind, shaking of the building, speaking in tongues), and the later ministry of the Spirit (cf. I Cor. 14 and Acts *in passim*). (d) There were both men and women in the apostolic company of the day of Pentecost (Acts 1:14, "with the women"). That women should receive the Spirit in the same measure as the men is, of course, a most unusual prophecy in the Jewish economy, although not completely without precedent, e.g., as in the case of Deborah. (e) With the coming of the Spirit which accompanied Peter's speech in which he invited the multitude to salvation. (f) Peter's expression, "even as many as the Lord our God shall call" (Acts 2:39), is parallel to Joel 2:32, "and in the remnant whom the Lord shall call." (g) Finally, in language that frequently paralleled Joel 2:30–31, Jesus Christ predicted the utter desolation of Jerusalem by the Romans. So, the day of Pentecost, with its effusion of the Spirit and its call to salvation, came in generous time before the fall of Jerusalem. Further, it is well-known that the Christians, recalling the prediction of their Lord, fled the city and were spared that terrible destruction.[9]

Joel 3:6–8. In verse 4 Joel mentions the cities of Tyre and Sidon, and the seacoast cities of Palestine. In verse 6 he charges them with carrying away the Jews as captives which they did. Then Joel predicts: "Behold, I will raise them out of the place whither ye have sold them, and will return your recompense upon your own head: and I will sell your sons and your daughters into the hand of the children of Judah, and they shall sell them to the Sabeans, to a people far off" (vv. 7, 8). When Alexander the Great marched down the coast of Palestine he decimated in order Tyre, Sidon, and Phoenecia. Thirteen thousand of the inhabitants of Tyre were sold in captivity. When Sidon was taken by Artaxerxes Ochus, 40,000 perished.[10]

Furthermore, the Jews in many cases were freed from their captors and "various parts of Philistia and Phoenecia were brought under Jewish rule."[11] Thus, both features of the prophecy were fulfilled, namely, that the enemies of the Jews would go into captivity, and that the Jews would be released and actually rule over them. The Sabeans were traders like the Phoenecians and Tyrians and ranged far and wide. Thus, the Tyrians were sold to the remotest of slave traders.

3. Amos

Amos 1:3–5. Amos predicts that the military strength of Damascus would be broken by "fire"—a symbol of a conquer-

---

[9] *Infra*, in the treatment of Zechariah.
[10] Historical details are given by Lange, Henderson, HBC, and JFB. HBC cites *Diod. Sic.* (xvii, 46) as authority for 13,000 Tyrians sold into captivity by Alexander.
[11] HBC. Pheiffer dates Joel about 350 B.C.

ing army—and that "the people of Syria shall go into captivity unto Kir." This was fulfilled by Tiglath-pileser who went up "against Damascus, and took it, and carried the people of it captive to Kir, and slew Rezin" (II Kings 16:9).

Fausset notes that there is a black marble obelisk found in the central palace of Nimrod that has on it the names of Hazael and Ben-hadad of Syria as tributaries of Shalmanubar, king of Assyria.[12]

Amos 1:6–8 declares that fire shall come upon Gaza, "which shall devour the palaces thereof," and that Ashdod and Ashkelon shall both suffer similar fates. Hezekiah lashed out against Gaza (II Kings 18:18), and in order, Sennacherib, Pharaoh-necho, and Alexander the Great attacked it. The other cities mentioned were attacked by Psammeticul of Egypt, Nebuchadnezzar, the Persians, Alexander the Great, and finally the Asmoneans.[13]

Amos 1:9, 10. This is a similar prophecy that a fire would come to Tyre and its palaces. The city of Tyre was literally burned by the missiles of Nebuchadnezzar.[14]

Amos 1:13–15. This is a prediction of fire upon the wall of Rabbah, the metropolis of the Ammonites. The extensive ruins of Rabbah have been discovered by Seetzen and Burchhardt.

Amos 2:1–3. Moab is also to experience a "fire," and the *judge* is to be cut off. Through some events not now clearly known the judge was substituted for the king. It is known that Nebuchadnezzar set up judges in Tyre after he captured it. At any rate Nebuchadnezzar utterly conquered Moab and

---

[12] JFB. He also agrees that Tiglath-pileser fulfilled the prophecy.
[13] JFB, Henderson.
[14] Cf. Feinberg, *op. cit.*, p. 44, HBC, and JFB. The latter says: "The Phoenecians had aided the Syrian Ben-hadad in his unsuccessful rebellion against Shalmanubar. But as yet Amos had no indication to suggest his prophecy of their coming doom . . . Sargon, according to Assyrian inscriptions, took Tyre and imposed tribute on Cyprus . . . . Many parts of Tyre were burned by fiery missiles of the Chaldeans under Nebuchadnezzar . . . . Alexander of Macedon subsequently overthrew it."

from then on it ceased to exist as a nation being finally taken over by the Arabs.

Amos 2:4, 5. The Jews are not to escape the fire either. And so, the palaces of Jerusalem and much of the city was destroyed by fire when it was conquered by Nebuchadnezzar in 586 B.C.[15]

Amos 3:12–15. Doom is here predicted for Samaria, and this doom was fulfilled when Shalmaneser took the city, and in the deportation by Esarhaddon. There has been much archaeological confirmation of the mention here of ivories with Samaria, and also the state of ruin of Samaria.

Amos 5:27 predicts a captivity "beyond Damascus." This, of course, was fulfilled in the Assyrian and Babylonian captivities that followed more than a hundred years later.[16]

4. Obadiah

Obadiah is a prophecy directed at the Edomites in which it is declared that (a) the heathen would conquer them, and (b) the Jews would conquer them. By substantial inferential reasoning, in the presence of no *specific* historical data, it has been demonstrated that Nebuchadnezzar conquered the Edomites. Subsequently it is known for sure that the Nabatheans inhabited the land. The Romans eventually thoroughly cleaned up any remaining traces of the Edomites, and they passed out of existence. Therefore, the prophecy that Edom would be conquered by the heathen and made insignificant has been fulfilled.

That the Jews conquered them is proved by reference to I Maccabees 5:3 and to Josephus' *Antiquities* (XII, 18, 1). They were attacked successively by John Hyrcanus and Simon of Gerasa. Therefore, the prediction that the Jews too would conquer them has been fulfilled.[17]

---

[15] Cf. II Kings 25:9, Feinberg, *op. cit.*, and KD.

[16] Amos 6:14 also is relevant here. This verse predicts a whole region to be inflicted with agony. This was fulfilled in the invasion of Tiglath-pileser.

[17] Greater details will be found in KD, and HBC.

Obadiah 17–21 has further interesting details. It states that although Edom shall perish, "upon mount Zion shall be deliverance, and there shall be holiness; and the house of Jacob shall possess their possessions" (v. 17). The Jews, though carried away captive, did return to Jerusalem and "possess their possessions." It further states that "the house of Jacob shall be a fire, and the house of Joseph a flame, and the house of Esau for stubble, and they shall kindle in them, and devour them; and there shall not be any remaining of the house of Esau." As mentioned *supra* after the return from the captivities the Jews did attack the Edomites and did subdue them, and eventually by the "mopping up" tactics of the Romans caused the house to disappear.[18]

Verses 19, 20 give a list of the territories that the Jews shall occupy. A very interesting list is given by Josephus[19] of the cities that the Jews occupied in the time of Alexander Jannaeus. It shows that upon the return of the Jews from captivity and subsequent times that they literally took over the general territory here indicated.

Obadiah 21, "And saviours shall come up on mount Zion to judge the mount of Esau; and the kingdom shall be the Lord's." The saviors (deliverers) commenced with men like Zerubbabel, but it was the Maccabeans who actually conquered the Edomites and delivered the Jews from them. Then Obadiah adds the amazing prophecy that this is entailed with the kingdom of God. And historically it is true that the inter-Biblical period was the great preparatory period for the advent of Christ.[20] Part of that preparation was the rise of the Asmoneans[21] and the conquest of Edom. The content of the

18 Many commentators quote Josephus' (*Bell. Jud.* IV, 9, 7) description of the terrible state of Edom after the conquest of Simon of Gerasa.

19 *Antiquities,* IV, 4, 4.

20 Cf. Breed, *The Preparation of the World for Christ.*

21 Agreeing with this interpretation is CB, Henderson, HBC in part, KD in part. The problem as to whether the inter-Biblical period completely exhausts the fulfillments of Obadiah is not our concern. KD say that it doesn't, and other commentators look for enlarged fulfillment in the Church.

"kingdom" is determined by the examination of the New Testament. But in summary, what Obadiah predicted came to pass. He predicted a conquest of the Edomites by the heathen and by the Jews, and that the Jews would be established in their land while the Edomites would cease to exist. So the Babylonians, Nabatheans, and Romans conquered the Edomites, as did the Asmoneans and Simon of Gerasa. Furthermore, the Jews did return from captivity, and did inhabit much of the land of Palestine again, and they did give birth to deliverers, and in the course of time Christ came preaching "repent for the kingdom of heaven is at hand."

5. Micah

Micah 1:6, "Therefore, I will make Samaria as an heap of the field, and as plantings of a vineyard: and I will pour down the stones thereof into the valley, and I will discover the foundations thereof." This prophecy was fulfilled in the capture of Samaria by Sargon in 722, although the ICC throws the verse forward to Maccabean times. Samaria was on a hill and the stones may be found today literally poured down the side of the mountain, and the foundations of the city will be found to be discovered, i.e., laid bare.

Micah 3:12, "Therefore, shall Zion for your sake be plowed as a field, and Jerusalem shall become heaps, and the mountain of the house as the high places of the forest." There is some disagreement among the interpreters as to whether this is to be looked upon as fulfilled in the destructions involved in the captivities or whether it is also predictive of the destruction of Jerusalem; and, if the prophecy were conditional and somewhat averted, or if the prophecy were genuinely fulfilled. If the prediction be taken in its most obvious sense that Jerusalem shall undergo a destruction like Samaria, then the prophecy was fulfilled in the near and remote future alike in sufficient degree to be taken as a fulfillment of the prophecy. Some commentators accept the report that Titus had Jerusalem literally plowed up and others consider it legendary.[22]

Micah 4:10, ". . . O daughter of Zion . . . thou shalt go even to Babylon; there shalt thou be delivered." This verse has caused many commentators considerable trouble as they reason that Micah should have restricted himself to Assyrians as they were the dominant power of the time. However, Fausset correctly remarks on this passage as follows:

> Like Isaiah, Micah looks beyond the existing Assyrian dynasty to the Babylonian, and to Judah's captivity under it, and restoration. Had they been, as rationalists represent, merely sagacious politicians, they would have restricted their prophecies to the sphere of the existing *Assyrian* dynasty; for Assyria was then in the meridian height of its power . . . . But their seeing into the far-off future of Babylon's subsequent supremacy, and Judah's connection with her, proves them to be inspired prophets. Not only so, but both contemporary prophets foretell the deliverance from Babylon as well as the captivity in it.[23]

An alternative view is that of Kleinert in Lange's Commentary, namely, that Babylon here refers backward to Nimrod and the ancient city of Babel as representing the anti-god forces, and Judah, the kingdom of God.

Micah 5:2, "But thou, Bethlehem Ephratah, though thou be little among the thousands of Judah, yet out of thee shall he come forth unto me that is to be ruler in Israel; whose goings forth have been from of old, from everlasting." Although the critics emend the text primarily from the way the Septuagint reads, they yet admit that Bethlehem is meant.[24] Furthermore, it is evident that Jesus was born in Bethlehem. Radical critics have tried to assert that Jesus was really born

---

[22] For, JFB; against, Henderson.

[23] JFB, *in loco*. So also Henderson. G. A. Smith considers the phrase "even to Babylon" a gloss. Why? Not on critical differences in texts, but upon rationalistic suppositions.

[24] Cf. ICC, *in loco*.

in Nazareth and raised there, and that the Bethlehem legend was attached to the Gospels to bring in another Messianic fulfillment. However, the vast amount of material concerning the census of Luke 3:1 ff. with the expectation that each man would return to his family town greatly strengthens the Gospel contention that Jesus was born at Bethlehem.[25]

Further, there is the statement of the Jews themselves that they expected their Messiah to be born in Bethlehem (Matt. 2:6).

6. *Nahum*

Nahum is a prediction and description of the destruction of Nineveh. To begin with, it is noteworthy that the ICC does not consider the prophecy *vaticinium post eventum*.[26] In that the prophecy is so graphic and so amazingly fulfilled it stands as one of the most unusual in Scripture.[27]

Nineveh was built on a plain with sluice canals running into the city. It was a magnificent walled city, wealthy and populous too. In the height of its military and economic glory Nahum predicted its ruin. The Medes approached the city and the battle followed. There were assaults and counter-assaults. What finally turned the "tide" was literally a tide of water for the river rose to a new level and washed away part of the wall. The attackers poured in and desolated the city, sacked it, and set it on fire.

Of special interest are the following:

1:10, declares that in a state of drunkenness the Ninevites would be destroyed. Part of the success of the Medes was due to the optimism of the Ninevites who assumed the enemy was permanently repulsed and gave themselves to drinking and feasting.

1:8, mentions that the city would perish by "an overrun-

---

[25] Cf. the evidence listed in Barton, *Archaeology and the Bible* (7th edition), Chapter XXIX.
[26] ICC, p. 275. The Latin means, "to prophesy after the events."
[27] For the following we rely largely on Lange.

ning flood" which we have already mentioned. Compare also
2:6, "The gates of the rivers shall be opened, and the palace
shall be dissolved."

3:3, refers to the number of persons that perished; 3:13
also refers to the fire that shall burn the city; 3:19 speaks of
the utter ruin of Nineveh, and so it was. It ceased to exist as
a world power.[28]

1:10. "It was related by Diodorus (II. 26) that the city was
taken by assault, when the besiegers heard from deserters
that carelessness and drunkenness prevailed in Nineveh"
(HBC).

3:11, "thou shalt be hid." It is well-known that Nineveh was
hid under mounds and had to be excavated.

7. Zechariah

The general tone of Zechariah 1:12–21 is that the future for-
tunes of the Jewish people were not going to be like the former with special mention made of the captivities. God's favor
and mercy is now going to be upon Judah and Jerusalem. This
prophecy has a general fulfillment in that from about 520
B.C., the date universally assigned to this prophecy, to A.D.
70, the city of Jerusalem and the Jewish people remained
intact in the land. Granted they had their difficulties with the
Seleucids and their glories with the Maccabees; nevertheless,
when Christ was born there was a Jewish commonwealth with
some genuine semblances of the older Mosaic system.

Quite specifically it states in Zechariah 1:16 that "My house
shall be built." This was in process and it was finished in the
sixth year of Darius (Ezra 6:15) or four years later. It also
states in Zechariah 1:16 that "a line shall be stretched forth
upon Jerusalem." This was fulfilled 70 years later when the

[28] Cf. HBC. "It should not be forgotten, that when the prophet wrote, the
world had never witnessed or imagined such an overthrow of a great city.
Nor could it have reasonably been anticipated that commerce would have
forsaken its old emporium . . . . The doom of Nineveh has been delineated by
one upon whom, besides the gift of prophecy, God bestowed the highest
poetical powers," p. 636.

city was rebuilt by Nehemiah (Neh. 6:15). In Zechariah 1:17 it reads: "My cities through prosperity shall yet be spread abroad," and this was certainly fulfilled by the time Christ was born when all Judea and Palestine were teeming with people.[29]

Zechariah 1:20, 21 mentions four carpenters and the four horns, the former to undo the work of the latter. The political empires prior to the captivities and during the captivities did wreak havoc on the Jews. But the tide is to be reversed and the Jews are going to be settled in the land. In historical succession the Persians, Greeks, Seleucids, Maccabees, and finally Romans held dominion in Palestine. Although the Jews suffered a good deal and had some most excruciating experiences, nevertheless they remained in the land and as noted *supra* had genuine semblances of a national life with temple, sanhedrin, capital city, priesthood, and sacrifices when Jesus Christ was born.

In Zechariah 2:4 the prophet predicts that Jerusalem shall be inhabited as a town without walls for the multitude of men and cattle.[30] Certainly, the struggle of the Jews in this time and the time of Nehemiah does not answer to the scope of this prophecy. Therefore, the fulfillment of the prophecy was projected further into the future and so finds its fulfillment in the populated land in the time of Christ as previously discussed *supra* in reference to predictions in Chapter I.

Zechariah 2:7 contains an invitation to Jews in Zion to deliver themselves. Some of the Jews for either reasons of health, family, or fortune had settled in the city. The city made at

[29] Cf. Perowne, *op. cit.*, on verses 16 and 17. Henderson, *op. cit.*, refers to Josephus' remark as to how Jerusalem had to keep building walls and expanding to care for its populations.

[30] The remarks on the predictive passages of this chapter in *The International Critical Commentary* exhibit a barren skeptical negativism. It reveals the hermeneutical bankruptcy of liberalism, and its incapacity to approach Scripture with a genuine measure of sympathy. One feels that such a man as Henderson is far closer to the spirit of prophecy and the actual nature of the book of Zechariah, than those scholars whose pens are so frequently dipped in the acid of skepticism.

least two efforts to arise and re-establish its former independence. Two or three years after this prediction such an uprising took place. The Jews that remained were caught in the maelstrom; those that heeded Zechariah fled and so profited.[31]

In Zechariah 2:10, 11 it reads: "Sing and rejoice, O daughter of Zion: for, lo, I come, and I will dwell in the midst of thee, saith the Lord. And many nations shall be joined to the Lord in that day." Though there might be partial fulfillment in the subsequent inter-Biblical period, the conclusion of Henderson is irresistible: "The divine residence here predicted, must be interpreted as that which took place during the sojourn of the Son of God in the land of Judea."[32] Furthermore, it was the direct result of the incarnation that led to the formation of the Church, and from the formation of the Church to the spread of the gospel among the Gentiles. Therefore, the "dwelling in the midst" must be the incarnation with "many nations joined to the Lord" through the preaching of the gospel in the Book of the Acts.[33]

Zechariah 3:8, "for they are men wondered at." The Hebrew original means "men of sign, or of portents, or of type." These men are the fellow priests of Joshua. One of the clearest teachings of the New Testament is that Christ is the fulfillment of the Levitical high priesthood, and that believers are a kingdom of priests. Whether these fellow priests of Joshua refer to Christ or to the believer-priests is not possible to prove. However, in either case it is a prophecy with a fulfillment that is reasonable and not forced or unnatural.

Zechariah 3:8, "I will bring forth my servant the BRANCH." That the Branch is one of the titles of the Messiah cannot be controverted. Some would insist that the prophecy

---

[31] Cf. Perowne, *in loco.*

[32] So agrees Talbot W. Chambers in Lange, and Keil and Delitzsch, and most of the conservative commentators.

[33] There could even be a token fulfillment of this in that Cyrus, Darius, Alexander, Ptolemy, Philadelphus, Augustus, and Tiberius sent offerings to the temple, in addition to the widespread proselyting that took place in the inter-Biblical period. Cf. Jamieson, Fausset and Brown, *op. cit.*

is only to the intent that the weak ruling house of Israel would be strengthened to carry on; others insist it is the Messiah. Certainly the movement of the prophecy is so striking, and the context so laden with "great salvation" that the Messiah is the only satisfactory interpretation of the Branch. In Jesus Christ we have the fulfillment of this prophecy. All that the prophecy calls for is found in Him. This is strengthened by the following verse.

Zechariah 3:9, "and I will remove the iniquity of that land in one day." Some think this refers to the cleansing of the land because the temple services are renewed; and others think that it refers to the release of the Jew from his oppressors (Henderson). However, in view of the Messiah prediction of verse 8, and the Stone prediction of verse 9, it is almost mandatory that the removal of the iniquity be the death of the Branch. The expression "in one day" is taken to mean "finished at once" (Keil and Delitzsch). One of the clearest doctrines of the Epistle to the Hebrews is that Jesus died once for all for sin. Therefore, the prophecy was fulfilled in the death of Jesus Christ at Calvary for He is the Branch of verse 8, and the Stone of verse 9.

Zechariah 6:8, "Behold, these that go toward the north country have quieted my spirit in the north country." The north country is Babylon, the archfoe of Israel at this time and since the captivities. The vision opens with four chariots sent to various parts of the earth, particularly north and south. Some commentators take the south country to be Egypt indicating that her power was to be broken also. Others take the four chariots as equal to the four powers of Daniel 2. If such interpretations are correct the prophecy stands uniquely fulfilled. However, returning to verse 8, it states that Babylon's power is to be permanently broken. The Babylonians twice revolted against the Persians and each time were put down. Never again did the Babylonians rise to world power and become a threat to the Jews. God's Spirit was then actually quieted in the north country in that the course of events was such that Babylon no longer became an oppressor of the Jewish people.[34]

Zechariah 6:9–15 is a marvelous Messianic passage. First, we have again reference to the Branch (v. 12), a Messianic title, and the prophecy here fulfilled in Jesus Christ. Secondly, there is the expression "he shall grow up out of his place." The exegetical evidence favors the notion of growing up in his natural abode rather than that of sprouting out roots from underneath. Thus, Jesus Christ was born of Jewish parents, in a Jewish city, under a Jewish covenant, and was reared in keeping with the Jewish law—all of these statements easily verifiable by consultation of the New Testament. Thirdly, it states "he shall build the temple of the Lord." Jesus Christ Himself declared that He was going to build a church (Matt. 16:18 ff.); this is restated by Paul in terms of a temple (Eph. 2:19–22); and by Peter in terms of a foundation (I Peter 2:5, 6). Fourthly, we read, "he shall bear the glory" of a king (v. 13). Certainly, one of the most patent truths of the New Testament is that Jesus had a supernal glory, e.g., His transfiguration (Matt. 17), and the declaration of John, "and [he] manifested forth his glory" (John 2:11). Fifthly, "he shall be a priest upon his throne" (v. 13). One of the most glorious affirmations of the Epistle to the Hebrews is that Jesus Christ is typified by Melchisedec, a king and a priest. So Christ was born of the tribe of Judah as a regal King, and saluted of God a High Priest after the order of Melchisedec (Heb. 5:10, cf. also 7: 1 ff.). Finally, "they that are afar off shall come and build in the temple of the Lord" (v. 15) is claimed as one of the results

---

[34] The abject spiritual poverty of radical criticism is again evident at this passage. The ICC substitutes Zerubbabel for Joshua for which there is not one iota of manuscript nor exegetical evidence; and then interprets the crowning as an abortive effort for the Jews to set up their own king. But the Persian secret police find out and Zerubbabel disappears, no doubt having been liquidated. Thus, a magnificent Messianic prophecy is robbed of all its glory by (a) forcibly altering the text, and (b) making tenuous and presumptuous statements about the activity of the Persian secret police.

of the "council of peace" (v. 13). What could be more fitting and stronger at this point than the words of Paul when he wrote, "But now in Christ Jesus ye who sometimes were far off are made nigh by the blood of Christ, for he is our peace, who hath made both one, and hath broken down the middle wall of partition between us" (Eph. 2:13, 14)?

In agreement with our announced principle we cannot appeal to Zechariah 9:1 ff. as fulfilled prophecy, but it does illustrate how precarious is the liberalistic and naturalistic position. So specific and so detailed are the predictive elements of this chapter that if the traditional date of Zechariah be sustained supernatural prediction is immediately verified. The radical critic must on *a priori* grounds, in this case equivalent to prejudice, date the passage after Alexander the Great. However, if some phenomenal archaeological find comes to light, the entire radical position could be upset. Certainly the last hundred years of archaeological research are such that it is only a profound prejudice that could declare *a priori* that no such find is even conceivable. If radical critics do this, then their subjective bias and bigotry of scholarship is evident. The conservative can appeal to the discoveries of manuscripts of Daniel and Isaiah in the Dead Sea cave as well as to the famous John Rylands fragment of John's Gospel that absolutely dated John's Gospel prior to the time set by certain radical critics.

Zechariah 9:9, "Rejoice greatly, O daughter of Zion; shout, O daughter of Jerusalem: behold, thy King cometh unto thee: he is just, and having salvation: lowly, and riding upon an ass, and upon a colt the foal of an ass." This is quoted in Matthew 21:4, 5 as fulfilled in the Palm Sunday entrance of Christ into Jerusalem. The Jewish authorities of the earliest times were unanimous in asserting its Messianic character.[35]

Although later interpretations vary, the Messianic concept

[35] There is a survey of the history of the interpretation of this text in Lange, *op. cit.*, p. 71. Efforts to evade the text have been made from Grotius on. The ICC is strangely silent at this point.

is central. Certain features of this verse stand out that make it very significant as related to Jesus Christ. The king of the Jews is here set opposite to Alexander the Great. (a) He is a Jewish king, and the royal line of Jesus Christ is verified by the genealogical tables of both Matthew and Luke. (b) He comes to the Jews for their help, and the ministry of Jesus Christ was to minister and give His life a ransom. This is the force of the expression "to thee," i.e., not only to the Jews but to help them. (c) The king is just, and so was the perfect life of Jesus Christ. (d) The king is "saved." If taken actively it refers to His utter consecration to the mission of His life; if taken passively it refers to His possessing salvation; in either case, the term is extremely felicitous of Jesus Christ. (e) He is afflicted, and affliction is one of the leading notions of the word "lowly." A more wonderful correlation of prophecy and fulfillment would be difficult to conceive. The Jewish commentators had extreme difficulty with the apparent incongruity of the terms "king" and "lowly." Yet in Jesus Christ we have One demonstrated to be king by virtue of the genealogical tables; One put to death with an inscription charging Him with being king of the Jews. Zechariah 9:9 clearly describes a suffering king; and a suffering king is exactly what Jesus Christ was. (f) The king comes riding upon an animal that is not a war horse. So Jesus Christ actually rode into Jerusalem upon such an animal and literally fulfilled this Scripture.

It could be argued that this was *artificially* fulfilled. That the last point could be artificially fulfilled is granted. Any person might take an animal so described and ride into Jerusalem. But the status of point (f) is seen in a completely new light if it is realized that *the preceding 5 points are not capable of artificial fulfillment*. When the text is examined we find it fulfilled point by point in the character and life of Jesus Christ.

Zechariah 11:1–14 certainly presents a most marvelous description of the relationship of the Messiah to the true flock and to the faithless flock. The first three verses refer to the desolation before the appearance of the Messiah. Commentators differ widely as to the specific reference, although the overrunning of the Roman Army of Palestine seems to be most natural, in view of the following verses. At least, there is a surface parallel between the advance of the Roman Army and the advance of the fire.

Zechariah 11:4 is an address to Zechariah in which he represents the Messiah. The command is to feed the flock. The fulfillment is the appearance of Christ, in Palestine as the promised Messiah, whose first message was "Repent for the kingdom of heaven is at hand," and who spent about three years of blessed sacrificial ministry among the people of Israel.

Zechariah 11:7 indicates that the Messiah actually fed the flock, the flock being defined as "the poor of the flock." This was fulfilled in first, the gathering of Jesus Christ of twelve ordinary men as disciples, and second, His great ministry to the people who were as a flock without a shepherd.

Zechariah 11:8–11 indicates that with some of the flock the relationship would be first strained, then turned to enmity. This was fulfilled in the constant antagonism manifested toward Christ by the officialdom of the Jewry at that time, and in turn the strong castigations of them by Jesus Christ in Matthew 23, ending with announcements of their destruction (Matthew 24, 25) with the kingdom being given to another nation. But Zechariah 11:11 reads in part "and so the poor of the flock that waited upon me knew that it was the word of the Lord." Thus, the dire predictions of our Lord as contained in Matthew 24 and 25, and prophetically in Zechariah 11:8–11, and fulfilled in the destruction of Jerusalem, did not fall upon the Christians. Fausset writes: "He had, thirty-seven years before the fall of Jerusalem, forewarned His disciples when they should see the city compassed with armies, to 'flee unto the mountains.' Accordingly, Cestus Gallus, when advancing on Jerusalem, unaccountably withdrew for a brief space, giving Christians the opportunity of obeying Christ's word, by fleeing to Pella."[36]

Zechariah 11:12 indicates that the price of the Jews for the service of the Messiah was thirty pieces of silver, the price of a slave. This is quoted by Matthew (27:5-10).[37] Here we have a matter most difficult to controvert. If the matter of the thirty pieces of silver existed in the text with no appreciable interpretative material in the context, Matthew could be accused of having forced the meaning of the verse. But the amazing thing is that, as has been indicated, the entire scope of the passage is (a) Messianic, and (b) deals with the most unsalutory relations between the Messiah and certain elements of the flock. Thus, the thirty pieces of silver form part of a Messianic passage that already has a marvelous fulfillment in Jesus Christ and His life and ministry. Therefore, the matter of the exact number of coins is of heightened significance. The parallels of Zechariah 11 with the life of Christ are certainly astounding.

Adding to what has been already said is the statement in Zechariah 11:13 that the money was to go to the potter. T. T. Perowne writes: "The 'thirty pieces of silver' were literally the 'goodly price' paid for Him, 'whom they of the children of Israel did value.' 'The Potter' was literally the recipient of it, as the purchase-money of his exhausted field for an unclean purpose."[38] Even more emphatic are the words of Keil:

> For by this very fact not only was the prophecy almost literally fulfilled; but, so far as the sense is concerned, it was so exactly fulfilled, that every one could see that the same God who had spoken through the prophet, had by the secret operation of His omnipotent power, which extends even to the ungodly, so arranged the matter that

[36] JFB, *in loco.*
[37] The problem of assigning it to Jeremiah is not our concern, but the difficulty is by no means insuperable.
[38] Cambridge Bible, *in loco.*

Judas threw the money into the temple, to bring it before the face of God as blood-money, and to call down the vengeance of God upon the nation, and that the high priest, by purchasing the potter's field for this money, which received the name of "field of blood" in consequence "unto this day," perpetuated the memorial of the sin committed against their Messiah.[39]

Zechariah 12:10, "And I will pour upon the house of David, and upon the inhabitants of Jerusalem, the spirit of grace and of supplications: and they shall look upon me whom they have pierced." This is quoted twice by John (John 19:37, and Rev. 1:7). The Jews had been a stout people before God. Periods of rebellion and apostasy mark their entire history. But the time shall come when a spirit of grace and penitence shall come upon them. Then they shall look to their God whom all these centuries they have so maltreated. They, by their various forms of impiety, have pierced God.

However, this general and metaphorical piercing of God has a specific and literal fulfillment in the crucifixion of Jesus Christ. To pierce means to put to death. Every effort to evade the full force of these words is proved futile.[40] Metaphorically, Jesus was pierced by the words, "crucify him"; literally, He was pierced and put to death by the nails and the spear. The passage has been taken as Messianic by the Jews from antiquity until present times. We concur with T. T. Perowne when he wrote:

> The Speaker is Almighty God. The Jews had pierced Him metaphorically by their rebellion and ingratitude throughout their history. They pierced Him, literally as the crowning act of their contumacy, in the Person of His Son upon the Cross.[41]

[39] KD, *in loco.*
[40] Cf. Lange and JFB, *in loco* where such efforts are examined and refuted.
[41] CB, *in loco.* It is interesting that the Jews tried many things to break the full force of the expression "whom they have pierced." The piercing of Jehovah does sound harsh. But, as Keil points out (KD, *in loco*) as soon as the incarnation comes into view the difficulty is immediately obviated. It

Zechariah 13:7–9. There is little doubt that the subject suddenly changes at verse 7 from a discussion of a false shepherd to the proclamation of the good shepherd, very much after the manner of chapter nine in which the Messiah-king is immediately introduced after a discussion of the heathen king, Alexander. Here is an amazing prediction that, viewed in the light of Old Testament revelation only, appears very strange. But when it is seen through the lens of New Testament truth it becomes an amazingly lucid passage.

First, the sword is a symbol of judgment. As Fausset says the sword is "the symbol of judicial power, the highest exercise of which is to take away the life of the condemned . . . . Not merely a show or expression of justice . . . is implied here, but *an actual execution of it on Messiah the Shepherd, the substitute for the sheep, by God as judge.*"[42] Here is presented the execution of a shepherd by the decree of God.

Second, who is this shepherd? He is "my fellow." There are those that claim the shepherd here is a bad character, but the remarks of Keil are conclusive to the contrary.

> No owner of a flock or lord of a flock would call a hired or purchased shepherd his "anity." And so God would not apply this epithet to any godly or ungodly man whom He might have appointed shepherd over a nation. The idea of nearest one (or fellow) involves not only similarity in

---

is one of those amazing unplanned coincidences of Scripture that reveal the omniscience of God behind the printed page.

The ICC states that (1) the day of mourning is future as is the appearance of the Messiah, and (2) the person pierced is looked upon as already extant at this time. In reply, it is to be noted that the evidence of the New Testament is completely *ignored*. Secondly, in Zech. 12:9 we have the expression "in that day" which is part of prophetic vocabulary which means "in some future time." Obviously, in the future time when the Jews shall look upon the Messiah and mourn they will already have pierced him. Granted, the appearance of the Messiah is future to the time of Zechariah, but it is past in terms of the time of the mourning. To ignore such an obvious explanation on the part of the ICC reveals either a willful effort to ignore all evidence to the contrary of its religious naturalism, or else its profound antisupernaturalistic prejudice which incapacitates it from an adequate treatment of the Scripture.

[42] JFB, *in loco*, italics are his.

vocation, but community of physical or spiritual descent, according to which He whom God calls His neighbour cannot be a mere man, but can only be One who participates in the divine nature, or is essentially divine. The shepherd of Jehovah, whom the sword is to smite, is therefore none other than the Messiah.[43]

Third, this verse is appealed to by Jesus Christ Himself as fulfilled in His death on the cross (Matt. 26:31, 32). He is the smitten shepherd; His disciples are the dispersed flock.

In the Old Testament picture the strange situation is presented in which the Lord rises up against His fellow with the sword. Yet as we read the life of Christ in the Gospels the skein is unraveled. Jesus of Nazareth, as the Messiah, is opposed by the Jews to the final measure of their request for His death. He is pierced and hung upon a cross until dead. Yet while being killed of man, He utters the cry, "My God, my God, why hast thou forsaken me?" It is the consistent testimony of the subsequent writers of the New Testament that although men put Christ to death, the hand of God was in it making an atonement for the sins of the world. The very fact that the threads of the Old Testament picture seem hopelessly tangled, and yet are so beautifully untangled in the life of Christ is further proof that beneath the letter of Scripture is the unerring guidance of the Holy Spirit.[44]

[43] KD, *in loco*. Other evidence to bear out this interpretation as the only permissible one will be found in JBF, Henderson, and Cambridge Bible. The remarks of the ICC to the contrary are quite anemic in view of the positive evidence suggested for Keil's interpretation.

[44] The ICC transposes this section back to 11:17. The Shepherd, in this interpretation, is not a genuine companion of God, but the object of God's indignation as a faithless shepherd. Thus, the ICC, in interests of its rationalism and skepticism, ignores at this point all the philological evidence to the contrary. It concludes its remarks by saying that "The words quoted from v. 7 by Jesus therefore, were not in a strict sense—he does not say they were —fulfilled in his arrest and the dispersion of his disciples, but here again an incident suggests a passage of which it serves as an illustration." P. 318. Of course, the admission of one genuine supernatural prediction would confound the entire rationalistic premises about Scripture. Therefore, *a priori*, all evidence for the same must be twisted or turned or in some sense robbed of its predictive element. Is this genuine "scholarly" objectivity?

8. *Malachi*

Malachi 1:2–5 declares that Edom will not be re-established but shall be permanently desolate. From the time of the Maccabees until today the land of Edom and the city of Petra have been desolate. First, three centuries before the Christian period Petra was occupied by the Nabatheans. It is apparent that Nebuchadnezzar had conquered the Edomites, thus making this possible. Second, they were attacked by Judas Maccabaeus (166 B.C.) and defeated. Later (135) John Hyrcanus completed the conquest and made them submit to circumcision and unite with the Jews. Finally, the entire countryside was laid waste by the onslaught of Simon Gerasa (A.D. 66).[45] According to the specific prophecy of Malachi, Edom, once desolated, never again regained her strength to become a power of any rank.

Malachi 1:11, "For from the rising of the sun even unto the going down of the same my name shall be great among the Gentiles; and in every place incense shall be offered unto my name, and a pure offering: for my name shall be great among the heathen, saith the Lord of hosts." Much has been made of the fact by some commentators, e.g., Edghill in particular, that the present tense of the verbs of this verse demands a realization of the prophecy at the time of the prophet, i.e., it is not a prediction of the future. But, the present or even past tense in prophetic language is not unusual. Further, Keil indicates that in Genesis 15:14 and Joel 3:4 the present participle is used for future events.

At this point, even the I.C.C. admits that the prophecy had no present realization for the Jews.

> At no time in the life of Israel could it be said with any shadow of verisimilitude that Yahweh was universally acknowledged as God. Nor is there any evidence that Judaism ever had any appreciable success among the na-

---

[45] For these details Cf. *The Cambridge Bible, Obadiah*, pp. 20–23.

tions at large in the propagation of its faith, even if any serious attempt at the conversion of the nations could be proven.[46]

Therefore, we must regard the verse as prophetic of the future. In particular the verse predicts the following: first, that the God of the Jews would be worshiped and adored by the Gentiles of all the earth. The Christian religion makes no pretense of inventing or discovering a new God, but professes to believe in the Jehovah of the Old Testament as equivalent to the Father of the New. Furthermore, the Christian church has spread around the world, forming the only genuine universal religion of mankind. Second, the true worship of God would be maintained among the Gentiles which, in turn, implies the cessation of Jewish institutions—a most amazing prediction from a Jewish prophet. The Christian turns to the Epistle to the Hebrews to prove that in the Christian Church is offered true prayer, true offering, and true worship.

Commenting on this passage Packard says:

> What an insight into the most distant future! How much is involved in this prophecy? The kingdom of God is taken from the Jews and given to the Gentiles, the abrogation of the old dispensation wherein the worship of the Father was confined to one place, the coming of the hour "when the true worshippers shall worship the Father in spirit and in truth"; the universal spread of Christianity.[47]

Malachi 3:1, "Behold, I will send my messenger, and he shall prepare the way before me: and the Lord, whom ye seek, shall suddenly come to his temple, even the messenger of the covenant, whom ye delight in: behold, he shall come, saith the Lord of hosts." Here again is a most amazing prophecy that when viewed in light of New Testament events is so remarkably fulfilled and interpreted.

---

[46] ICC, *in loco.* For survey of theories cf. Edghill, *op. cit.*, p. 333 ff.
[47] Lange, *in loco.*

First, a messenger shall come before the Messiah; so, a most remarkable and unusual personage, John the Baptist, appears. His entire life is one of a strong, fearless, devout prophet. His one great message is to tell Israel that her Messiah is about to appear.

Second, he was to prepare the way for the Messiah, and this he did by his great message of repentance, and the multitude that followed him were baptized.

Third, while the messenger is preparing the way the Messiah is to appear, i.e., "The Lord . . . shall suddenly come." Thus, Jesus Christ appeared in the midst of John's ministry.

Fourth, the Messiah is "the Lord . . . the messenger of the covenant," yet the coming of the Lord is verified by the Lord who says, "he shall come, saith the Lord of hosts." What strange words—the Lord shall come, and the Lord shall send the Lord! Yet, the pages of the New Testament make it all so clear. The Father sends the Son. Jesus of Nazareth was God manifest in the flesh, and so was the Lord who is the One who said, "he shall come, saith the Lord of hosts."

Furthermore, this coming One is the "messenger of the Covenant," and so it is clearly stated in the Epistle to the Hebrews that Christ is the mediator of a New Covenant (Heb. 8:6). Therefore, in the ministry of John the Baptist, in the incarnation of Christ in God, in the appearance of Christ while John is yet preaching, in the mediatorship of Christ, and in the distinction between the Father and the Son, every essential point of this prophecy is remarkably fulfilled in the New Testament.

Malachi 4:5, "Behold, I will send you Elijah the prophet before the coming of the great and dreadful day of the Lord: and he shall turn the heart of the fathers to the children, and the heart of the children to their fathers, lest I come and smite the earth with a curse."

This is quoted in Matthew 11:14, and Mark 9:11, 12 as fulfilled in John the Baptist. First, Christ says that John is not literally Elijah, but the spirit and power of Elijah, thus permitting history to interpret prophecy. Second, the question needs to be asked if the fulfillment is genuine. Could the answer be anything but yes in view of the facts: (1) that John the Baptist came to minister not of judgment but of Him who brought grace and truth, and (2) that John the Baptist worked a remarkable spiritual revival upon the nation of Israel as indicated in Malachi 4:6?

This again illustrates how a prophecy, generally and somewhat blurred in nature, is so marvelous particularized and sharpened by its fulfillment.

In concluding this section on prophecy we wish to point out the radical treatment of Zephaniah's three short chapters. A history of the critical evaluation of Zephaniah will be found in the ICC and the present status of opinion in Pheiffer. Out of the 53 verses in the English translation, 40 have been rejected as not coming from Zephaniah. For example, Eichorn and Theiner reject 2:13–15; Oort rejects 2:7–11 and 3:14–20; Stade denied all of chapter 3 and 2:1–3, 11; Schwally rejected 2:5–12 and 3:1–20; Wellhausen rejected 2:2, 3; Budde rejected 2:4–15, 3:9, 10, 14–20; Davidson rejected 3:10, 14–20; Nowach rejected 2:3, 7a, c, 8–11, 3:14–20; S. A. Smith rejected 2:8–11; Driver rejected 3:18–20, 2:7b, 11, 3:9, 10; Marti rejected 2:3, 8–11, 15 and all of chapter 3; Cornill rejected 2:7–11, 3:14–20; Van Hoonacker rejected 2:7–10, 11; and Beer rejected 2:7a–10, 15, 2:1–3, and all of chapter 3.

If this above information is charted so as to show visually what each critic accepts or rejects, it will be apparent that there are wide divergences as to where the scissors should cut and where they should not. To try to refute criticism by showing the divergences of the critics is not the most substantial type of refutation; but on the other hand such a procedure reveals (1) that much of critical activity must be rather arbitrary, and (2) that if the critic wishes to call his work scientific he must use the word rather loosely.

Summary: We have now passed in review (1) the argument for prophecy; (2) refutation of objections to it; and (3) a list of fulfilled prophecies from the Minor Prophets. These examples by no means exhaust the amount of evidence available. We believe then, by a fair and honest inspection of the data just presented in the paragraphs above, there is sufficient evidence made apparent that the prophets of the Old Testament were imparted a wisdom and knowledge which was not their own. The necessary and valid conclusion is that the religion of the Old Testament was supernaturally given by God to the prophets.

This is the seal of divine omniscience upon the pages of the Holy Bible.

CHAPTER IV

SUPERNATURAL VERIFICATION THROUGH MIRACLES

DEFINITIONS OF MIRACLES frequently express the general apologetic orientation or philosophical orientation of the definer. Hume, and much of modern philosophy with him, defined miracles as a *violation* of natural law. Any such definitions that emphasize the words *violation* or *contradictory* or *in opposition to* prejudice the case immediately against miracles. Rather than trying to give a precise definition of a miracle we shall concern ourselves with the elements that any definition of a miracle must reckon with.

First, a miracle must be a *sensible* event. It has been argued at length that a miracle is a miracle whether man sees it or not, or even if man could not see it. God could work a change in the constitution of an atom that would be too small to detect, yet be a genuine act of God's power; and He could work it a thousand miles from anybody. However, for the serviceability of miracles to mankind, such discussions are not practical although the answer one way or the other may have immense theoretical interest. The miracles we *know* of so patently on the pages of the Bible are miracles that are sensible, i.e., they are presentations to the eye or ear. This means that seldom is the recognition of a miracle a matter of lengthy *inference*. There is considerable difference between the statement "that dress is green," and "the earth revolves around the sun." The first statement is verified by direct visual presentation; the second by a long chain of inference. Miracles are more or less direct presentations, and therefore are either directly perceived as miracles or are immediately inferred as such.

Secondly, the miraculous is such as to *strongly* and *clearly* suggest the presence of the supernatural. Granted, at times the phenomenal may appear as miraculous and the miraculous as phenomenal. An elevator once plunged forty stories and the operator was standing on the one square foot that was not crushed to bits. It was phenomenal but not miraculous. To grant a point, if an earthquake loosened the stocks in the Philippian prison (Acts 16), then a phenomenon had appeared as miraculous. But there is such a variety and number of Biblical miracles that in many cases we know it is not the phenomenal appearing as the miraculous, e.g., when a leper is instantly cleansed or a blind man is instantly given sight or a crippled man runs, leaps, and walks. But the *qualia* of the miraculous is of such a nature as to *strongly* and *clearly* suggest to the human mind the presence of the supernatural.

Thirdly, the miraculous is done within a redemptive context. This may be stated various ways. It may be said that miracles have an ethical or moral quality; or that miracles are part of covenantal revelation; or that miracles accredit the message of the messenger. The general notion is that miracles are not like the tricks of a magician. They do not appeal primarily to human curiosity, nor are they efforts at entertainment. Miracles, therefore, are part of the context and fiber of the Christian conception of redemption.

Two other observations are pertinent at this point. First, not all supernatural acts of God are classed as miracles. For example, although regeneration is supernatural it is not miraculous although in popular speech we speak of the "miracle of the new birth." The reason apologists do not consider the new birth or inward empowerments of the Holy Spirit or other such answers to prayer as miracles, is that the supernatural act of God is not sensible. We may read in the Scripture that the new birth is a supernatural act and we may experience unusual changes in habit and personality from it, but as an act of God in itself it is not sensible and therefore not classed as a miracle.[1]

Secondly, Christian apologists are divided as to how a miracle is to be related to natural law. One group insists that miracles are a type of law with which we are not familiar, but nonetheless, a type of law. This view is defended by such men as Alexander in his *Evidences of Christianity* and by Carnell in his *Introduction to Christian Apologetics*. The argument is that miracles must not be classed as contrary to natural law and so made to offend science, but rather they are law-obeying activities of God in which God uses the laws and materials at His disposal. According to Carnell if the scientists work hard enough on miracles they might conceivably find the underlying law. By so doing he wishes to put the miraculous right in the lap of the scientist.

Another group views miracles as acts of creation. Neither group would rule out the coöperation of the supernatural with the natural in performing a miracle. For example, an earthquake could have been caused by God, which in turn, acting like an earthquake, started from ordinary causes, would have loosed the bars in the Philippian prison. Or, perhaps, there were extremely disposing circumstances for the dividing asunder of the Red Sea. But the second group argues that a miracle is essentially a free sovereign act of God like creation.

We appreciate the good will of the first group in their effort to classify a miracle within the order of law and so preserve its scientific respectability. But we feel that such a definition of a miracle is not possible. A law in science is a uniformity, a regularity, a periodicity, a generality. To assert that miracles are a function of a higher law or law at all is to use the word

[1] Cf. C. W. Rishell, *Foundations of the Christian Faith*, pp. 212-213.

law in a different sense, therefore, than its customary usage in science. If miracles are a function of law, such laws have none of the usual characteristics of scientific law. It is conceivable that a miracle is a law in that, in a given situation X, God will perform the miracle Y; i.e., in certain circumstances, the love of God compels God to do a miracle. But those situations are solely the property of God and we can form no regular hypothesis about such a higher law. In agreement with Machen we assert that a miracle is an act of creation. It is a given, transcendent, supernatural act of God's power. If a miracle reflected law (as used in natural science) how do we by that law *predict, organize,* or *render intelligible* a given experience? or experiences? Into what set of axioms do these laws fit, and how are they assimilated into our body of scientific data? Mozley, in his great work *On Miracles* ably supports this contention of ours (preface to the second edition). However, Bett, *The Reality of the Religious Life,* argues very forcibly for the opinion that miracle is law-abiding. What Bett actually affirms is that in the total picture miracles are not queer events, logical contradictions, or out-of-place occurrences. This is precisely what we argued for in both Chapter I and Chapter II. Within the context of the Christian system, miracles are credible. To assert, however, that they are not functions of some yet unknown law, is not to assert that they are queer events in the total picture. In the scope of divine providence miracles *naturally* belong. But to try to reduce miracle to law is to use law other than it is used in science. What makes miracles credible is not that they are law-abiding to some law yet unknown and perhaps even unknowable, but that they fit so well and admirably into the plan and purpose and execution of redemption.

I. MIRACLES AND WORLD VIEW

Older works on evidences proceeded on the basis of common sense realism. Seldom did treatises on metaphysics or epistemology preface their remarks, and when they did, they usually reflected common sense realism or Lockian empiricism. But certainly since the turn of the century, and especially since the epochal work of Orr, *The Christian View of God and the World* (even though Orr himself failed to work out metaphysical and epistemological details), the problem of evidences cannot be developed apart from the world-view considerations. The essential problem is no longer, e.g., can we prove by ordinary historiographical methods that Jesus called Lazarus out of the grave. It is now apparent that every historiographer works with a formulated or assumed world view which governs completely what he admits as historical fact. Therefore, the Christian debate over miracles must be in terms of (1) the conceivability of the supernatural, and (2) if the supernatural is conceivable it is therefore possible for sound historiographical methods to prove that Jesus called Lazarus out of the grave as recorded in John 11.

Our thesis at this point is this: *Miracles must be seen within the Christian context if they are to be given a fair hearing.* The general thesis in endeavoring to establish a supernature and therefore the conceivability of miracles was the theme of the second chapter, and that argument will not be repeated here. It is our contention here that *miracles appear as credible facts within the Christian system.*

It may be safely asserted that a hypothesis does not receive fair treatment if viewed disconnected from its system, and further, that any hypothesis proposed must make peace with the system that it is associated with—even to revolutionizing the system, e.g., Copernicus and Einstein. It is therefore impossible to see miracles in the Christian perspective if viewed *only* as problems of science and history, i.e., to use only historical and scientific categories for interpretation. It is not asked that miracles be accepted blindly simply because they are associated with the Christian system; nor do we argue in a circle asking one to view miracles from the Christian position to see them as true when the Christian system is the point at issue. *No hypothesis in science is confirmed until tentatively accepted as true.* The tentative acceptance does not prove the hypothesis but it is absolutely necessary to test the hypothesis.

Consider the claims of Galileo, Kepler, and Newton about the solar system. Are their propositions correct? We can know *only* if we assume them provisionally to be true, then make a typical logical statement: If P, then Q. If P (the earth goes round the sun), then Q (the stars must be infinitely remote and have a parallax). But if the hypotheses of these men are scoffed at *the scoffer has no means of knowing if they are true or false.*

The conclusion at this point is as follows: *Logically* a given proposition will only be confirmed or falsified if placed within the system and tested for assimilation within the system; *scientifically* a given hypothesis must be assumed as true to confirm or disprove it; *psychologically* there must be sympathy and understanding on the part of the thinker if he is ever to really understand what another thinker proposes.

Negatively, it does great injustice to the Christian doctrine of miracles if the unconvinced person refuses to *logically* put the miracles within the Christian system and perspective; *psychologically* to view them only with disdain and unbelief; and *scientifically* to stubbornly refuse to even grant them provisional status as facts.[2]

Positively, when miracles are interpreted in terms of the Christian system they appear as true propositions, i.e., they fit coherently into the system.

Miracles will always fare poorly in deliberations *if* treated only as problems in science and history. The axioms of science

[2] H. Straton indicates the psychological refusal of the modern man to even give miracles a provisional status as fact when he writes: "The modern mechanistic world in which we live is one whose climate is *singularly unresponsive* to any and every account of miracle." *Preaching the Miracles of Jesus*, p. 13. Italics are ours. This volume also has an excellent annotated bibliography on miracles.

and history are not readily assimilable to miracles because of the very nature of a miracle. That is, both science and history work on the axiom of *continuity* and the miracle is essentially a *discontinuity*. Therefore, additional axioms are necessary to overcome in science and history the strong prejudice that is continuously met in philosophy, science, and history. These axioms are part of the Christian system, and it is these axioms that re-enforce, fortify, and interpret the *factual* claim to miracles.

It is the Christian system with its axioms, for example, that causes a Christian scholar to look seriously upon the Christian miracles and yet be as sceptical as a naturalist about other so-called miracles. That is to say, it is the moral and spiritual *setting* and *character* of the miracles that causes the Christian scholar to consider them as historical facts. Apologists have various ways of stating this conviction which we may frame as follows: *Biblical miracles are viewed as facts by Christian scholars because the miracles fit into a grand, spiritual, ethical, redemptive system.*[3] Hume is neither the first nor the last to set miracles cleanly out of the Christian setting. An article in the *Hibbert Journal* sets miracles in a distinctly pagan setting.[4] The Christian rightfully objects that miracles must not be refuted by (1) a definition of miracles that makes them appear obviously impossible, and (2) isolating the Christian miracles completely from their Biblical setting.

Machen argued correctly when he reasoned that "the possibility of miracle, then, is indissolubly joined with 'theism.' Once admit the existence of a personal God, Maker and Ruler of the world, and no limits, temporal or otherwise, can be set to the creative power of such a God. Admit that God once

---

[3] Cf. Straton, *op. cit.*, p. 14; C. S. Lewis, *Miracles*, *op. cit.*, *in passim;* F. F. Bruce, *Are the New Testament Documents Reliable?* p. 61; J. O. F. Murray, "The Spiritual and Historical Evidence for Miracles," *Cambridge Theological Essays*, p. 319.

[4] H. H. Dubs, "Miracles—A Contemporary Attitude," *Hibbert Journal*, 48: 159–62, January, 1950.

created the world, and you cannot deny that He might engage in creation again. . . . In one sense . . . miracles are a hindrance to faith—but whoever thought to the contrary? It may certainly be admitted that if the New Testament had no miracles in it, it would be far easier to believe. The more commonplace narratives have little value. The New Testament without the miracles would be far easier to believe. But the trouble is, would it be worth believing?"[5]

At this point we remind the reader of points discussed in the first chapter, namely, the cardinal points of the Christian system. Each one needs to be related to the problem of the miraculous. For example, the Christian believes in a free, sovereign, omnipotent God—free to do what He wills; sovereign to do what He wills, being responsible to Himself alone; and omnipotent to perform what He wills. He also believes that God is loving, merciful, and kind, seeking man's redemption, salvation, and good. This involves man's involvement in sin, his blindness, and his rebellion.

Miracles thus form part of the plan of redemption. To man in sin they are a means of breaking through to him, for he is encased within the two shells of ignorance and rebellion. Miracles are displays of omnipotence dispelling both ignorance and rebellion. But they are not sheer displays of power, but are deeds of mercy and love. They·are not deeds performed to gain money, or political advantage, or personal gain or selfish vain-glory. They are not, by any means, entertainments to gain the acclaim of the populace. They are acts of divine grace to relieve human suffering, to dissipate doubt, and to prompt faith.

To isolate miracles from their redemptive setting and to strip them of their ethical chaste nature, and treat them coldly as academic problems of either history or science is to

[5] Machen, *Christianity and Liberalism*, pp. 102–103.

misrepresent them and to actually caricature them. They must be seen in the shining of the light from the pages of Holy Scripture, their natural environment.

Miracles are also possessed of great revelational value. (1) In the tenderness of Jesus Christ in healing the sick we see the *love of God* revealed. His deeds of healing are love deeds and proclaim to man that the heart of the Eternal is wonderfully kind. (2) In the miracle we see the *power of God* revealed. Here is a God greater than disease, greater than death, greater than Nature. Each miracle is a testimony of the sovereignty and omnipitence of God, therefore, miracles. (3) Miracles reveal, as Mullins correctly reasons, we believe, the relationship of the spiritual to the material.[6] First, the miracle reveals the priority of the spiritual. It is God working on nature or Spirit working on matter. Miracles are a wonderful corrective in a century in which the spiritual is looked upon as some anemic nothingness compared with the definiteness and substantiality of the physical. If the physical yields to the power of the spiritual, the superiority of the spiritual stands revealed.

Furthermore, miracles prove that the customary duality of matter and spirit is not the highest truth. We do, in practical experience and for reasons of debate, make a distinction between the material or physical or natural and the spiritual or mental. But the operation of spirit on matter in a miracle proclaims not only the superiority of the spiritual but that spirit *can* influence matter. The revelational value here for creation and the mind-body problem is potentially very great. Thus, Mullins judges that "miracles do not disturb but unify the world order. They proclaim that the dualism of matter and spirit is not the highest truth. They show that these two things are somehow under the control of one."[7]

[6] E. Y. Mullins, *Why Is Christianity True?* p. 183.
[7] *Loc. cit.*

II. Miracles Authenticate the Christian Message

It has been argued from the earliest days of the Church that miracles authenticate the message of the messenger, and this is not to be refuted simply because trite or traditional. This feature appears in Roman Catholic, Eastern Orthodox, and Protestant apologetics. *If* man is in sin; *if* great theological propositions are difficult of proof; *if* subjective conviction is slippery grounds—what better method of convicting men of the truthfulness of theological claims is there than supernatural verification?

A. *Jesus Christ appeals to His miracles as His divine authentication.* In John 5, Jesus speaks about the various ways by which the Jews can know that what He claims is true. One of the most amazing series of claims ever made by Jesus is found in John 5, where He is accused of making Himself equal with God (v. 18). Jesus, rather than correcting this as a false assumption, proceeds to show how correct their inference was (vv. 19 ff). Then at the conclusion of the claims He indicates how the truth of the claims can be verified, e.g., God bears witness to Him, John the Baptist bears witness to Him, and the Scriptures bear witness to Him. However, He also claims that His *works* (His deeds, His acts) also bear witness: "The works which the Father hath given me to finish, the same works that I do, bear witness of me, that the Father hath sent me" (v. 36).

In John 10, the Jews directly ask Jesus to tell them plainly if He is the Messiah (v. 24). Jesus answered them directly by saying: "I told you, and ye believed not: the works that I do in my Father's name, they bear witness of me" (v. 25). This is followed by a discussion of the Good Shepherd. At the conclusion of which He says: "If I do not the works of my Father, believe me not. But if I do, though ye believe not me, believe the works: that ye may know, and believe, that the Father is in me, and I in him" (vv. 37–38).

In John 2 is recorded the miracle of turning water into wine, and John comments by saying that "This beginning of miracles did Jesus in Cana of Galilee, and manifested forth his glory; and his disciples believed on him" (v. 11).

In John 14 is the famous discourse on heavenly mansions. Jesus makes the astounding claim that whoever knows Him, has known the Father. He invites the disciples to believe that this is so simply by His own saying so. But, if they hesitate He says, "Believe me for the very works' sake" (v. 11).

In the events recorded in Luke 7 we find John the Baptist in prison, and in a state of confusion. He is not sure whether Jesus is the Messiah or not. He sends a delegation to Jesus who asked Him if He be the coming Christ or not (v. 20). Then Jesus "cured many of their infirmities and plagues, and of evil spirits; and unto many that were blind he gave sight" (v. 21). Having performed these miracles Jesus then turns to the disciples of John the Baptist and says: "Go your way, and tell John what things ye have seen and heard; how that the blind see, the lame walk, the lepers are cleansed, the deaf hear, the dead are raised" (v. 22).

In Matthew 9 is another event of significance. A man sick of palsy is brought to Jesus, and rather than saying to him "Arise and walk" he says, "Thy sins be forgiven thee." The scribes considered this blasphemy, and Jesus knowing their disputations asked them: "Wherefore think ye evil in your hearts? For whether is easier, to say Thy sins be forgiven thee; or to say, Arise and walk? But that ye may know that the Son of man hath power on earth to forgive sins, (then he saith to the sick of palsy,) Arise, take up thy bed, and go unto thine house" (vv. 4–6). Jesus very clearly here reasons that the power to heal directly and immediately as He alone was able means that He has the authority to forgive sins. The power of working miracles demonstrated His authority in the spiritual domain.

Not only is it clear that miracles authenticated the message of Jesus, but it is clear that miracles did the same for the Apostles. Although the book of Acts is not replete with miracles like the Gospels, nonetheless they are there. Further, they are of a variety too—miracles over disease, miracles over nature, and miracles of providence. These powers accompanied the apostles, to demonstrate to the people that heard them that their message was truly God's message. This is certainly the clear meaning of Hebrews 2:4 which states that God bore witness to the preaching of the apostles with "signs and wonders and with divers miracles, and gifts of the Holy Ghost, according to his will."

There is a further consideration at this point that is worthy of serious examination. *In view of the tremendous claims of Christ, miracles become a moral and ethical necessity.* Jesus Christ claimed to be the Son of God; to possess prerogatives that belong to God alone (John 5); to be the One who determines whether a soul goes to Heaven or Hell; to be the Saviour of the world; to be the Light of the world; to be the Bread of life; to be the Good Shepherd; and to be the Messiah. These claims are greater than we have ever read of any human being ever having made.

Certainly if these claims were true, and we were angels or demons, agents to whom the world of spirit is the world of sight, we would know them directly and need no secondary type of proof. But to the contrary, we are human beings existing in flesh with powers dimmed by infirmity, and with hearts darkened by sin. Such enormous claims cannot be decided by us by an act of pure intuition. Such limited, confused, and darkened creatures need a type of demonstration that is lucid and unequivocal. Miracles are the appropriate demonstration.

It is common knowledge that demented people will make unusual claims. A demented person may be very terrifying or comical as he makes his enormous claims even to deity itself. How then shall we tell the true Son of God from some demented person? How shall we say that our faith in Christ is warranted, but faith in some impressive but demented pseudo-Messiah is gullibility? Very obviously, the ability to perform the miraculous clearly differentiates between the true Messiah of God and the host of deluded or demented individuals who have paraded themselves as great ones from God. We, therefore, consider it a moral and ethical obliga-tion of God, that if Christ be the Son of God He make it so known that never will Christ be in competition with a de-mented or deluded person, and that never can we be accused that our faith in Christ as the Son of God is pious gullibility. We believe (in part) that God has protected His Son by the defining and clarifying power of miracles.

Bishop Butler has observed that much philosophical de-bate may arise over miracles *on the theoretical level.* Philos-ophers may have a variety of reasons as to why miracles did not happen, and why even in the providence of God they should not happen. But, Joseph Butler observes, there can be no objection to miracles from *practical* considerations. Cer-tainly, there was no better means available to God to impress on the minds of the people, Jews and Gentiles alive in the first century A.D., the divinity of the Christian religion than by miracles. There is no better method of impressing a large num-ber of illiterate or semi-literate peoples, few of which have the time, mentality, or background to follow any sustained philo-sophical argument, than by the miraculous. The use of the miraculous to authenticate the message of Christ and His apostles was the most practical and appropriate for the situ-ation no matter what sophisticated arguments may be brought against it.

B. *Miracles are an intricate part of the record which would become meaningless without the miracle.* Older synoptic crit-ics of a modernistic bent considered it a feasible task to go through the Gospels and shave off the miracles much like warts and leave the fabric of the record intact. For different reasons conservatives and form-critics have joined together to renounce this as an impossible effort. The miraculous is part of the very fiber of the record that cannot be cut like a superficial growth and an extraneous and imposed body of material. Miracles inhere vitally in the records themselves, and if deleted render the record unintelligible.

Around many miracles are certain events *before* and *after*. The former set the stage for the miracle, and the latter deal with the consequences that follow from it. If the miracle is pruned off, the material before and after is left dangling in mid-air.

For example, by a comparative study of the Gospel accounts it is evident that the raising of Lazarus in John 11 is the event that actually set off the series of events that led to Jesus' death.[8] Now, if there had been no raising of Lazarus there would have been no special inciting of the Jews at this time, and with no inciting of the Jews, no plan and no crucifixion. The raising of Lazarus is part of the very fiber of the account.

One of the most graphic narratives in the entire New Testament is the record of the healing of the blind man in John 9. If the blind man had not been healed there would have been no testimony from him, no stir among the people, no disquietude of the Pharisees, and no examination first of the blind man's parents and then of the blind man. All the subsequent action and talk after the event would be meaningless, unless there were first the healing.

The same situation obtains in the book of Acts. In Acts 4 is the inquisition of the apostles. It was produced by a huge multitude that gathered around Peter and John. Why did they gather? They saw the lame man healed by Peter "walking and leaping and praising God" (Acts 3:8). No healing, no exciting of the people; no exciting of the people, no preach-

[8] Cf. John 11:53, "From that day forth they took counsel together for to put him to death."

ing; no preaching, no arrest. The miracle is indispensable to the entire series of events.

Consider too, the accusation against Jesus that He was in league with the Devil (Matthew 12). The charge was that He worked His miracles by the power of Satan. The counter-charge of Jesus was that if any person attributed the love and benevolence of God manifested through His Holy Spirit to the master spirit of all evil, hatred, and murder, such a person had committed an unforgivable sin. But the charge and the counter-charge without the miracles are meaningless. If the Pharisees wished to oppose Jesus, the obvious accusation would have been that he was a fake or that his miracles were fakes. But the evidence of miracles was so incontestable that another expedient had to be resorted to, to quell their significance.

C. *The miracles and the words of Christ are wonderful and perfect counterparts.* It would be a most distressing experience if a man should appear of great spiritual power and magnetism of speech whose life should be marred and marked by gross iniquity; it would be even more distressing if a man with power to work great miracles should have a foul, dirty mouth. One of the easiest ways of identifying fakes and deceivers is by the inconsistency of word and life. But compare the matchless correlation of the word and works of Jesus. No man that has ever lived, if the record be true, has ever said such glorious, such spiritual, such theologically profound words as Jesus Christ; and equally so, no man that has ever lived has ever lived a life filled with such great miracles of love, mercy and tenderness. If Jesus spake great words with no miracles, we might call Him a great prophet or a religious genius and stop there; and if Jesus worked great miracles, but had nothing really to say, he would confront us with an imponderable enigma. But notice how easily we expect such glorious words from one who can work such marvels, and how readily we believe in the marvels of one who can speak such words. From our vantage point the intersection of the evidence from the wonderful words of Jesus and the magnificent marvels is incontestable. As Mullins comments, the miracles "were the deed of which the gospel was the word."[9]

D. *The miracles of Christ have adequate and sufficient testimony to establish them as historically real.* As we indicated in our definition of miracles, miracles are sensible events, events that are manifest or evident to the eyes or ears or sense of feeling. They are not hidden interior works that are matters of a long chain of closely reasoned inference. Miracles are discovered, i.e., made aware to human beings, by presentation to the senses, e.g., the cleansing of the skin of a leper, the restoration of a shrunken limb, or the restoration of sight to a person congenitally blind.

If miracles are capable of sensory presentation, they can be made matters of testimony. If they are adequately testified to, then the recorded testimony has the same validity for evidence as the experience of beholding the event. No matter what Hume said at this point, *legal procedure in thousands of courts of the world, as well as scientific historiography,* is conducted on the grounds of reliable testimony by word of mouth or by written document. For purposes of *evidence* the courts treat the testimony of a man who saw a crime as if the court itself saw it, if they have no reason to doubt the integrity of the witness. Furthermore, the mere passage of time does make them increasingly difficult of examination. But once an event is recorded reliably in document form, the reliability of the document is not at all changed by the mere passage of time.[10] If the raising of Lazarus was actually witnessed by John and recorded faithfully by him when still in soundness of faculties and memory, *for purposes of evidence,* it is the same as if we were there and

---

[9] *Op. cit.,* p. 181.
[10] Cf. R. S. Foster, *The Supernatural Book,* p. 227; M'Ilvaine, *op. cit.,* pp. 170, 172, 206–207.

saw it. By examination of the Gospels, the following reasons may be employed to prove to us that the miracles are subject of adequate and reliable testimony.

1. *There were many miracles performed before the public eye.* Jesus healed in the cities, at the busy corners, when surrounded by a mob, when speaking before multitudes in the open or in a house. They were not for the most part done in secret or seclusion or before a select few. Most of them were public property, as it were. There was every occasion and opportunity to investigate the miracle right there. No effort is made to suppress investigation. Such clear, open, aboveboard activity is good evidence of actual occurrence.

2. *Some miracles were performed in the company of unbelievers.* Miracles are always popping in cults that believe in miracles. But when the critic is present the miracle does not seem to want to occur. But the presence of opposition or of critics had no influence on Jesus' power to perform miracles. More than once, right before the very eyes of His severest critics Jesus performed miracles. Now certainly, to be able to do the miraculous when surrounded by critics is a substantial token of their actual occurrence.

3. *Jesus performed His miracles over a period of time and in great variety.* The impostor always has a limited repertory and his miracles are sporadic in occurrence. Not so with Jesus. His miracles were performed all the time of His public ministry from the turning of water to wine in Cana to the raising of Lazarus. Further, He was not limited to any special type of miracle. Sometimes He showed supernatural powers of knowledge, such as knowing that Nathanael was hid in a fig tree; or he showed power over a great host of physical diseases—blindness, leprosy, palsy, fever, insanity, and death itself; or He was able to quell the elements as He did in stilling the waves and the wind; or He could perform acts of sheer creation as when he fed thousands of people from very meager resources.

Imposture on this scale is impossible. The more times He healed, the more impossible it would be if He were an impostor. Further, it is incredible to think that for three and one-half years He maintained one consistent imposture. The number of miracles, their great variety, and their occurrence during all His public ministry are excellent evidence that Jesus actually performed the miracles the Gospel writers record.

4. *We have the testimony of the cured.* Many times when Jesus healed, it is recorded that the healed person went broadcasting far and wide that he had been healed, even in those cases where Jesus cautioned the person or persons against it. There was the banquet that Lazarus attended and at which he readily could have given his personal testimony (John 12:1, 2). There was the blind man of John 9 who said "whereas I was blind, now I see" (v. 25). Nor are we to minimize the afterglow, as it were, of the life of Christ. Certainly, the report of His miracles found their way all through the hamlets and villages of Palestine, e.g., Paul tells Festus that the things about Christ were not "done in a corner" (Acts 26: 26). Consider too, that two of the Gospels were written by men who were not eyewitnesses, so available was the data of the life of Christ. Thus, part of the reason of the sudden and energetic growth of the Church in Acts was memory of the marvelous life and miracles of Jesus Christ. The result of the personal testimonies of the many who were healed, as they spoke to their loved ones, their relatives near and distant, and their townspeople, cannot be ignored in accounting for the great success of the preaching of the gospel in the Book of Acts.

5. *The evidence from the Gospels cannot be undone by appeal to the pagan miracles.* Miracles are believed in non-Christian religions because the religion is already believed, but in Biblical religion miracles are part of the means of establishing the true religion. This distinction is of immense importance. Israel was brought into existence by a series of

miracles; the law was given surrounded by supernatural wonders; and many of the prophets were so indicated as God's
spokesmen by their power to perform miracles; Jesus came
not only preaching but performing miracles; and the Apostles from time to time were able to work wonders. It was the
miracle authenticating the religion at every point. "All the essentials of Hinduism would, I think, remain unimpaired if
you subtracted the miraculous, and the same is almost true
of Mohammedanism," writes Lewis, "but you cannot do that
with Christianity. It is precisely the story of a great Miracle.
A naturalistic Christianity leaves out all that is specifically
Christian."[11]

Pagan miracles lack the dignity of Biblical miracles. They
are frequently grotesque and done for very selfish reasons.
They are seldom ethical or redemptive and stand in marked
contrast to the chaste, ethical, and redemptive nature of the
miracles of Christ. Nor do they have the genuine attestation
that Biblical miracles have. Therefore, to examine some pagan miracles and show their great improbability, and then to
reject all miracles on that ground is not fair to Biblical miracles. "To infer that all so-called miracles are spurious because
many are found to be so is a *non sequitur* and an abuse of reason," writes Foster, "to write down a list of gross and miserable superstitions and blazing impostures, and then classify
all supernaturalism as *ejus dem generis*, is a species of logical
knavery not respectable among honorable thinkers."[12]

E. *There is no adequate evidence contrary to miracles.*

The Christians were soon persecuted, and underwent trial
by fire, sword, and dungeon. At such occasions the possibility
of recanting or exposing something as fake are at a maximum.
But there is no record of any Christian ever renouncing Chris-

---

[11] Lewis, *op. cit.*, p. 83.
[12] Foster, *op. cit.*, p. 223. For other references to refutation by appeal to
pagan miracles see G. P. Fischer, *The Grounds of Christian and Theistic Belief*, Chapter X: and J. B. Mozley, *On Miracles*, Lecture VIII. B. Warfield,
Counterfeit Miracles has some valuable data on ecclesiastical miracles.

tianity, when so persecuted, on the grounds that the miracles claimed by Christianity are fake.

Consider the case of Judas Iscariot. When he went to betray Christ what could have been more damaging than the first-hand evidence that the miracles of Jesus were fakes or impostures or tricks. On this score the mouth of Judas is sealed. All he can do is tell the Jews where Jesus prayed, and what a tribute to Christ by such a betrayal!

That Jesus was hated by many of His fellow countrymen is a matter of Gospel record. The same is true of the infant Church. Yet the inhabitants of Palestine who had sufficient motive in their hatred and sufficient proximity to the life of Christ have never written a line in denial of a single miracle.

On the other hand, some of the very opponents of the Christian faith admitted that Christ performed miracles, e.g., Celsus, Hierocles, and Julian the emperor.

Summary: It has been the main contention of this chapter that miracles do fit as facts within the Christian system, or, if we assume the truthfulness of the Christian system, there is no longer any question as to the factuality of miracles. Within the Christian system miracles (1) are conceivable in view of our basic set of convictions, and (2) are proved to have occurred by consideration of history and fact. The positive evidence is for their occurrence; the appeal to the contrary is inconclusive. But we have been arguing *within* the boundaries of the Christian faith. At this time we must meet the objections of those on the outside and to this task we devote the next chapter.

*   *   *

Special Note

Allan Richardson in his *The Miracle-Stories of the Gospels* rejects the evidential interpretation of miracles on the grounds that the people of Jesus' day expected miracles from remarkable personalities and hence the miracles of Jesus would carry little evidential value. However, Richardson does accept the historical occurrence of miracles. In defense of the evidential interpretation of miracles we assert:[13] (1) The verses we cited *supra* clearly teach that miracles were performed by Christ and His apostles as evidences of their divine mission and message. Granted that miracles were easier to believe then than now, still nobody went around ancient Palestine every day restoring sight, cleansing lepers, raising the dead, as Jesus Christ did. Even though those people more readily believed miracles, the miracles of Christ could not but have had a remarkable effect upon their mentality. Let the reader of the Gospels note well the number of times we are told either that great multitudes followed Jesus, or, how His fame spread throughout all the surrounding countryside. (2) Richardson does give theological value to the miracles, i.e., they show the redemptive presence of God. They are signs of the coming of the kingdom of God. Is this not merely putting the miracle in its theological setting? Who denies that the evidential interpretation denies the theological nature of miracles? And, after all his exposition, has he, nevertheless, affirmed the evidential value of miracles even though he has framed the question around a Biblical-theological context rather than a metaphysical-evidential one? (3) But even so, if people in Jesus' day looked upon miracles differently from the way we do, that does not hinder us from seeing miracles in terms of our view of Nature and scientific law, and hence seeing their enormous evidential value from such considerations.

[13] To our way of thinking Mozley's arguments for the evidential value of miracles is crystal-clear. *On Miracles,* Lecture I, "Miracles Necessary for a Revelation."

CHAPTER V

REBUTTAL TO THOSE WHO
DENY MIRACLES

I. Science Has Not Successfully Denied the
Factuality of Miracles

SCIENTISTS OPPOSE MIRACLES ON THREE COUNTS: 1) Science has not experienced miracles; 2) miracles contravene natural law; 3) the universe that the scientist works with does not seem to be friendly to miracles.

The first accusation is neither here nor there. Science cannot discover miracles for the obvious reason that miracles happened in a once-for-all redemptive movement of God in history, and miracles are therefore in the past. They are matters only of historical science, i.e., they are matters for those who weigh evidence, documents, and testimony. It is therefore not possible for scientists to reënact the crossing of the Red Sea, or the floating of an axe head, or a sudden cure of leprosy.

In reference to the second objection, we affirm that the objection is actually a definition of a miracle even though a rather poor one. The relationship between natural law and miracle is not that of contradiction, but of transcendence. Obviously, a miracle is something quite different from the usual routine of Nature.[1] To refute a philosophical position by de-

---

[1] The writer is aware of the arguments made for a spiritualistic metaphysics on the basis of proposed indeterminacy in atomic physics, or the proposed spontaneity of atomic particles, or the statistical formulation of modern physical laws, but he does not consider them as serious data for a spiritualistic metaphyics or a physical basis of the miraculous.

nying a definition is hardly a reasonable procedure. Ordinarily, storms are not quelled or waves stilled by the spoken word of a man, but by meteorological forces. The very basis of the detection of the miracle is its *super*-natural and *transcendent qualia.*

The most a scientist could say at this point is this: Events with the *qualia* of a miracle are not found in the customary, daily routine of science, nor are they deducible from any of the usual axioms of any of the sciences. To assert that miracles *cannot* happen is to take *philosophical* ground. This introduces the third opposition of science.

Ultimately the belief or denial of miracles is a matter of world view. Carnell is correct when he writes:

> If we cast our problem in any lower dimension than a strife between a supernaturalistically conceived and a naturalistically conceived *einheitliche Weltanshauung,* we can be assured that we are not grappling with the issue of miracles in its true proportions. To state the crux of the issue in boldest relief: Is the *Almighty* in sovereign control of all reality or are the *immanent laws?* Is the *mind of Christ* the *Logos* of things, or the mind of *autonomous man* the basis of all meaning? These questions state our problem in its proper breadth of importance.[2]

Granted that science does not occasionally confront a miracle; granted that miracles do not accord with the pragmatic rules of scientific procedure, neither of these demonstrates the *inconceivability* or the *impossibility* of miracles. A scientist can only assert the inconceivability and impossibility of miracles by *extrapolating* his science into his philosophy. At that point, the matter of miracles is no longer a scientific problem but is a broader philosophical one. Our comments at this point are:

[2] E. J. Carnell, *An Introduction to Christian Apologetics,* pp. 243–244. Italics are his.

A. If the scientist takes the *axioms* of his science and makes them *first principles* of philosophy, he is engaging in metaphysics as much as any other competent philosopher.

B. The principle by which miracles are ruled out is the principle of the uniformity of Nature. This principle in point of historical origin is part of the theism of the Scholastics and was invoked to show that an orderly God has an orderly universe; and there is no single experiment or method of experimentation to prove the principle. It is pragmatically verified and is not a demonstrable scientific axiom. The uniformity of Nature is, therefore, as much a theistic assumption as it is naturalistic. In the theistic system it is the expression of the fidelity of God to Creation. But this fidelity does not rule out miracles. Lewis' words at this juncture are worthy of quoting:

> But if you admit God, must we admit Miracle? Indeed, you have no security against it. That is the bargain. Theology says to you in effect, 'Admit God and with Him the risk of a few miracles, and I in return will ratify your faith in uniformity as regards the overwhelming majority of events.' The philosophy which forbids you to make uniformity absolute is also the philosophy which offers you solid grounds for believing it to be general to be *almost* absolute. The Being who threatens Nature's claim to be omnipotent confirms her in her lawful occasions.[3]

C. The scientist must assume, further, the truthfulness of some form of *scientism*. If he does he must assume that

1. This is a determined universe in all levels

2. That all the forces at work are "scientific" forces.[4] Both of these assumptions are extremely tenuous.

What science may say is this: The report of miracles must

---

[3] Lewis, *op. cit.*, p. 128. Italics are his.

[4] If naturalism's metaphysics is punctured so is its scientism, and a metaphysics in which miracles are conceivable is a very credible option. Besides splendid refutations in the philosophic tradition of naturalism cf. Lewis, *op. cit.*; Straton, *op. cit.*, pp. 16–17; Richardson, *op. cit.*, p. 173 ("The skepticism of the modern mind concerning the Gospel miracles actually arises not

be considered suspect *unless* valid and cogent reasons be given that would cause us to consider the report as trustworthy. We agree that all miracle reports be treated with great suspicion and doubt; we also agree that there are adequate historical and philosophical reasons for considering seriously the *factuality* of Christian miracles.

II. Historical Criticism Has Not Successfully Denied the Factuality of Miracles

From the early attack of Gospel miracles in the sixteenth century until today there has been one series of assaults upon the factuality of New Testament miracles. We judge that this assault is not successful.

A. The assault is frequently made in the interest of some very definite philosophical position (agnosticism, skepticism, pantheistic determinism, deism, materialism, religious modernism, or naturalism). Part of the modern mentality is the stubborn and negative attitude about miracles and it is in large part of philosophic origin. Thus, the critic commences his study with a closed mind on the subject. "Nothing is so unscientific," writes Lunn, "as the closed mind, and unfortunately the typical modernist embarks on this research with his mind already closed to the possibility that miracles occur, and are the work of supernatural agencies."[5]

Every critic is a philosopher and a philosopher of history and he approaches the problem with his philosophic prejudices.

> If the past years have taught us anything at all, [writes Parvis] they have taught us that the work of the New Testament critic . . . involves not only historical method

---

from any historical understanding but from a garbled view of the 'conclusions' of 'science' and physical science at that" p. 174); T. S. Farmer, "Physical Science and Miracle," *Journal of the Transactions of the Victorian Institute*, Vol. 80, 1948.

[5] Arnold Lunn, "Miracles—The Scientific Approach," *Hibbert Journal*, 48: 242, April, 1950.

but also the philosophy of history. History must be viewed as consisting not merely of occurrences but of events, which are occurrence plus meaning.[6]

Therefore, if the critic is a religious naturalist he will elect any number of avenues of escape from the patent miracles of the Gospels. The factuality of miracles is ruled out *a priori* on the grounds of a previously accepted naturalistic philosophy.

To this position we state: Religious liberals "kill" the facts to make their philosophy consonant with all of experience. On the other hand, it is our conviction that if the religious naturalist would see miracles from the perspective of a religious transcendentalist he would see both the *reasonableness* and the *factuality* of miracles.

B. Most modern critics of the Gospels assume a very agnostic attitude toward the historical validity of the Gospels, which agnosticism we declare is untenable.[7] We do so for the following reasons:

1. *The Book of Acts stands firmly against any "evolution" of the life of Christ.*[8] Ten days after the ascension Peter preaches a theological and miracle-working Christ. For form-criticism to survive it must break the back of the essential historicity of the book of Acts and Luke's qualifications as a historian. *How does form-criticism do this?* It does it by treating lamely the lives of the Apostles the same way it treats the life of Christ! The movement that first apotheosized Christ, in turn glorifies the disciples! This religious creativity has to compound itself at this point or all is lost. The apotheosizers

---

[6] M. M. Parvis, "New Testament Criticism in the World-Wars Period," *The Study of the Bible Today and Tomorrow*, p. 73.

[7] We assume at this point the reader's acquaintance with synoptic criticism—the general outlines of its history and its current schools of thought, and the significant literature on the subject. We shall treat as a class all forms of agnosticism concerning the Gospel record of Christ (e.g., religious liberalism and form-criticism).

[8] As we shall deal constantly with form-criticism we refer the reader to L. J. McGinley, *Form Criticism of the Synoptic Healing Narratives* for a magnificent bibliography, a good historical discussion of its origins, a description of its leading beliefs, and trenchant criticisms.

of Christ must now be apotheosized by the next generation! Certainly, this is pure *ad hoc* reasoning to keep a defective hypothesis alive.[9]

2. *The historical, geographical, personal, and cultural* (material and social) *references of the Gospel writers and the book of Acts reveal their high fidelity to these types of facts.* In connection with this, two things may be said:

a) Sir William Ramsay has indicated the extreme difficulty of falsifying such details or creating them from imagination. This can mean only that the writers were familiar with these details firsthand and were not men of Asia, Greece, or Rome rewriting Palestinian history. The geography of Palestine, the archaeology of Palestine, the history of Palestine have been gone over repeatedly and the fidelity of the Gospel writers to these matters is unimpeachable. "The description [by the Gospel writers] of the land in which He lived and the people whom He encountered—a land and people never seen by many of the early Christians—*has never been convicted of an inaccuracy.*"[10] The possibility of imaginative composition of Gospel events by other than Palestinian that is true to the facts is very remote.

b) If these men prove to be accurate in these details then their *general sense of fact and judgment* stands vindicated and it is not possible to call them bungling peasants.

[9] If any reader wishes to see how Acts embarrasses form-criticism and how this type of criticism can escape Acts only by lamely attributing the same myth-making to the Apostles as well as to Christ, let him read M. Dibelius, *A Fresh Approach to the New Testament and Early Christian Literature,* pp. 257 f., for his treatment of Acts.

[10] McGinley, *op. cit.,* p. 10, italics are ours. "Wendt acknowledges that the Acts of the Apostles is 'an historical work of invaluable worth.' Sir William Ramsay . . . asserts as the result of the most careful examination that 'Luke's history is unsurpassed in respect of its trustworthiness.' Even Eduard Meyer . . . acknowledges that St. Luke's history is 'one of the most important works which remain to us from antiquity.'" D. M. McIntyre, *Some Notes on the Gospels,* p. 29. Shotwell's opinion is: "Luke, as the *Acts of the Apostles* show, was an educated man who compiled his history out of various sources, was accurate in geography and painstaking, and his work stands equally alongside the best pagan histories of his times." Quoted by W. Smith, *The Supernaturalness of Jesus,* p. 55. Cf. A. T. Robertson, *Luke the Historian in the Light of Research.*

3. *Synoptic critics must ignore completely the united testimony of the Early Church.* In their agnosticism they must reject completely the testimony from Clement of Rome onward. This is a serious charge and not to be shaken off lightly by synoptic agnostics.[11]

4. *There is not enough time for the supposed remarkable evolution of the life of Christ to take place.* Jesus died about 30 A.D. Some scholars date either James or Galatians around 45 A.D. All admit apostolic writings by 50 A.D. If a lowly humanistic religious teacher be transformed into a majestic Christ the transformation must have the following characteristics—*all of which are extremely doubtful possibilities.*

a) It had to be an *incredibly rapid* change, for in a scant twenty years at the *maximum* it is complete.

b) It had to be unusually uniform, for no alternate testimonies are found, and no evidence of evolution is discoverable.

c) It had to be done in full knowledge of the original eyewitnesses and apostles—as it was complete by 50 A.D.[12]

5. *Problems of criticism of the Synoptics does not mean agnosticism of their historical validity.* Granted it might not be

---

11 "The information furnished by Irenaeus, Tertullian, Clement of Alexandria, Origen, and the Muratorian fragment, concerning the traditional origin of the Gospels, is passed by without reference [by form-critics]. Justin's observation that the Gospels are Apostolic Memoirs is mentioned merely to reject it as misleading." McGinley, *op. cit.*, p. 22.

12 On two occasions Filson has indicated that it was simply impossible for such a tremendous transformation to take place in such a short time. Cf. Floyd V. Filson, "How I Interpret the Bible," *Interpretation*, 4:182, April, 1950; and "The Central Problem Concerning Christian Origins," *The Study of the Bible Today and Tomorrow*, pp. 340–341. McGinley states that there is only *fifteen years* for the active evolution of the life of Jesus into the Synoptic picture. *Op. cit.*, p. 24. Within thirty years the Christ of theology was accepted in Rome. McGinley further indicates that the bitter enemies of Christ and the Church would certainly have resisted and condemned such an evolutionary development. C. C. Torrey has written: "Each of the four Gospels is plainly written . . . for Jewish readers; no one of them steps out of the atmosphere of Palestine even for a moment . . . The 'Church' of the Gospels is that of the first chapters of Acts, with no slightest trace of later development . . . There is not a word in any of the four books that might not have been written within twenty years after the death of Jesus." Quoted by McIntyre, *op. cit.*, p. 10.

possible to work out a uniform theory of the synoptic problem. That impossibility does not *mutatis mutandis* argue for a skepticism about the life of Christ. Baillie accuses the form critics at this juncture. After indicating their basic assumptions he writes:

> Thus the Form Critic often tantalizes us by stopping short with the question: *What did the primitive community mean by this story?* He stops short (why?) of the much more important question . . . *What did our Lord mean* when he said or did this thing?[13]

To reduce all to the *Sitz im Leben* is not adequate. To show differences of approach, of presentation, of detail is not equivalent to breaking the force of historical validity in the Gospels.

6. *The integrity of the apostles must be denied by form-criticism.* As previously indicated the Early Church not only transformed Jesus into the Messiah but the Apostles into wonder-workers. In order to do this the integrity of the Apostles must be challenged.

a) Because in their lifetime they did not faithfully represent the true life of Christ.

b) In their lifetime they permitted a willful distortion of the life of Jesus. In the frequently quoted words of Vincent Taylor: "If the Form-Critics are right, the disciples must have been translated to Heaven immediately after the resurrection."[14]

c) Jude presents a fateful fact to form-criticism. *Jude is the brother of James and therefore a brother of Christ.* Whether the picture of a naturalistic humanistic Jesus is correct or the theological Christ is correct, *in neither case could anybody*

---

[13] D. M. Baillie, *God Was in Christ,* p. 56. Italics are his. Baillie lists the *a priori* assumptions of Form criticism to be: (1) that all Gospel material is in a readily distinguishable form; (2) that the Gospel writers had no other interest than homiletical; (3) that in the time of the formation of the tradition, eyewitnesses were absent; and (4) that the thing which provoked the incidents in the Gospels were not events in the life of Christ but in the life of the church—the *Sitz im Leben.*

[14] Quoted by McIntyre, *op. cit.,* p. 10, fn.

claim to be the blood relative of Christ without that being the actual fact.

7. *There is no evidence of any genuine evolution in the Gospels or in the New Testament or in the Early Church.*

a) The so-called Liberal interpretation of the Gospels in which a naturalistic Jesus could be separated from a theological Christ is now defunct.[15]

b) Form criticism itself has proved that the earlier strata contain the same theological Christ as the later ones.

c) Discoveries of papyri of the Gospels forces the dates of all the Gospels back into the first century.

In essence, the form critics have created an *artificial hiatus* between the actual life of Jesus and both the early Church and the New Testament records. Into this artificial hiatus they throw all the evolution of the humanistic Jesus into a theological Christ. The only evidence for this is a *sociological theory of legend genesis and development.* By locating all in this unknown fictitious hiatus they have taken impregnable ground, for no evidence can be found to the contrary. But by the same token—no concrete evidence can be marshalled for them. It is like the naïve evolutionist who, when asked where life came from, says: "From the stars." His statement is as impossible of refutation as it is of demonstration.

8. *Finally, the emergence in the documents of the theological Christ, and the emergence in history of the Christian church, stand as magical and mysterious if the form critics or synoptic agnostics are correct.* The pressing question as to whence comes this tremendous creative force is left unanswered. The proposed answer of an emergence from a social

---

[15] Richardson, *op. cit.*, p. 170. F. F. Bruce, *op. cit.*, p. 33. For a masterful history and analysis of form criticism cf. N. B. Stonehouse, "Jesus in the Hands of a Barthian: Rudolph Bultmann's Jesus in the Perspective of a Century of Criticism," *The Westminster Theological Journal*, 1:1–42, November, 1938. Richardson, in his *The Miracle-Stories of the Gospels* says that the "one thing which we cannot do is to invent a picture of Jesus which professes to be based upon the 'facts' which the Evangelists record yet ignores their interpretation of them, for fact and interpretations are indissoluble and together constitute 'history,'" p. 125.

milieu is hardly adequate. *Genius is always highly personal.*
Who were these geniuses who could write the world's greatest
literature, the world's greatest Life, the world's greatest love
story, the world's greatest theological treatises, yet pass by
unnoticed, or at least unrecorded? If a social milieu could
produce the literature of the New Testament we have a type
of phenomenon as distressing of explanation as the miracles
critics endeavor to explain away.[16]

Our conclusion can only be this: *Synoptic agnosticism*[17]
*is not possible and the New Testament Gospels stand histori-
cally reliable including the miracle story.*

III. THE OPPOSITION TO MIRACLES FROM PHILOSOPHY HAS NOT BEEN SUCCESSFUL.

The denial of miracles by philosophy has been essentially
in terms of some type of *determinism.* It may be a *physical determinism* that rules out miracles as in materialism or naturalism. It may be a *logical determinism*[18] that forbids miracles

[16] "Indeed, the theory of the collective origin of the synoptic tradition
would suppose that there arose almost spontaneously an intense faith in the
divinity of a crucified Jew, a complete and sublime system of dogma and
moral, an organized cult life—all without the dominant personal influence
of Jesus, or even of Paul, since it prevailed at Rome before his advent. Such
a proposition contradicts everything we know of the primitive communities."
McGinley, *op. cit.,* p. 7. C. H. Dodd vigorously rejects the notion that "the
whole great course of Christian history is a massive pyramid balanced upon
the apex of some trivial occurrence." *History and the Gospel,* p. 109. He repeatedly argues in this book that the Gospels and the Epistles depend upon
the essential facts of the life of Christ and that it was not possible for it to
be otherwise. Cf. pp. 71, 72, 82–84, 109–110.

[17] Cf. the very strong words against synoptic agnosticism by Richardson,
op. cit., pp. 170–171; Filson, "How I Interpret the Bible" ("the longer I
study the more convinced I am that the gospel stands or falls with the statements that Jesus lived, that we know the essentials of what He said and did,
and that we have a substantial outline of how the church took form," p. 182);
D. M. Baillie, *op. cit.,* p. 58. Turning back on form Criticism Joblin writes:
"Form criticism has convinced me that Mark was in the direct current of
the living tradition when he gathered the material used and treasured by the
Church in which he lived; in other words, the work of the Form critics has
moved the Gospel records *into the stream of history* rather than out of it."
Op. cit., p. 47. Italics are ours. Worthy of special mention is the strong position of W. Manson in *Jesus the Messiah* for reliable data on Jesus, and trenchant criticisms of Form criticism and Gospel agnosticism.

[18] A. S. Farrar, *Critical History of Free Thought,* considers Spinoza the
founder of all objections *a priori* of the inconceivability of miracles, pp. 160–
161.

as in pantheism and Absolute Idealism (Spinoza, Hegel). It may be an *ethical determinism* that rules out miracles as inconsistent with the nature or purposes of God as in various idealisms, deism, and religious modernism. Our notations, in a word, are as follows:

A. Our reply to physical determinism, and all forms of scientism is that the self-transcendence of man over matter, instinct, and stimulus shows that there is *more* to reality than cause and effect.[19]

B. Our reply to logical determinism is of much the same order. Novelty, creativity, and freedom are facts not assimilable to logical determinism.

C. Our reply to idealism and religious modernism is:

1. An optimistic anthropology must be assumed along with a defense of the moral continuity of man with God, and a definition of sin that is essentially inconsequential. We do not believe that the facts justify such interpretations. The realistic attitude toward sin is a healthy sign in certain places of modern theology.[20]

2. The genuineness of the claim of revelation in the Scriptures must be by-passed and ignored by idealism and religious liberalism.

In general, we reply to all of them that *facts* are not to be "killed" by philosophies. If miracles are matters of sane, credible historical *fact*, then philosophers must not "kill" the facts to maintain their systems, but they must adjust their philosophies to the facts. If miracles have the same type of credible evidence that permits a historian to believe in the existence of the Hittites, or Alexander the Great, or the Theban Empire; and if the attack upon the miracles is shown to be unsuccessful, then miracles stand as part of the body of fact that every

---

[19] This has been masterfully done by R. Niebuhr, *The Nature and Destiny of Man.* All other arguments against naturalism may also be invoked at this point.

[20] Surveying this modern emphasis of realistic theology on the profound nature of sin is Mary Thelen's *Man as Sinner.*

philosopher must insert in his metaphysics. Miracles are ignored frequently today by philosophers, not upon the basis of a lengthy, detailed, genuine historical investigation, but on the grounds of the deep, abiding prejudice of modern man who believes in some form of scientism or determinism and so rules out the transcendent *a priori*.[21]

In conclusion, philosophy has not broken the force of the evidence for miracles because: (1) proposed metaphysical systems are not faithful to *all* the facts; or (2) it willfully ignores the entire concept of revelation and its verification in contrast to creating a metaphysical system by dialectics or analysis, etc.; (3) or it is not true to human nature in its transcendence or sin in its rebelliousness and darkness; or (4) it constructs metaphysics prior to noting the sound historical evidence for miracles, and then in turn rules out miracles *a priori*.

One of the most profound and confusing prejudices of modern man is that he believes that one is scientist *or* Christian, that one affirms the uniformity of nature *or* else demands a hodge-podge, that one is intellectual and naturalist *or* emotional and religious. Orthodox Christians believe in the uniformity of Nature for all practical purposes of science; they believe in revelation verified by the most active and highest use of man's intellect; they believe that emotion must be previously verified by sensible and rational evidence; they believe that a man may be scientist and Christian.

[21] For example, Lewis accuses modern man of ruling out miracles because modern man thinks he has found the real story of the universe in atoms, time and space, or economics and politics. *Op. cit.*, p. 119. Murray indicates that the rejection of miracles by modern man is just as much metaphysical and philosophical as the man who accepts them, i.e., it is not modern man as scientific and Christian as dogmatist and metaphysician. "The Spiritual and Historical Evidence for Miracles," p. 313. Bruce declares that if the historical evidence for miracles is good, a historian will not refuse them on *a priori* grounds. *Op. cit.*, p. 60. Speaking of the closed mind of a person given to scientism, Lunn writes: "The determination to regard the natural order as a closed system is a dogma which is completely sterilizing in its influence on research. An analogous dogma would have been equally fatal to astronomical research." *Op. cit.*, p. 243.

IV. MODERN PSYCHOLOGY CANNOT DISCREDIT THE MIRACLES

Psychology has suggested many reasons to doubt the actual occurrence of the miracles recorded in the Gospels.

A. *Psychologists have said miracles are faith cures.* It is well-known to psychologists and to the medical profession that many ailments of patients are functional or hysterical, and no medicine or operation will cure them. The mental cause of the ailment is so great as to actually create genuine symptoms. Such people have been cured by psychiatry, hypnosis, or unusual unexpected experiences, or by religious conversions. It has been argued that Jesus was such a magnetic or dynamic personality or such a natural born personality-psychologist that He could dispel these hysterical or functional symptoms by His own ability. Now we would not argue that there were no cases of hysteria or functional disorders among the multitudes Jesus healed, but to consider all such miracles as faith cures is not possible. The healing of congenital blindness or leprosy cannot be so accounted. Further, there is the nature miracle which is inconceivable as a faith cure, not to mention the inconceivability of raising a person from the dead by faith cure. No genuine opposition can come from this consideration.

Garvie's objections against Matthew Arnold's theory that miracles are faith-cures are: (1) Modern science does not admit a wide enough scope for faith-cures to cover all the miracles of the Gospels. (2) Faith-cures cannot account for nature-miracles. (3) The theory is overburdened by having to insist on the self-deception of Jesus and of the multitudes.[22] Besides this Richardson indicates that the concept of faith-cures was not known in Jesus' time.[23]

B. *We could not tell a miracle if we saw one, is another objection from psychology.* That is to say, it would be of such

---

[22] A. E. Garvie, *A Handbook of Christian Apologetics*, p. 74 ff.
[23] *The Miracle-Stories of the Gospels.*

a nature that we could not make heads or tails out of it. It would be so utterly novel as to be incomprehensible. But surely, if such be the objection what do we do to medical science and its amazing cures? Years ago when peritonitis reached a certain stage, the person bloated up and died; but now, where death once was inevitable, miraculous recoveries are made with penicillin. Consider too, the marked changes that can be made in human personality by adequately treating people with endocrine gland deficiencies. Dull, moronic people can be made normal, bright and cheerful. Consider too the progress in other sciences. The unusual, the remarkable, the unexpected is daily routine reading in scientific reports. Hume's objection, then, that we could not tell a miracle if we saw one would not only rule out miracles, but also (1) any possibility of recognizing a miracle drug or cure in medicine, and (2) new and great discoveries in other sciences.

C. *Psychologists have thrown grave doubt over man's powers to adequately report events.* Psychologists have set up mock situations and have had subjects write down what happened. The contradictions and uncertainties recorded by the subjects has been a staggering blow to the so-called reliability of the human person as an observer. The same general skepticism has been applied to the recorders of the Gospel.

It is not our purpose to controvert the empirical findings of psychology as to the matter of degree of reliability of witnesses. The data can be found in any text on applied psychology. However, two observations must be made at the outset. (1) Law courts have not stopped functioning in spite of what the psychologists have said. No other means has yet been devised to replace the data that can be gleaned from a witness's account. Evidently law courts assume that such witnessing is not quite as unreliable as some would make it out to be. (2) The psychologist is apt to prove too much. If car A struck car B and killed Mr. C, the subsequent investigation might turn up such conflicting reports: Car A was going

30 mph—car A was going 40 mph; car A signaled before turning—car A did not signal; car A was straddling the white line
—car A was not straddling the white line; car B rammed into
car A at full tilt—car B screeched its wheels, the brakes were
applied too hard, etc., etc. Now, if we were to judge that an
event laden with contradictions could not occur, said accident could not have occurred. But the smashed cars and the
dead Mr. C. argue to the contrary. In spite of divergence of
reports certain data are agreed on by all. Hence, a limitation
must be set upon the supposed unreliability of witnesses. Does
not the psychologist himself who performs the experiment
assume that he is pretty reliable? If he took his conclusions too seriously he would have to throw his own experimentation out, for he, too, is a witness to psychological experiments. And how could he test the reliability of witnesses
in some mock accident if he did not assume that he had seen
what did happen so as to check the reliability of the witnesses?

In reference to the Gospel accounts, we are not limited to
one witness or a few witnesses or one miracle or a few
miracles. There were numerous miracles seen by a great number of people. The increase in the number of witnesses and
miracles highly increases the possibility of the miraculous
occurring. One or two healings under dubious circumstances,
with few witnesses, would not be readily acceptable to any
conservative. But the gospel record is filled with miracles of
every description performed within the eyesight of hundreds
and at times thousands of people. No doubt can be cast upon
the miracles then on the recent studies in reliability in reporting events.

Consider too, the chasteness, sobriety, and general reliability of the accounts. When it comes to faithfully reporting
geographical data, historical data, and cultural data, the Gospel writers have never been successfully accused of a blunder.
As literary documents, in spite of form criticism's assertion

that the Gospels are *Kleinlitteratur* ("sub" literary documents)
the Gospels stand as some of the finest literature human hands
have written. Luke's Gospel has been called by some the most
beautiful book in the world. The evidence of the geographical, historical, cultural, and literary competency of the Gospel
writers lends great weight to their authority in recording the
miracles.

D. *Psychologists have asserted that miracles are contrary
to experience.* This objection has been steadily repeated since
first announced by Hume. What this amounts to is a definition
of a miracle in reverse; or, it amounts to a garbled definition of
a miracle. It is a miracle's ability to arrest the mind, to startle
the imagination, to appear totally unique, *that makes it function as a miracle.* If it did not have this psychological *sting,*
it would not do what it is supposed to do. A miracle is *supposed to be* different from usual, ordinary, customary experience.

Now, if a man asserts that he will believe nothing that is
not customary, he has put out the eyes of science. Certainly,
no valid objection can be made against miracles on the ground
that miracles are so different from what we usually experience, and, at the same time, not urge the same objection
against the novelties of science. The only respectable objection is the objection of the naturalist or materialist who, on
stark metaphysical grounds, affirms that this is not a miracle-
permitting universe.

Supernaturalists have noted that there is a steady loss in
western culture of any appetite for the supernatural or transcendental. The supernatural and transcendental is getting
ruled out with a dogmatism that is no more blind and emotional than that which moderns are accustomed to attribute
only to medieval theologians. The antisupernaturalist insists
that in spite of what the supernaturalist says, and in full disregard of what the supernaturalist denies, that the issue is over
(1) modern, scientific, educated, enlightened mentality with a

universe of law, order, dependability, and regularity, as over-against (2) a narrow, dogmatic, bigoted, obscurantist mentality with a universe that is magical, irregular, and untrustworthy. There has dropped out of modern mentality a genuine spirit of open-minded inquiry. Miracles are condemned as inconceivable before there has been any of the usual investigations that characterize open-mindedness, a spirit of impartiality, or free inquiry. Supernaturalists believe in science, education, enlightenment of mentality as much as antisupernaturalists. They further believe to a very large measure with the antisupernaturalist that this is a universe of order and dependability.

Summary: It has been our purpose to establish the world view that makes miracles conceivable, to discuss the historical reasons for their being factual, and to rebut efforts either to deny their conceivability or factuality. If our purpose has been accomplished, our Christian faith stands wonderfully verified as the religion of God. *It bears the imprimatur of the supernatural, the miraculous.*

CHAPTER VI

THE VERIFICATION OF CHRISTIANITY BY THE SUPERNATURAL CHARACTER OF ITS FOUNDER

THE LIFE AND CHARACTER of Jesus Christ is the holy of holies in the history of the world," wrote Philip Schaff;[1] and if this is true his further judgment cannot be resisted: "Blessed is he who from the heart can believe that Jesus is the Son of God, and the fountain of salvation."[2] There is no doubt that if the Gospel record be recognized as sober history, every person with the ability to see the implications of such an admission must also admit the divinity[3] of the Christian religion, and that Jesus Christ is the greatest man that ever lived. However, ignoring for the moment the testimony of the gospel record, it is true that historical record bears witness to the conviction that Jesus Christ is the greatest man that ever lived.[4] Speaking of the greatness of Jesus, Schaff writes

---

[1] Philip Schaff, *The Person of Christ*, p. 1.

[2] *Ibid.*, p. 3.

[3] In this chapter we are using the word divinity in its older and genuine sense as pertaining to God. It is used parallel to the Greek word *theotes* and *theiotes*. The general thesis of this chapter is similar to what has been called the apologetic of the incarnation, or to those works that rest the case for Christianity in the nature of Jesus Christ, e.g., A. M. Fairbairn, *A Philosophy of the Christian Religion*, and A. B. Bruce, *Apologetics*.

[4] H. G. Wells writes: "When I was asked which single individual has left the most permanent impression on the world, the manner of the questioner almost carried the implication that it was Jesus of Nazareth. I agreed." Then after a very complimentary discussion of the historical greatness of Jesus, Wells asks where Jesus stands in history when strictly judged by a historian's standard. The answer is "By this test Jesus stands first." H. G. Wells, "The Three Greatest Men in History," *The Reader's Digest*, May, 1935, p. 12 ff.

that "this Jesus of Nazareth, without money and arms, conquered more millions than Alexander, Caesar, Mohammed, and Napoleon; without science and learning, He shed more light on things human and divine than all philosophers and scholars combined; without the eloquence of schools, He spoke such words of life as were never spoken before or since, and produced effects which lie beyond the reach of orator or poet; without writing a single line, He set more pens in motion, and furnished themes for more sermons, orations, discussions, learned volumes, works of art, and songs of praise, than the whole army of great men of ancient and modern times."[5]

Yet, how paradoxical are our history books! The greatest man that ever lived is scarcely given a passing reference in our world history books—usually less than a page. Frequently that description is of a humanistic Jesus who could hardly have caused a ripple in the stream of human history, let alone changing its great course by digging new channels with nail-pierced hands. The philosophers are no less innocent, for although from Jesus stems two thousand years of constant philosophical activity, the histories of philosophy either skirt Him entirely or give Him space far in contradiction to His actual impact on history. Casserley, *The Christian in Philosophy*, gives clear evidence of the major role that Christ through Christian philosophy has played in the history of philosophy. Again the philosophical position of Jesus, so to speak, is usually set forth in concepts dictated by religious liberalism, and the judgment of Fairbairn goes unheeded that "it is not Jesus of Nazareth who has so powerfully entered into history; it is the deified Christ who has been believed, loved, and obeyed as the Saviour of the world."[6]

Our thesis is not merely that the great historians admit that Jesus is the greatest man that ever lived, but that *He is unique*

[5] *Ibid.*, pp. 29–30.
[6] *The Philosophy of the Christian Religion*, p. 15.

and therefore incomparable. The Christian gets his cue from the great scene of Revelation 5, in which the entire world is searched for a man to take the book of the future from the hand of God. No man is found worthy, and as John weeps, he is told that the Lion of the Tribe of Judah is worthy to take the book. Here is Jesus Christ not only as great, but as *unique, incomparable, peerless, matchless.*

The first thesis, namely, that the Gospels are reliable history may be doubted; the second, that Jesus is the greatest man that ever lived, cannot. Testimony from many sources to the unexcelled greatness of Christ will be found in abundance in such treatises as Schaff, *The Person of Christ,* and R. L. Woods, *Behold the Man.*[7] The very serious question of this chapter is to what degree the greatness of Jesus depends upon the historical person described in the Gospels.

I. THE GOSPEL PICTURE DEFENDED

It is now admitted that the effort to find two very distinct strata in the Gospels (a stratum of the theological Christ, and a stratum of a human Jesus) is impossible. The picture of the Gospels is uniformly both the human Jesus and the theological Christ. It is the thesis of the believer that this is a true picture. The purpose of a hypothesis is to make meaningful individual phenomenon. The germ-theory of disease is almost universally accepted, because it renders so many thousands of our experiences meaningful. In science a hypothesis which has a very close connection with fact, experience, and experimentation is held as true or valid. The conservative argues in this manner: If we assume the doctrine of the incarnation, that Jesus is God the Son robed in human nature,

---

[7] Schaff has a bibliography of books which deal with greatness of Jesus; and has in great detail the famous testimony of Napoleon. Woods has over four hundred testimonies about Christ with full bibliographical references. An older work much like Woods is J. H. Whitmore, *Testimony of Nineteen Centuries to Jesus of Nazareth* (1889). The testimony is documented. Robert Speer's *Studies of the Man Christ Jesus* is a beautiful analysis of the many wonders of our Lord's personality and character.

the data of the Gospels becomes meaningful. That is to say, between the hypothesis of the incarnation and the actual facts of the Gospel record there is an amazing agreement. The only procedure is to ask ourselves this question: *If God became incarnate, what kind of man would He be?* It is the contention of the believer that the life of Jesus Christ answers these questions in such a compelling and convincing manner that the deity of Christ must be admitted.

The picture of Jesus in the Gospels is declared to be correct by the Catholic Church, Oriental Orthodox Church, and orthodox Protestant Churches. These affirm that His greatness is due to the fact that He is exactly what the Gospels say He is.

Religious liberals, atheists, and unbelievers will admit the greatness of Jesus, but deny the full validity of the record. Their common thesis is that a uniquely good man in the hands of well-meaning but imaginative disciples or religious community becomes a Son of God with miraculous powers. The *divinely unique* and *supernatural* is contributed by His disciples or the religious community.[8]

Let us first realize that we have few *a priori* notions about our Lord's incarnation. We cannot decide what century He should be born in, or what country, or what state in life, or with what physical features. There are no well-known rules about incarnations. That is to say, there can be no formal objection to Jesus' claims solely on the grounds that He was born in Palestine during a certain century and of poor parents. Nothing in the nature of things tells us whether He should have been born in a palace or a stable, or as to whether His father should be a musician or a carpenter. Perhaps in the inscrutable divine counsels there are reasons, but we are ignorant of them. Therefore none can form any sort of *a priori* prejudice against the incarnation from such considerations.

---

[8] Fairbairn has described in vivid, graphic terms the orthodox and the liberal pictures of Jesus. Cf. *op. cit.*, p. 7 ff.

It reminds us of Kierkegaard's discussion of "The Moment." God has to grant the conditions; man cannot manufacture them. So it is with the incarnation. The terms of it God alone can prescribe. We can discover the conditions of the incarnation only after it has happened.

A. *If God became a man we would expect His human life to be sinless.* We cannot conceive an incarnation in which the human nature assumed could involve the divine nature in a transgression or fault. If a man refuse to grant this on metaphysical grounds affirming that if so held it would deny the reality of the human nature, he certainly must admit it on ethical grounds. However, it is the uniform testimony of the New Testament that Jesus Christ was sinless, blameless, and faultless, and believing Christians of all ages would heartily assent to Schaff's affirmation that "in vain do we look through the entire biography of Jesus for a single stain or the slightest shadow on His moral character. There never lived a more harmless being on the earth. He injured nobody, He took advantage of nobody. He never spoke an improper word, He never committed a wrong action."[9]

The language of the New Testament is restrained and adulation is missing. Pilate could find no fault with Him, and admitted in so many terms that the death penalty was a trumped-up charge. He admitted that he could find no fault in Jesus, and his wife warned him that Jesus was a just man. Both the Roman centurion and the thief on the cross acknowledge His moral dignity, and the multitude give Jesus a left-handed compliment by saying that He trusted in God. Judas admits that he betrayed innocent blood and "even dumb nature responded in mysterious sympathy; and the beclouded Heavens above, and the shading earth beneath, united in paying their unconscious tribute to the divine purity of their dying Lord."[10]

John the Baptist could find no sin in Christ to be confessed;

[9] *Op. cit.,* p. 32.   [10] *Ibid.,* p. 35.

Paul admits that Christ "knew no sin"; and Peter affirms that Christ "did no sin, neither was guile found in his mouth"; and John makes it clear that Jesus is the only man who has ever lived who has the moral purity and worth to take the sealed book from the Father's hand.

How our Lord is to be contrasted with great saints and mystics! To them confession of sin, and painfully laborious efforts toward saintliness were daily fare. In fact, the closer to God the more vivid becomes their consciousness of sinfulness. Jesus possessed perfect sinlessness and purity not by struggle, privation, asceticism, or pilgrimage. It was His by birth and nature. Jesus never could have written Romans 7 with its terrible inner moral struggle; nor could Jesus have died like saintly Augustine, by daily reciting on his deathbed the penitential Psalms coupled with confession of sins. Our Lord never confessed sin, never admitted a need of repentance, but appeared at all times as a man possessing perfect moral purity. We marvel at such giants as Luther and Calvin, yet there seems a genius in Augustine that looms greater than Luther or Calvin. Going from the writings of Augustine to Paul, we feel that "lo, a greater than Augustine is here," for deeper than the deepest in Augustine are the depths of Paul. Yet in going from Paul to Jesus we feel we have left lowlands for Himalayan peaks. The great saints of the Old Testament— Abraham, Moses, David, or Isaiah—are but trophies of forgiving and empowering grace, whereas Jesus towers over them needing neither forgiveness nor the sanctifying grace mortal sinners require.

I think it would be no exaggeration to affirm that those who criticize the moral perfection of Christ are either moral anarchists, e.g., Nazis and Communists, or quibblers, e.g., those who object to His cleansing the Temple, or sending the pigs down the slope into the water, or in cursing the fig tree.[11]

---

[11] C. F. Rogers, *The Case for Christianity*, p. 99 ff., defends the morality of such actions in some detail. Richardson, *The Miracle-Stories of the Gospels* defends the sending of the pigs into the lake, pp. 72–74.

There He stands, *sinless*. Whatever men may claim for being great, this is one thing they cannot. They may be brilliant or strong, fast or clever, creative or inspired, but not *sinless*. Sinless perfection and perfect sinlessness is what we would expect of God-incarnate, and this we do find in Jesus Christ. The hypothesis and the facts concur.

B. *If God were a man we would expect Him to be holy.*[12] By sinless we mean the absence of moral blemish, and by holiness we mean the positive presence of spirituality. If God were incarnate we would expect Him to be the model of piety, spirituality, and holiness. Jesus, if admired for nothing else, is admired for the religion He practiced. Even those who reject His transcendence, the religious liberals, find in Him the greatest example of genuine personal holiness. His prayer life was deep, spiritual, and beautiful. His speech was clean, chaste, and honorable. His attitude toward God the Father was one of deep respect, profound trust, and always reverent, chaste, and proper. His teaching about the spiritual life was that which emphasized the ethical, the inward, and the pure in contrast to the external, the empty ritual, and the hypocritical. To hundreds of thousands of Christians, Jesus led the one perfect life of piety and personal holiness on the sole consideration that He was God-incarnate.

Such a personality, possessed of moral purity and perfect piety, who stands in such a marked contrast to His earnest, but erring disciples, is no fiction of the imagination. "It seems absolutely incredible" writes Garvie, "that any one of the disciples, or several in concert, or the Christian community could have first invented and then depicted the personality of Jesus as it appears in the Gospels."[13] Here again the hypothesis of the incarnation is adequately supported by the

[12] Schaff, *op. cit.*, says that as great a miracle as is Jesus' sinlessness, greater is His positive virtue "which rises in magnitude as we contemplate the positive side, namely, his absolute moral and religious perfection," p. 41.
[13] A. E. Garvie, *A Handbook of Christian Apologetics*, p. 98.

facts, i.e., the pure, beautiful moral purity and holiness of the Jesus of the Gospels.

C. *If God were a man we would expect His words to be the greatest words ever spoken.* What is great literature? great oratory? The famed eloquence of one generation often appears stilted and artificial to another. Great music, great poetry, great literature is great because it speaks to something universal in human nature. Because it does this, it is able to stand the test of time. The simple plots of the opera have a perennial appeal to audiences because they are so human. They represent identical situations that endless human generations experience. Shakespeare appeals to us because he has so magnificently caught the universal in human nature and experience. He said beautifully, masterfully, what each of us already has experienced and known, but has failed to find the right pool of words to dip our pen into and so tell it.

Statistically speaking, the Gospels are the greatest literature ever written. They are read by more people, quoted by more authors, translated into more tongues, represented in more art, set to more music, than any other book or books written by any man in any century in any land. But the words of Christ are not great on the grounds that they have such a statistical edge over anybody else's words. They are read more, quoted more, loved more, believed more, and translated more because they are the greatest words ever spoken. And where is their greatness? Their greatness lies in the pure, lucid spirituality in dealing clearly, definitively, and *authoritatively* with the greatest problems that throb in the human breast; namely, Who is God? Does He love me? Does He care for me? What should I do to please Him? How does He look at my sin? How can I be forgiven? Where will I go when I die? How must I treat others?

No other man's words have the appeal of Jesus' words because no other man can answer these fundamental human questions as Jesus answered them. They are the kind of words and the kind of answers we would expect God to give, and we who believe in Jesus' deity have no problem as to why these words came from His mouth.

D. *If God were a man we would expect Him to exert a profound power over human personality.* At no point is the bankruptcy of behavioristic psychology and all impersonal, pseudo-scientific psychology, so evident as in the realm of human personality. Personality is distinctly a spiritual and religious concept and not a scientific one, and therefore psychologists are caught in a dilemma of trying to understand a spiritual entity by recourse to non-spiritual categories. One of the greatest impacts among human beings is the impact of personality upon personality. Most human beings are rather ordinary in their impact on other human beings. True, there is always influence, but seldom *impact*. Here and there is a remarkable preacher, general, professor, artist, politician, or executive who has the power of personality impact. One cannot help but feel that General MacArthur and Prime Minister Churchill are men whose personal presence is dynamic.

If God were a man we would not only expect Him to be sinless and holy, but to possess personality *in its most profound essence* which would in turn manifest itself in its impact upon His contemporaries. Whether Jesus be man or God, whether the Gospels be mainly fiction or fancy, certainly a historic person named Jesus gave certain men such an impact as to be unequaled by far in the entire annals of the human race. After nearly two thousand years the impact is not at all spent, but daily there are people who have tremendous revolutionary experiences which they associate with Jesus Christ, be He dead or risen in Heaven.

The personality of Jesus is without parallel. It is unique and incomparable. Wherever He is, He is the Master. When surrounded by hungry multitudes or by hating Pharisees, when questioned by clever theologians or besought by stricken sinners, whether examined by stupid disciples or by a Roman governor, *He is the Master.* When He asks men to leave all and follow Him they do, or else leave Him broken-hearted. If they betray, they commit suicide. But His grip on men is not fanatical. It leads men to deeds of ethical quality and great self-sacrifice.

Nowhere does Jesus as an incomparable personality reveal Himself as in His suffering. His ministry commenced with forty days in the fierce suffering of temptations. In His three years of public ministry He suffered from poverty, from hunger, from weary journeys, from the cruel accusations of His enemies, and from His misunderstanding loved ones. But as His decease approaches, the intensity of His own feelings increases, and His words are weighted with sorrowful premonitions.

The last days on earth commence with a picture of spiritual agony and mental anguish without parallel in all human history—*Gethsemane.* Midst olive trees, night shadows, and drowsy disciples, a spiritual Armageddon is fought with sweat, blood, and agonizing prayer. Pure, holy, piety beams forth as well as complete, and magnificent consecration to God. Then follows arrest, abuse, mistrial, lying accusations. Next came the cruel, heartless words, "Crucify him." Amidst the swirl of human passions—hatred by the Jews, fear by the disciples, cruelty by the soldiers, callousness and fear of Caesar by Pilate, morbid curiosity by Herod—Jesus alone is possessed of calm. He alone is the master of passion, of heart, of tongue, and of will.

Listen to His words as He dies; watch Him as the life-blood flows from His veins. He pauses to forgive a penitent thief and open Paradise's gates to him; He remembers His dear mother and gives orders for her care. When the effects of loss of blood, shock, exposure, and torture finally make their demands felt, He cries "I thirst." As the inward spiritual sufferings reach a climax, He recites the words of a great Old Testament saint, and as He feels life ebbing surely and steadily toward that last moment of consciousness before the silver thread is snapped, He, in an act of pure and holy piety, commends His departing soul to God. With one last burst of energy, knowing the full meaning of the cross before its inexhaustible meaning was grasped by human consciousness, He cries, "It is finished." This is how the greatest human Person that ever lived, died; and He died like no other man ever has.

How futile it is for scholars to ransack Greek, Roman, and Jewish literature to find so-called parallels to Jesus' words. Is it not already a confession of the greatness of Jesus to even feel required to find parallels to His words? Was it not the greatness of Jesus which has informed us as to how tremendous certain truths are, which truths have already been said by others? It is the great personality behind the words of Jesus that we must never lose sight of, for it was that personality that made His life and His words so great.

To the believer in the integrity of the gospel record, there is no answer to be found by involved investigation, for it is on the surface of the record. Jesus Christ as the God-man is the greatest *personality* that ever lived, and therefore His personal impact is the greatest of any man that ever lived. This is true no matter how one construes the synoptic problem.

E. *If God were a man we would expect supernatural doings: 1. Being God alone would involve some tokens of the supernatural; 2. Certainly God owes it to man that there is no possible mistake at such a tremendous point.* At every step of His life, Jesus Christ confronts us with the supernatural. He was born by a supernatural birth; He was protected by supernatural ministrations of angels; He possessed supernatural knowledge; He could do supernatural things. He could order Nature, and Nature obeyed. He could speak to disease and it fled. He could confront the dead, and bring the departed back.

The believer believes that Jesus must, of necessity, have

worked the miraculous. Such important and impressive claims
need more than ordinary means of impressing us with their
truthfulness. The miracles are not warts or growths that may
be shaved or cut off, leaving the main body of the gospel
record untouched. Garvie very strongly insists that "a Christ
who being Son of God, and seeking to become Saviour of
men, [and] wrought no miracle, would be less intelligible and
credible than the Jesus whom the Gospel records so consistently present to us."[14] Mozley argues very much to the
same intent in his first lecture *On Miracles.* No mere philosophical speculation, no inferential judgment, no appeal to
innate ideas, can carry the burden of this assertion. The human mind cannot be accused of incredulity or excessive skepticism to demand more than usual methods of verification at
this point. Nor is the Gospel record lacking in the strongest
type of verification of the theological claims of Jesus Christ
as the Son of God.

Supernatural characteristics were part of His own person.
When men sought to kill Him He could pass by them untouched (Luke 4:29, 30); on one occasion His preincarnate
glory shown through His human body (Matthew 17, the
transfiguration);[15] and on three occasions in His earthly ministry, God Himself spoke from Heaven words of divine approval. We cannot decide *a priori* how an incarnate God
would be made manifest, but there is certainly nothing lacking or disappointing in the evidences of divinity in the gospel
records in reference to Jesus Christ.

This is the watershed of all human opinion—is this divinity
the elaboration of the religious community as all unbelief
must affirm, or did it actually characterize Jesus Christ? The
Christian affirms confidently that Jesus, being God the Son,
there is nothing incredible or inherently irrational or para-

---

[14] *Ibid.,* p. 73.
[15] Cf. Wilbur Smith, *The Supernaturalness of Christ,* Chapter V, "The
Unique Transfiguration of Christ," in which the evidential value of this
event is set forth.

doxical in the supernatural elements of our Lord's earthly life. The hypothesis that He is the Son of God is amply verified by the presence of the supernatural in His life.

F. *If God were to become a man we would expect Him to manifest the love of God.* Certainly if God is love, then Christ must exhibit that love as no other man has ever exhibited it if He be God Himself. Who could ever controvert the claim that in the recorded life of Jesus Christ we have the supreme example of pure, unsullied, unselfish divine love? Where in all history is there a man whose touch upon the life and heart of the sinful, the brokenhearted, the contrite, the despised, the poor, is so tender, so loving, so gentle? Who is it but Christ that has taught us to be kind and gentle to the downtrodden and to the fallen? Who is it but Christ that alone is called the Friend of sinners? In spite of all progress of social theory and development of democratic thought, nothing yet surpasses the life of Christ as an inspiration to humanity to be humane to itself.

The supreme act of love and manifestation of love in Christ was without question His death on the cross. Is there anything in all recorded history like His death? Read the gripping description of our Lord's death by a man who knew through study and experience its great meaning:

"While Jesus suffered the agony of seeing sin seemingly tie the very hands of the Father from delivering Him from death, He bore it to free our souls. He hung in mortal pain by His loving arms held fast to the tree, that we might be sure in the hour of death of dropping into 'the everlasting arms.' He died with this agonizing *why* upon His lips, that we might die with no question upon ours.

"That startling cry, misunderstood then as now, made the spectators shudder. One last upward look, one last word of prayer, and the death of deaths has come! Forward falls the brow, thorn-scarred and bloody! The noblest, purest soul that ever dwelt in human body is gone! The lifeless form hangs

limp on the Tree of the World's Shame! The Author of Life
is dead!

"Never again could crucifixion have such a victim! Never
had death such prey! Loving hands that had wrought in every
possible good, their work is done! Poor blood-stained limbs
that in love trod so many a weary mile while serving man,
their last step has been taken! Great busy brain through
which had pulsed the thoughts of the Infinite, its thinking is
over! World-embracing heart beating in rhythm with the
measureless love of God, the Roman spear will soon lunge
needlessly into thy divine tenderness! Farewell, Sovereign
Soul through which Deity surged and suffered in quest of a
lost humanity! O world of my sin, the sin of the world has
slain the Son of God! What a Cross! What a death! What a
love! 'My God! My God! Why didst Thou die for me?' "[16]

G. *If God were to become a man, He would be the most
divine man that ever lived,* i.e., He would be unique and incomparable. Jesus Christ is not a great man among great men.
He is uniquely the greatest man of all history. This can be
easily verified from the mouth of atheist, infidel, and unbeliever, not to mention the enormous testimony from the Christian church. Very obviously, if Jesus Christ is God incarnate
there is no mystery as to why He is the greatest man of all
history. Notice the nature of this greatness: *it is precisely because His life is so divine.*

At this point of the argument the *background* of Jesus must
be presented. Whether we fully believe the reliability of the
Gospels or not, it will be admitted by all that Jesus was born
in Palestine of poor parents; that He had none of the advan-
tages of wealth; that He was not learned or schooled either
by Jew or Greek; that He had no opportunity or occasion
at any time to contact some remarkable source of mental,
philosophical, or scientific body of knowledge.

Yet this Galilean rustic proclaims Himself to be the Son of

[16] B. Champion, *More Than Atonement,* p. 188-189.

God, the Light of the World, and after 1800 years,[17] His claim is still accepted by hundreds of thousands of people in the most enlightened countries of the world. That a Galilean carpenter should so claim to be the Light of the world, and be so recognized after so many centuries, is best explained on the grounds of His divinity.

H. *If God were a man we would expect His personality to be true humanity.* Only God could tell us what a true man should be like. Certainly there are anticipations of the perfect man in the piety of the Old Testament. First and foremost must be a complete God-consciousness coupled with a complete dedication and consecration of life to God. Then ranked below this are the other virtues, graces, and attributes that characterize perfect humanity. Intelligence must not stifle piety, and prayer must not be a substitute for work, and zeal must not be irrational fanaticism, and reserve must not become stolidity. In Christ we have the perfect blend of personality traits because as God Incarnate He is perfect humanity. Schaff describes our Lord in reference to this point of our discussion as follows: "His zeal never degenerated into passion, nor His constancy into obstinacy, nor His benevolence into weakness, nor His tenderness into sentimentality. His unworldliness was free from indifference and unsociability, His dignity from pride and presumption, His affectibility from undue familiarity, His self-denial from moroseness, His temperance from austerity. He combined child-like innocency with manly strength, absorbing devotion to God with untiring interest in the welfare of man, tender love to the sinner with uncompromising severity against sin, commanding dignity with winning humility, fearless courage with wise caution, unyielding firmness with sweet gentleness."[18]

Conclusion: The believer considers the evidence conclusive.

[17] Cf. C. A. Row, *A Manual of Christian Evidences,* Chapter I.
[18] *Op. cit.,* p. 64. At this point Speer, *op. cit.,* must be mentioned for a painstaking analysis of the virtues of Christ's personality.

Granted that Jesus is the Son of God, all the various features
of His life so follow. His sinlessness, His holiness, His magnificent words, His dynamic personality, His supernatural characteristics, His love, and His greatness, all naturally and
necessarily follow from His divinity.

II. REBUTTAL

That the New Testament in all its parts considers Jesus
divine can no longer be questioned. To use the Ritschlian
expression, Jesus has had the *value of God* to millions of believers, whether He actually possesses divinity or not. The
liberal and unbeliever denies the metaphysical deity of Christ.
Can such an assertion bear the weight of the case it must
seek to defend? We think not. Unbelief cannot make good its
case for the following reasons:

A. *There is no time for any evolution of the conception of
Jesus.* It is embarrassing at least for the critic who remains
within the Christian Church to charge Jesus with delusion or
deliberate falsification. Critics have preferred to lay the onus
of misrepresentation on the religious community that trans-
muted this human spiritual genius into a divine supernatural
Lord. Obviously this took time. But when we look for the
time element it cannot be found.

To begin with, earliest Church history, apart from the erring
Ebionites, recognizes a divine Christ. From Acts through
Revelation Christ is presented as divine. It was formerly
thought by critics that the Gospels could be excavated in
such a way as to reveal the original layers of history, as depict-
ing a human but remarkable spiritual personality. Now, except for incurable old fashioned liberals, it is conceded that
the Jesus of Mark is as divine as the Logos of John.[19] As the
documents of the New Testament stand, there is not the
slightest chance of recovering a strata untouched by super-

[19] For a scathing rebuke of the liberal effort see A. M. Hunter, *Interpreting the New Testament*, p. 49 ff.

natural conceptions of Jesus. The evolution from a human, natural Jesus to a divine supernatural Lord had to take place between the life of Christ and the writings of the New Testament. But as we showed in our discussion of the miracles and the resurrection there is no time for this. Paul was converted about 33 A.D., and certainly the testimony of Paul is that Christ is divine. At this point there was never any debate between Paul and any disciples. In the authentic writings of Paul we have authentic opinions of the Church which force the issue back to at least 33 A.D., which leaves three years for this transmutation to take place. This is tantamount to admitting that from the day of Pentecost the Church was in possession of high Christology.

Then we are faced with the problem of deciding where the disciples got it. Either they got it directly from Christ or they imagined it themselves. If they got it from Christ, then we either have to admit the truthfulness of the New Testament Christology or impugn the person of Christ. If we impugn the person of Christ, we must admit that what on the one hand appears to be the holiest, godliest, divinest man that ever lived is also guilty of the grossest misrepresentations in all of human history. But if we charge the transmutation to the disciples then we must admit that they had such views right from the start. The authentic epistles of Galatians, Romans, and Corinthians will tolerate no other conclusion. The rugged facts of the case indicate no other possibility than this: That the disciples had a notion of Christ's divinity which they got directly from Christ. Then again we are caught in a most vexing dilemma if we deny the truthfulness of it: We must admit that the holiest, godliest, divinest Man that ever lived is at the same time the most pretentious falsifier that ever lived. The case for unbelief cannot be made.

B. *There is no variation in the picture of Jesus.* We have already indicated that all the documents of Christianity point to a divine Messiah. The Jesus of the Gospels is a divine Lord

and Saviour. Further, we have indicated that it is impossible
to recover a pure historical section of the Gospel which presents a human but spiritual man. *If we deny the divinity of
Christ and the presence of the supernatural, where do we get
the picture of the Jesus we think actually existed?* We get it
out of our own heads dictated by our own metaphysical and
religious convictions; we do not get it out of the Gospels. The
Christ of atheism, of liberalism, and of Barthianism is not the
Christ of the historical documents.[20] There is not a shred of
evidence that such a Christ lived. The Christ of these men is
a hybrid combination of accepted segments of the Gospel
narrative patched together with religious and metaphysical
opinions. The documentary evidence weighs like lead against
the unbeliever at this point.

C. *Although there are four Gospels, it is one Personality
presented.* Critics present the Gospels as a series of disassoci-
ated fragments. This is especially true in form-criticism. But
what should be a very vexing phenomenon to form-criticism
is that the Christ of the four Gospels is the same Christ. The
content of the Gospels varies, the length varies, the perspective varies, many of the details vary, but *it is the same Person
throughout.* It is not possible that out of fragments, myths,
legends, snippets, parables, and wonder-stories should emerge
that same divine picture. Form-criticism has an impossible
burden to bear at this point, as does all agnostic synoptic
criticism. Hunter's criticism of form-criticism is that "scepticism has vitiated [it] almost from the start."[21] The two mistakes of the form-critics which he specifically names are (1)
they completely ignore the traditions of the early post-apos-
talic Church as to the composition of the Gospels; and (2)
they have a "willful disregard of the existence of eye-witnesses
in the early Christian communities."[22]

[20] Says A. M. Hunter very strongly in *Interpreting the New Testament.*
[21] *Ibid.,* p. 39.
[22] *Loc. cit.*

In Hunter's remarkable book he defends the general authenticity of the Gospels. The *facts* of the Gospels created the *faith;* not the *faith* the *facts.* He gives three reasons for believing this: (1) The entire atmosphere of the Gospels is first century Palestine; (2) the gospel record is built upon the gospel message (*kerygma*) which can be traced back to within a few years of the crucifixion; (3) the gospel writers all appeal to the Old Testament as containing the prophecies which in turn were fulfilled in Christ. This must mean that the *facts* were prior to the faith and controlled the faith, else the Church would never have been able to get away with such claims. His conclusion is then that "all these considerations point in one direction. The Gospel is rooted in history."[23]

D. *Remarkable personalities are behind remarkable movements.* One of the weaknesses of modern studies in the history and sociology of religion is to become overly engrossed in the contribution that a cultus or a culture makes to a religion, with an almost stupid forgetfulness of the power and function of dynamic religious personalities. In much of New Testament criticism great personalities like Jesus, Peter, and Paul, are almost dropped out of the picture and replaced by religio-sociological forces. We do not deny that cultures and civilizations have certain "spirit of the times" or "moods," but great human achievement is always from great human personality.

Very clearly one of the chief issues in gospel criticism is whether the dynamic of Christianity stems from the *sitz-em-leben* (the social situation) or from Jesus Christ. It is our contention, which we believe is supported by all historical analogy, that the moving power behind the Christian movement was not some religio-sociological condition obtaining in ancient Palestine, *but the personality of Jesus Christ Himself.*

The previous point and this one when forged together make

---

[23] *Ibid.,* pp. 47–48. He is substantially joined in this position by C. H Dodd, *History and the Gospel.*

a powerful refutation of agnostic synoptic criticism. The Gospels in all their variety do present one consistent picture of the personality of Jesus Christ; and in accord with historical analogy great movements are engendered by great personalities. Consider the time of the American revolution. No matter how great the politico-sociological situation was with opportunity, it took great men like Washington, Jefferson, and Franklin to manage it the right way. Grant was made a great general by the situation of the Civil War. Other generals had similar opportunities but he had the specific cluster of characters that made him a great general of that hour. But as a President he had the tremendous opportunity of rebuilding the American unity. As a President he was one of our least successful men. The great generals of World War II were not simply made great by remarkable opportunities. The war situation permitted the expression of their greatness.

It is hard to understand a radical critic who will believe that there was more power for good, more strength for love, more spirit of holiness in a religio-sociological[24] movement in Palestine than in a great, dynamic spiritual personality. If the analogy of history means anything at this juncture it is all for the conservative, and none for the radical critic.

Conclusion: We have argued that both the gospel record and human history have presented Jesus Christ as the greatest human being who has ever lived. This is exactly what we would expect if He were God incarnate, and so the New Testament claims stand substantiated; namely, that Jesus Christ is great because He is supernatural. Next, we argued

---

[24] Hunter, *op. cit.*, accuses the form-critics of being greatly disconcerted over the authenticity of some little phrase in Mark, yet will swallow huge quantities of religious sociology about early Christianity for which there isn't a shred of historical evidence. Furthermore, the effort of the form-critics (Bultmann in particular) to 'de-mythologize' the New Testament could easily backfire into a 'de-mythologizing' of the form-critics. If the world view and cosmology of the first century Christians colored their theology, why do not the same considerations about twentieth century world views and cosmology invalidate form-critics' theological views?

that any effort to rebut this claim was unsuccessful. The burden of denial is far greater than that of assertion. *Christianity then stands verified by the supernatural character of its Founder.*

CHAPTER VII

SUPERNATURAL VERIFICATION THROUGH THE RESURRECTION OF CHRIST

I. The Importance of the Resurrection

THE RESURRECTION is *the* miracle of the New Testament.[1] It corresponds to the miracle of the exodus in the Old Testament. The deliverance from Egypt supernaturally brought into existence the Hebrew people as a separate nation with a distinct sense of destiny, and the exodus was followed by a burst of revelation equaled only in Scripture by the life and work of Jesus Christ. There were the giving of the law, the tabernacle and all its details, the priesthood and its regulations, and the offerings. The Ten Commandments were prefaced by a reference to the mighty deliverance of Israel from Egypt (Exodus 20:2). Just as the exodus was the supernatural seal of the Old Covenant so the resurrection of Christ is the supernatural seal of the New Covenant, or as Hamilton states it: "It constituted the Imperial Seal of the Lord God Almighty on the life, work, and teaching of Jesus of Nazareth."[2]

A. It was *the personal miracle of the Messiah,* attributed jointly to the Father (Romans 6:4), to the Spirit (Rom. 8:11), and to the Messiah Himself (John 10:18). No other miracle possessed the element of the supernatural as did the resurrec-

---

[1] The classic treatment of the resurrection is that of W. J. Sparrow Simpson, *The Resurrection and Modern Thought.* His bibliography contains individual lists of works in English, German, and French. Cf. pp. 463–464.
[2] F. Hamilton, *The Basis of the Christian Faith* (third edition), p. 285.

tion. Whereas other miracles which the Messiah performed were for others or *about* Himself, e.g., the miracle of the tax money found in the mouth of a fish, the resurrection was *the miracle of His Person.* The resurrection *powerfully* declared Jesus to be the Son of God (Romans 1:4). In His Person He has "the power of an endless life" (Hebrews 7:16), and is a priest "made higher than the heavens" (Hebrews 7:26).

B. This miracle of the resurrection is *a major cog in the plan of redemption* whereas the other miracles of our Lord and His disciples are secondary and ancillary to the plan of redemption. The healing of a leper had its place in showing the love, power, and goodness of God as well as revealing the Person of the Messiah; but it was not an integral part of the transaction of redemption. The resurrection with the incarnation and atonement is planted at the very heart of the gospel and plan of redemption. So crucial is the resurrection to the writers of the New Testament that Peter attributes all the blessings of redemption to it (I Peter 1:3); Paul avows that without it the work of Christ is undone (I Cor. 15:17), and that the confession of the resurrection is integral to salvation (Romans 10:9, 10), something not directly true of any other miracle. Ramsey's fine comment at this point is that "the classic enemies—sin and death—could be dealt with only by a mighty blow, a blow which the death of the Messiah Himself alone could strike."[3] It is Filson's observation that the resurrection of our living Lord "guarantees to eschatology an essential place in Christian outlook and thought."[4]

C. The resurrection of Christ is *the seal of our resurrection.* The healing of sick people does not warrant us in believing that Christ will heal each of us today, nor did the resuscitation of Lazarus guarantee our immortality. It is the resurrection of Christ as *firstfruits* which alone opens the grave—

[3] A. M. Ramsey, *The Resurrection of Christ*, p. 11.
[4] F. V. Filson, "The Focus of History: The Resurrection in Biblical Theology," *Interpretation*, 2:37, April, 1949.

in anticipation—to the believer and unto life eternal. Because
He arose, we shall arise (cf. Romans 8:11).

D. The resurrection of Christ *possesses great evidential
value*. This resurrection was not a resuscitation but a resurrection to immortality and incorruptibility. It was a physical
glorification. Our future resurrection bodies will be like
Christ's is *now*. If a man were publicly put to death and in-
terred in a grave known to a competent body of men, and if
he appeared with (1) appropriate evidence that he was the
same person as was put to death, but (2) possessed new and
unusual powers and characteristics, it would be evident that
he had been raised from the dead by the power of God.

Certainly Jesus was put to death in a great public execution known to such historians as Tacitus and Josephus.[5] The
execution was in the capital of the Jewish commonwealth
under the direction of the Roman governor and his soldiers, in
co-operation with the highest Jewish authorities, and during
one of the great religious seasons. Jesus certainly died. The
swoon-theory is an outright evasion of the record through
willful intention and without a shred of historical validation.
According to the Gospels the grave-owner was known, the
type of burial is known,[6] its location was known. When Pilate
set a watch over the grave he indicated its locality to friend
and foe alike.

When Jesus appeared after His burial He was able to prove
to His disciples that He was the same one put to death. There
were the personal reassurances of personal conversation, the
marks of the crucifixion unchanged by the transformation of
His body, the performance of the miraculous, and the familiarity of His features. As Orr remarks these appearances
were not fleeting glimpses of Christ but "prolonged inter-
views."[7]

[5] Tacitus, *Annals*, XV, 44; Josephus, *Antiquities*, XVIII, 3.
[6] See pictures of such in G. Barton's *Archaeology and the Bible* (seventh edition), figures 238 and 264.
[7] James Orr, *The Resurrection of Jesus*, p. 145.

Our Lord's ability to appear and disappear, to pass through barred doors, and to ascend into the sky proved Him to be in a transformed state of existence. His eating of food proved that He was more than spirit or phantom. As the record stands untampered in the New Testament, Jesus Christ was raised from the dead and *is therefore the Son of God,* and, *the religion he taught is the God-given, God-sanctioned religion.* Although it might be psychologically possible to admit a resurrection and deny any metaphysical importance to it, it is impossible to see how logically this could be the case. If Jesus Christ be risen from the dead—risen in the full sense of being transformed so as to be immortal and incorruptible, the Christian religion which he taught is God-given, and therefore Paul is correct when he informs the Athenians that all men are under obligation to believe it (Acts 17:31). This is the evidential value of the resurrection of Christ.

II. CLASSIFICATION OF THE EVIDENCE

Throughout the previous pages there has been a rather large *if* in the mind of the reader—IF Christ be risen. The change from the *if* to the *now* is a matter of amassing evidence to show that the proposition claimed is a proposition of fact.

A. *Philosophical evidence.* It might seem strange to speak of the philosophical evidence for the resurrection from the dead of Jesus Christ. But if the works of the opposition be read it will be discovered that *it claims philosophical reasons for not accepting the resurrection.* Bowen directly claims that "we must recognize that our *Weltanschauung* must be for all of us a valid ground for disbelief in many things which ancient testimony urges upon our credence."[8] If the radical critic may claim philosophical grounds for the proof of the impossibility of the resurrection, the believer may assert philosophical grounds for its occurrence. If the assumption of the uniformity of nature rules out the resurrection, the assumption

[8] C. R. Bowen, *The Resurrection in the New Testament,* p. 62.

of the Christian Biblical Trinitarian Theistic philosophy rules
it in. "Christian theism is Resurrection theism," writes Ramsey.[9] We believe that by following the rigorous methodology
developed by philosophical investigations over the centuries,
and in conjunction with the unique data of the Bible, we can
construct a Christian theism. Among our postulates of Christian theism are these two: (1) God is free and sovereign to do
what He wills, and, (2) God is omnipotent so that He can perform what He is free to do, and wills to do. Putting it in
Bible terms we have the words of Paul to Agrippa: "Why
should it be thought incredible with you, that God should
raise the dead?" (Acts 26:8). Christian theism is philosophical
evidence for the resurrection because it grants the metaphysical conditions that would make such an act in this universe
both conceivable and possible. If the unbeliever may appeal
to his philosophical structure to deny the resurrection, we
appeal to ours to maintain it.

B. *Theological evidence.* If any miracle be proposed to me
for belief, the first thing I should ask is this: "Does this event
fit into any pattern or scheme of events of profound philosophical or religious importance?" One of the reasons why
numerous self-appointed Messiahs, miracle-workers, and di-
vine-healers have no staying power is that there is no depth
of significance to their accompanying religious beliefs; and
to the opposite, one of the reasons that *supernatural* Christianity has appealed to a great body of educated and intellectual men in every century of the Christian era is that the supernatural in Christianity is associated with such a magnificent set of theological tenets. Part of the evidence for the
resurrection is that the resurrection *does fit into a religious
system of profound metaphysical and religious significance.*

The last part of the first half of the twentieth century has
witnessed a plethora of books and periodical articles on the
philosophy of history. The professional historian, the profes-

9 *Op. cit.,* p. 10.

sional philosopher, and the professional theologian have produced works in this field, e.g., Toynbee, Löwith, Brunner, Baillie, Schweitzer, Butterfield, Niebuhr, Berdyaev, Sorokin, and Collingswood. One of the most important facts emerging from this welter of articles and books on the philosophy of history is a new and fresh appreciation of the historical nature of the Christian religion and Augustine's *City of God.* What Hegel tried to do for philosophy, i.e., give it historical rooting, the Bible had already done for religion, and Augustine for Christian theology. It is now felt that there is something *fake* or *artificial* about a metaphysical system constructed like Plato's or Aristotle's or Locke's or Descartes' which may be good ontological studies or epistemological analyses but are bereft of *historical connection.* Yet the universe and human life are historical to the very root. Part of the tremendous appeal of the Bible is that it is not a collection of religious propositions put together like Spinoza's *Ethics,* or a profound analytical work like one of Kant's famous *Critiques;* rather, the Biblical religion is strung out on a rope of time just like the universe and human life is. It has a *tangency* to reality which mere metaphysical analysis or synthesis lack.

It is currently seen that Biblical theology is theological history, and historical theology. Christian doctrine is metaphysics in historical garb. Casserley[10] makes some strong observations at this point. He affirms that modern studies of the philosophy of history might so revolutionize our thinking that all philosophy will be divided up between pre-philosophy of history period and the philosophy of history period. To him Christianity is metaphysics in historical form. Many of our great Christian doctrines are also great historical events. This shows the integration of Christianity with fact and the universe. *Hence, the resurrection of Christ fits into the total*

---

[10] J. V. L. Casserley, *The Christian in Philosophy,* p. 66 ff. Cf., *"The Bible writes metaphysics as though metaphysics were history,"* p. 66. Italics are his.

structure of Biblical theology, namely, that great acts of history share in the great doctrines of theology.

The resurrection is a historical-theological truth like the incarnation and atonement, and it is integral to the very plan of redemption. The Christian doctrine of salvation calls for it, and demands it. We may therefore boldly say that *the theological structure of Christianity is evidence for the resurrection*. By the resurrection of Christ sin and death are overcome, the infinite merit of the atonement is made available and the future resurrection of the blessed is sealed.

C. *Biblical evidence.* The Christian philosophy of religion (Biblical theism) makes the resurrection conceivable as a possible fact of history; Christian theology makes it a necessity in the plan of redemption; and the Biblical documents give us the historical reality of it. The resurrection of Christ is therefore conceivable, necessary, and actual.

1. *Old Testament evidence.* Christ died and rose again according to the Scriptures. The apostles turned to the Old Testament for evidence of the resurrection because Christ had so taught them to look for Him in the Old Testament. According to the Christian exegesis of the Old Testament, the resurrection was predicted long before it was claimed by the apostles as a fact. The many verses appealed to by the Apostles from the Old Testament will be found in most works on the resurrection and need not detain us here.[11] However, most works on the resurrection fail to deal with the *types* of the resurrection in the Old Testament, e.g., the budding of Aaron's rod, the wave offering, the offering of Isaac, as well as the typical significance of Melchisedec. Granted that there is not as much evidence from typology as we could wish, nonetheless it is there to some measure and adds its testimony to the resurrection chorus. But we repeat that according to the Christian exegesis of the Old Testament, prompted by Christ

---

[11] Cf. Ramsey, *op. cit.*, Chapter II, "According to the Scriptures," and Filson, *op. cit.*, p. 30.

Himself (Luke 24:25–27, 48), the resurrection was predicted long before it occurred. It must be kept in mind too that our Lord appealed to the experience of Jonah as typical of His own, and furthermore that Paul distinctly affirms that the Jewish mind is blind when reading the Old Testament until illuminated by the Holy Spirit (II Cor. 3:14, 15).

2. *The evidence of Christ.* Taking the Gospel record as faithful history there can be no doubt that Christ Himself anticipated His death and resurrection, and plainly declared it to His disciples, e.g., John 2:19–21, Luke 9:22, Matt. 12:40, Matt. 16:21, Mark 8:31, and Matt. 20:19.[12] The gospel writers are quite frank to admit that such predictions really did not penetrate their minds till the resurrection was a fact (John 20:9). But the evidence is there from the mouth of our Lord that He would come back from the dead after three days. He told them that He would be put to death violently, through the cause of hatred, and would rise the third day. All this came to pass.

3. *The evidence from the Gospels and Acts.* Although there is variation in detail there is concurrence of fact among the writers of the Gospels and Acts that Jesus rose from the dead. The most cursory reading of the Gospels reveals the fact that the Gospels deal with the death and resurrection of Christ in far greater detail than any other part of the ministry of Christ. The details of the resurrection must not be artificially severed from the passion account. As Dr. W. M. Smith[13] has indicated, we know what city Jesus died in, the numerous details of the events and conversations of His trial and death, and the historical personages. We know where, when, why and how He died. We know who got His body and under what circumstances and where it was laid. The Gospel writers continue the account—no thanks to our chapter divisions—with

---

[12] See the fine lines at this point by Wilbur Smith, *Therefore Stand*, p. 363 ff., and in Sparrow Simpson, *op. cit.*, Chapter I, "Our Lord's Predictions of His Resurrection."
[13] *Op. cit.*, p. 359 ff.

the same wealth of detail about the resurrection. They concur in asserting that: (1) it took place on the first day of the week; (2) it was first discovered by the women; (3) the stone was rolled away when the women arrived; (4) angels were present; (5) Jesus appeared to different individuals at different times as well as to groups of individuals; and that (6) He gave every evidence of being their Master of pre-crucifixion days, still possessing power to perform the miraculous, as having a body characterized by some sort of substantiality, and yet having a new set of supernatural characteristics.

4. *The evidence of the remainder of the New Testament.* In Acts 1, Luke tells us that Jesus showed Himself alive by many infallible proofs (*en pollois tekmeriois*), an expression indicating the strongest type of legal evidence. We have our Lord appearing and then ascending in this chapter. There are the personal appearances He made to Stephen and to Paul. The apostles commence preaching the resurrection in Acts 2, and so do throughout the rest of Acts.[14] It is referred to constantly by the writers of the Epistles; it is made the point of a special discussion in I Cor. 15;[15] and Jesus again appears alive in Revelation.

D. *The evidence of Church history*

In both ecclesiastical history and creedal history the resurrection is affirmed from the earliest times. It is mentioned in Clement of Rome, *Epistle to the Corinthians* (A.D. 95), the earliest document of church history and so continuously throughout all of the patristic period. It appears in all forms of the *Apostles' Creed* and is never debated.

E. *Inferential evidence*

A great deal of ingenuity has been exercised by apologists in demonstrating that even if the reliability of the Gospel rec-

---

[14] "The number of times the Resurrection is referred to in the book of Acts will amaze anyone who has not given this particular point serious consideration." W. M. Smith, *The Supernaturalness of Christ*, p. 191.

[15] Sparrow Simpson, *op. cit.*, Chapter VIII, "St. Paul's List of Witnesses." Also Chapter XIV, "The Resurrection in the Acts."

ord be debated, the course of events of church history were such that only the resurrection can adequately explain them. Generally speaking this inferential evidence follows these lines: (1) It is argued that the Early Church spread so phenomenally only on the explanation that it was given great power and boldness to witness through the resurrection; (2) that the personal lives of the apostles themselves can only be adequately explained by the transforming power of the resurrection; (3) Paul's conversion is accountable only if the resurrection were real; (4) the problem of the empty tomb resists any solution save the actual resurrection;[16] and that (5) there was no possibility of any fraud because the tomb was known both to friend and foe. Furthermore, nothing would have stamped out Christianity so fast as to produce the crucified body of Jesus Christ. There is a wealth of material on the inferential evidence for the resurrection which is ably and scholarly marshalled. We refer the reader to such treatises.

The Christian accepts the resurrection of Jesus Christ as a historical fact. He finds it conceivable because of his Christian theism; its rationale is found in his Christian theology; and its historicity is proved by an unbroken, extensive testimony from the Old Testament predictions through the pages of the New Testament record, and into Church history in the writings of the Fathers and in the earliest creeds.

III. The Impossibility of the Position of Unbelief

There are certain phases of the study of the resurrection which have reached a point of almost mutual agreement by all concerned. These matters need not be rehearsed at any great length. First, it is generally agreed that the New Testament belief in the resurrection is belief in the *physical* transformation of the crucified body of Jesus. A theologian may

---

[16] For example, a great deal is made of the details about the garments of our Lord found in the tomb, especially the napkin (John 20:7).

try to spiritualize the resurrection, but the New Testament in its plainest reading teaches the physical resurrection of Christ. For example Peter remarks that "him God raised up the third day, and showed him openly; not to all the people, but unto witnesses chosen before of God, even to us, who did eat and drink with him after he rose from the dead" (Acts 10:40, 41). Obviously, eating and drinking with a spirit is an impossibility. Secondly, it is generally agreed that the belief in the physical resurrection is universal in Christian literature—in the Gospels, in the Epistles, in Revelation, in the earliest patristic writings, and in the earliest creeds. No longer is it possible to consider the resurrection as an encrustation upon a simple humanistic Jesus. If form-criticism has served any purpose it has served to show that the supernatural element and the resurrection of Christ are deeply embedded in the Christian tradition from the first.[16a] Thirdly, the older method of granting that part of the record is historical and part is fictional is for the most part deemed unsatisfactory. It has become evident that if certain minimal historical facts be granted, the logic of the believer in the resurrection is impossible to parry. For this reason practically all of the older efforts to explain away the resurrection by recourse to the swoon theory, wrong-grave theory, telegraph theory, stolen body theory, etc., are beside the point, abortive; therefore we will not spend any time rehashing these theories so ably refuted in the other good evangelical literature.[17] This does not mean that from time to time one of these buried theories is not resurrected by some unbelieving scholar. Fourthly, it is agreed by all that the prob-

[16a] Cf. Filson, *op. cit.*, and William Hallock Johnson, "The Keystone of the Arch," *Theology Today*, 6:12–24, April, 1949, in which this assertion of mine is thoroughly substantiated.

[17] Wilbur M. Smith has written much on the resurrection and his writings are a good source of basic data on the subject. Cf. the chapter on the resurrection in *Therefore Stand* and in *The Supernaturalness of Christ*. In his article, "Why This Resurrection Emphasis," *His*, 8:2 ff., March, 1948, he has an annotated bibliography on the resurrection with an outline of all occurrences of the resurrection in the New Testament. He lists the outstanding books on the resurrection in his article "In the Study," *Moody Monthly*, 52:471–72, March, 1952.

lem of the resurrection of Christ either for or against is directly involved with (1) one's basic philosophical convictions, (2) one's formulation of the essential nature of the Christian religion, and (3) one's theory of the general credibility of the Gospels, which involves, in turn, one's solution to the synoptic problem.

Most of the evangelical treatises on the resurrection deal with the positive evidence, e.g., the empty tomb, the appearances, or the transformed lives of the apostles. This task has been done so many times before it need not be repeated here. Our approach shall be different. We shall *presume* the resurrection to be true according to the testimony we have already presented. We shall endeavor to show that the propositions that unbelief must maintain in opposition are too weighty with difficulties to stand.

Reconsider the solid, unbroken, unequivocal testimony of the documents to the resurrection. If we take the Gospels as they are, we find Jesus referring to His resurrection long before His actual death. This is especially true, if there are two cleansings of the Temple of which the one in John 2 is at the first of our Lord's public ministry. Then, there is the record of the resurrection in each of the Gospels. Many more references occur in the Epistles as well as in Revelation. The resurrection is mentioned frequently in Acts, in patristic writings, and in the creeds. From the standpoint of historiography this is amazingly sustained testimony. To controvert it, unbelief must maintain the following propositions:

A. Unbelief must state that the Gospel account of the resurrection is *completely* unreliable. Unbelief must not simply state that there are difficulties or problems or some confusion in matter of fact.[18] Such problems beset *all* historical inquiry.

___

[18] On such matters cf. Orr, *The Resurrection of Jesus,* in which he cites some blatant "contradictions" in standard historical works which everybody acquainted with the facts knows are not contradictions at all but complexities of a historical event which if divers elements are told in isolation only appear to be contradictory. All the facts put together render the apparent contradictions intelligible, p. 89 ff.

The entire evidential value of the record of the resurrection must be *annihilated*. This is not too easy a thing to do, if for no other reason than from the very diversity of the accounts. If all the accounts read ape-like, the same, the simple, artless, propaganda nature of the record would be manifest. But one of the vexing elements of synoptic criticism is that the Gospels will follow each other line upon line, yet in another passage will differ a great deal. Sometimes the difference is so slight, e.g., the form of the verb or the use of a synonym, that it is beyond us how to account for such exactness of expression yet with the insertion of such a trivial variation. Why do they seem to copy each other and yet not follow through with a good job of it? There appears to be but one answer: *the four writers, whoever they were, whenever they wrote, appear to be working with one common body of tradition from their own individual perspectives and sources of information.* The phenomenon of marked similarity, usually attributed to borrowing or use of common documents, may also point to common source of tradition. Relative independence of labor with marked identity of fact is one of the surest signs of genuine historical data. But at this point unbelief must reverse the usual law of historical evidence and assert the uniformity of mistake. That the writers of the Gospels were sincere, earnest men of high motivation, writing with no desire to defraud or deceive, is admitted by most critics. Yet if unbelief is to have its way, certain factors of delusion were at work so strongly that all the goodness and earnestness and common sense of these men were convulsed.

To be fair to all parties, one cannot impose a standard of historiography upon the synoptic writers that would end all historiography. Seldom is any historical event recorded just as it happened with all the details, with complete absence of conflicting testimony, with no confusion of data. Historians are constantly rewriting history and undermining previously accepted historical authorities. A certain amount of leeway must be granted in all historiography. Precision is the ideal, but the nature of the historical task prevents history from coming anywhere near the precision of the physical sciences. Let the resurrection narratives be judged by generally practiced rules of historiography, not by standards to which few if any historically recorded events attain. If this is done the case against the resurrection is lost. The *entire* record of the resurrection must be *completely* broken if the case for unbelief be maintained, for the data is such that if one crack be left unsealed, it is hard to keep the resurrection out of the realm of historical factuality.

B. Unbelief must *completely* destroy the witness of the Book of the Acts. The first chapter contains a record of the risen Christ, and the sermon in the second chapter boldly declares it. Besides this are the many other declarations of it in the rest of the text. Unbelief must make two affirmations and make them incontrovertible: Unbelief must deny both the historicity of Acts 1 in which the risen Christ talks to His disciples then ascends into Heaven, and the claims of such men as Peter, John, and Paul that Jesus did arise. Taking Acts as is, less than two months after the crucifixion, Peter preaches his Pentecostal sermon and none *deny* the *facts* he proposes.[19] Unbelief must make *complete* desolation of Acts 1 and 2. As Orr writes, "The assumption, practically of the hostile critics of that testimony is that the Church had no history; that it knew nothing, really, of its own past; that myths and legends grew up in rank abundance and were everywhere received."[20]

---

[19] In reference to the debate over the so-called "early chapters" of Acts, C. H. Dodd in his remarkable work, *The Apostolic Preaching and its Development*, believes in their general historical reliability and represents faithfully the *early* belief of the Church. He writes: "In short, there is good reason to suppose that the speeches attributed to Peter in the Acts are based upon material which proceeded from the Aramaic-speaking Church at Jerusalem, and was substantially earlier than the period at which the book was written . . . The first four speeches of Peter cover substantially the same ground. The phraseology and the order of presentation vary slightly, but there is no essential advance from one to another. They supplement one another and together they afford a comprehensive view of the content of the early *kerygma*." Pp. 20–21.

[20] Orr, *op. cit.*, p. 144.

Unbelief must affirm that either Luke repeated material that was utterly without foundation or that he manufactured it. As we indicated in our treatment of the miracles, form-critics must give Acts the same type of sociology-of-religion treatment they gave the Gospels. Unless the testimony of Acts is silenced, all radical criticism of the Gospels is meaningless as far as trying to deny the supernatural in Christianity is concerned. But here again, just as there must have been unanimity of deception and delusion about the supernatural elements in the Gospels, the same must now be said of the Book of Acts. Thus the same religious social conditions must now be stretched over the life of Christ and the early years of the Church, and the fabric is scarcely substantial enough to stand this much of a stretch.

Again, the radical critic has to deny the general data of the Book of the Acts, namely, that in Jerusalem there was a Church presided over by the followers of Jesus and thronged with thousands of believers; that if one wished one could have talked to Peter or John or Mary or James; that meetings of a larger nature were held for disputations (Acts 15); and that all along the disciples taught and preached the resurrection, *right in the city of the death and resurrection of Christ*, and surrounded by the same people who put Jesus to death, who could wish for *no greater thing than to be able to substantially deny His resurrection.* This could have been done if Christ were not risen "by taking a few minutes' walk to a garden just outside the city walls,"[21] comments Beasely Murray.

Yet unbelief cannot deny that there was a Church there. It cannot deny that it grew and grew. It cannot deny that it preached the resurrection. Yet unbelief must state that the cardinal truth of the resurrection was not probably fictional, or likely fictional or possibly a misinterpretation of other data; but *it must annihilate completely and successfully* the witness

21 *Christ Is Alive*, p. 35.

of Acts. It must call Acts a propaganda work bereft of serious historical validity.

Without question critics do this.[22] But do they do it successfully? Where in Acts is a palpable historical blunder? Where in Acts is a mistake in geography? in manners and customs of Jew or Gentile? Where in Acts is it unequivocally proved that Luke mentions some nonhistorical personage or event? The critic must assert that (1) even though the author of Acts had an amazing sense of historical, geographical, and cultural fact, (2) he was a theological bungler. The author of Acts could use the correct terminology of Roman officials— a most severe test for historical accuracy, could use accepted medical terminology (debated by Cadbury), could correctly describe the geographical features of Paul's journey, could give an amazingly accurate account of an ancient shipwreck, and yet be childishly naïve theologically. This is a very heavy load for radical theories to carry.

At the conclusion of a historical study of British works of merit on the Book of Acts, Hunkin concludes that the following propositions would be accepted "by the great majority of British scholars: (1) That the Acts is a product not of the second century but of the first: (2) That there is a strong probability that the author of the 'we' sections is the author both of Acts and of the third gospel; (3) That he possesses a great deal of accurate information with regard to St. Paul's journeys, some of it being first-hand: (4) That whatever be his sources for the early chapters of the Acts these 'Scenes from Early Days' are well chosen and consistent and give a picture of the march of events which at any rate, on the whole, are correct."[23] This measured judgment derived from the best of

---

[22] Cf. Foakes Jackson and Kirsopp Lake, *The Beginnings of Christianity: The Acts of the Apostles*, 5 vols. A. M. Hunter's estimate of this work is that it is "vitiated by an unwarranted scepticism." *Interpreting the New Testament*, p. 107. Speaking of the status of Acts he says further that "the work of Ramsay and Harnack has convinced most critics that within his limits Luke is an honest and trustworthy historian," p. 111.

[23] J. W. Hunkin, "British Works on the Acts," Jackson and Lake, *op. cit.*, II, 433. For a conservative introduction to Acts which is scholarly and abreast

British scholarship certainly increases the impossible load that unbelief must endeavor to carry.

C. Unbelief must destroy completely the evidential value of Paul. Certainly at the commencement, two things stand out: (1) Most of the radical critics will accept the major epistles of Paul as being authentic and written at approximately the traditional dates, *viz.* Romans,[24] Galatians, I and II Corinthians. Most scholars will also accept Ephesians (with some reservations), Colossians, Philippians, and Philemon as Pauline. It is only in reference to the Pastorals that there is anything like unanimity of belief among radical critics. Suffice to say we have documents of Paul considered authentic in which the fact of the resurrection is clearly stated; and, just as important, certain autobiographical statements of Paul. (2) Paul was an orthodox Jew who hated Jesus and the Church before his conversion. The thesis that Paul was a true child of orthodox Judaism astutely defended by Machen in *The Origin of Paul's Religion* has been redefended by a work which should prove a classic in Pauline studies, namely, Davies, *Paul and Rabbinic Judaism.* Hunter observes that the current trend in Pauline studies is entirely away from the idea that Paul was either (i) the founder of Christianity or (ii) a radical innovator.[25] Both of these assertions are reversals of radical critical interpretations of Paul, and substantiate the position of the believer, and pose vexing problems to the unbeliever.

Certainly Paul's great mind was not stupified in reference to the resurrection. Having come from Judaism to Christian-

---

of modern scholarship see F. F. Bruce, *The Acts of the Apostles,* and also see his Tyndale Lecture, *The Speeches in the Acts* in which the reliability of said speeches is defended.

[24] C. H. Dodd, *op. cit.,* p. 14, indicates that the importance of Romans is that in it Paul had to bear witness to universal Christian truth as it was to a church he did not found. What he appeals to in Romans must be common Christian data.

[25] Hunter, *op. cit.,* pp. 71–73.

ity, he was more than interested in the fact of the resurrection and grounds for belief in it. When Paul and Peter got together a few short years after Paul's conversion "they did not spend all their time talking about the weather."[26] Apart from the references throughout his epistles to the resurrection, there is the amazing evidence of I Corinthians 15:1 ff. The first thing to note of this chapter is that it can hardly be dated after A.D. 55,[27] and if there is any value at all to the effort of Knox, *Chapters in the Life of Paul,* to glean the chronology of Paul's life solely from the epistles, the time is greatly reduced. At most there are twenty-five years from the death of Jesus to I Corinthians 15. Sparrow Simpson[28] makes five observations of this account: (1) It is not a narrative but a veritable list; (2) it was not Paul's list but one handed on to him from the apostles; (3) by use of the Greek words it proposes to be chronological of nature; (4) the purpose of the list was not apologetic; and (5) it appears to be an official list.

This list, although written after A.D. 50, possesses the evidential value of the time of Paul's conversion about A.D. 33. As Beasley Murray observes,[29] Paul's conversion and resurrection faith, which he shared with all Christians, is near enough to be reliable and to be free from legendary accretions. This is difficult data to controvert. Paul was no spineless yielder to Jerusalem authority as a study of Galatians reveals. Paul believed in a personal manifestation of the risen Christ to himself; he believed in the fact of the resurrection; he accepted an official list of the appearances of Jesus. All this can be dated within twenty-five years of the resurrection.

[26] Dodd, *op. cit.,* p. 16.

[27] A. E. Barnett, *The Making and Meaning of the New Testament,* p. 50.

[28] Sparrow Simpson, "Resurrection of Christ," *Dictionary of Christ and the Gospels,* II, 505. As can be expected there is a list of radical critics whose only answer to this damaging evidence is that it is a gloss. Such critics are listed in C. R. Bowen, *The Resurrection in the New Testament,* p. 7 fn. But where did the data of the list come from? and how did it get into an authentic epistle with no protest?

[29] Beasley Murray, *op. cit.,* p. 49. Cf. also, "To speak of the 'legends' of the resurrection at so early a date as this reveals an utter lack of historical perspective." P. 51 fn.

To controvert Paul's evidence at this point one must first believe (1) that by some means or other, which radical scholarship has never demonstrated with any degree of unanimity among its own critics, the Early Church, including the very disciples themselves, came to believe mistakenly in the resurrection,[30] and that (2) they could make such a good case out of a mistake or delusion that neither friend nor foe could controvert it or perhaps in case of believers even suspect it to be false, and (3) that Paul had not the opportunity or will or means to investigate the resurrection. For unbelief to make its case, it must not prove this to be probably true, nor indicate that the evidence is tenuous—*it must do a work of complete demolition.* As long as the evidence has any substantiality to it the possibility of the factuality of the record is great. Therefore complete demolition is called for.

Added to the testimony of I Corinthians 15:1 ff. is the data of Galatians.[31] Paul made several trips to Jerusalem. The optimum date for his conversion is about A.D. 33. Paul was not only conversant with the apostles themselves but with many from the Church of Jerusalem, especially Mark and Barnabas. *With these friends there is no record of any disagreement about the content of the Gospel.* Further, Paul lived and moved in a great company of people, Christian and non-Christian. Goodwin in an appendix to *A Harmony of the Life of Paul* has a list of over one hundred and fifty people associated with Paul as gleaned from Acts and the Epistles. In Romans 16:7 we have the remarkable assertion that Andronicus was converted before Paul, as well as Junia, for he says of them that they "were in Christ before me." From such contacts Paul picked up a great deal of the life of Christ, more than is usually

30 Bowen, *op. cit.*, p. 4, indicates how much of modern opposition to the resurrection is "old stuff," which may be found in Trypho or Celsus or Porphyry and adds "nothing is more sobering for the modern critics than a study of the fathers."

31 Radical critics have tried to show that the biographical data of Paul as found in Acts and the Epistles is a hopeless snarl. Cf. D. W. Riddle, "Reassessing the Religious Importance of Paul," Willoughby, editor, *The Study of the Bible Today and Tomorrow*, pp. 314–328.

recognized. Stewart in *A Man in Christ*[32] collates all the evidence of Paul's knowledge of the character, life, and teachings of Jesus, as well as the parallels of thought and expression. C. H. Dodd remarks that "It would, however, be rash to argue from silence that Paul completely ignored the life of Jesus and His preaching; for, as we have seen, that preaching is represented only fragmentarily, and as it were accidentally, in the epistles. That he was aware of the historical life of Jesus and cited His sayings as authoritative, need not be shown over again."[33] Dodd also indicates that Paul received the gospel not later than seven years after the death of Christ. "Thus Paul's preaching represents a special stream of Christian tradition which was derived from the main stream *at a point very near its source. . . . Anyone who should maintain that the primitive Christian Gospel was fundamentally different from that which we have found in Paul must bear the burden of proof.*"[34]

If there were no resurrection it must be admitted by radical critics that Paul deceived the apostles of an actual appearance of Christ to him, and they in turn deceived Paul about the appearances of a risen Christ to them. How difficult it is to impugn the evidence of the Epistles at this point when they have such strong validation as authentic!

D. Unbelief is caught in a dilemma between the natural and the supernatural elements in the Gospels. All efforts to prove that Jesus never lived simply do not gain any real hearing. Even such a critic as Foakes Jackson is very harsh against those who would make Paul and not Jesus the founder of Christianity. He is very insistent that behind the Gospel records stands the wonderful person of Jesus.[35] Some of the most radical and skeptical historians will admit the historicity of Jesus. The radicals among the form-critics grant that Jesus

[32] P. 286 ff.
[33] *Op. cit.,* p. 28.
[34] *Ibid.,* p. 16. Italics are ours.
[35] *The Life of St. Paul,* pp. 16–17.

actually lived and that some of the data of the Gospels came out of actual history. Now link this up with the almost universally accepted conclusion among synoptic critics that it is not possible to locate a gospel-strata containing a simple, human Jesus. The theological Christ and the supernatural miracle are buried inextricably in the documents.

Unbelief now has the task of deciding what is historical and what is not. If it boldly says: "everything supernatural and theological about Jesus must go," then synoptic criticism has become artificial, dogmatic, and naturalistic. Under such a procedure, even if the supernatural is there, such a highhanded criticism would cut it out. But if the approach is not a highhanded skepticism and naturalism, success is impossible. Such an approach has the enormous task of stamping out every single spark of the supernatural. If the issue is over the existence of the supernatural, very obviously such an approach has made the conclusion its major premise. In short, before the criticism actually begins, the supernatural is ruled out. All of it must go. The conclusion is not therefore purely a result of openminded study of the supernatural, but a conclusion dictated dogmatically by an antisupernatural metaphysics. On what other basis could critics *completely* rule out the supernatural in a document that admittedly has historical value? What principle is to decide where history leaves off and fiction begins?

Granted, the case for unbelief may boldly state that it accepts a combination of the (1) uniformity of nature with the (2) immanental activity of God, and so claim to have just and adequate grounds to rule out the supernatural *a priori*. But the troublesome record remains with the supernatural deeply entwined with the natural, and of such a nature and in such a setting, as to constantly impress its truthfulness on a considerable body of erudite men of every generation. As long as this is true, the case for unbelief must have a restless sleep. In spite of the vicious attacks on the resurrection, new books by competent scholars which defend the resurrection keep appearing.

E. The case for unbelief must controvert the testimony of Hebrews, Petrine epistles, Johannine epistles, and Revelation as to the resurrection of Christ. This testimony is both in terms of affirmations of the resurrection and pronouncements of either the deity or Lordship of Christ. Unbelief must state that (1) either these men so named did not write said works or if they did (2) they handed down a belief they uncritically accepted. That is, critics accept the thesis of S. J. Case, *Experience with the Supernatural in Early Christian Times*, that the supernatural was "in the air" as it were, and people breathed it in uncritically as if it were part and parcel of the universe itself. However, it must be admitted that the supernatural is in the New Testament like sparks from a forest fire, and it will take a great deal of water to dampen them all and put them out.

Unbelief must repudiate the significance of James. Paul tells us that one of the special manifestations of the risen Christ was to James (I Cor. 15:7). This James is traditionally identified with the James of the Jerusalem Church (Cf. Acts 15:13, and Galatians 2:9); with the James of the Book of James, who in turn is identified as a brother of our Lord. It is quite a task to declare that a blood-brother of Jesus Christ —most scholars repudiate the "cousin" interpretation—who was head of the Church at Jerusalem, and the author of a canonical book, is a bit of fiction. But this is precisely what radical criticism must do.

Unbelief must repudiate the evidence from the writings of Peter.[36] It must, to defend its position, believe that the postapostolic Church was so gullible and non-historically minded

---

[36] Speaking of the authorship of I Peter, Hunter, *op. cit.*, observes that "With Selwyn's arguments [for the Petrine authorship of I Peter] at his back, no one need be ashamed of avowing his belief that Peter stands behind this notable letter." P. 113. Selwyn is the author of a learned and outstanding commentary on Peter (1946).

that such pious misrepresentations went undetected. But if it is granted that Peter did write I Peter, then Peter must be branded as a bungling enthusiast mistaking fancy for fact. The situation is even more extreme in Second Peter, wherein Peter gives his personal reminiscences of the transfiguration, and that Jesus told Peter about His own death during the post-resurrection conversations of Christ with His disciples. Unbelief has to root all of this out, e.g., by denying the Petrine authorship of Second Peter.

F. Unbelief has to deny all the testimony of the Fathers commencing with Clement of Rome's *Epistle to the Corinthians,* formerly dated as early as A.D. 70, but now usually around A.D. 95 and following through the testimony of the other apostolic fathers. It must assume that these men either did not have the motivation or the historical standards to really investigate the resurrection of Christ. The Fathers, considered by the Eastern Orthodox Catholic Church and by the Roman Catholic Church and Anglican Church as authoritative or highly authoritative, respected by the Reformers, and given due weight by all theologians, *are written off the record by unbelief.* They are deemed trustworthy for data about apostolic or near-apostolic theology, yet in matters of fact they are not granted a shred of evidential testimony. But this must be, or unbelief cannot make its case stick.

Conclusion: We have presented the positive evidence of the resurrection and the impossibility of making a case against it. The burden of unbelief is too great to carry. But one point may be urged against all that is said, namely, that all the evidences come from Christian sources. The New Testament admits this, for Peter says that "God raised [him] up the third day, and shewed him openly; not to all the people, but unto witnesses chosen before of God" (Acts 10:40, 41). Previous writers on this subject, e.g., William Milligan, *The Resurrection of Our Lord,* tell us the spiritual impossibility of unbelieving eyes beholding the risen Christ. Only those within the boundary of the kingdom of God could behold the King in His glory. But this does not prejudice the evidence of the resurrection if it can be shown that in other matters these men were trustworthy and dependable. The fact that a musician performs before his own family does not *necessarily* mean he is a poor musician because he plays before a prejudiced audience.

If the resurrection of Christ is, as the incarnation and atonement are, a historical-theological truth, it can only be seen as truth when seen with the eyes of God. The thrust of this chapter is to the intent that he who sees with the eyes of God is not bankrupt of evidence to know for sure that what he sees actually is. We can drive no man to faith by pure historical considerations. We can only drive him to the place of decision.

CHAPTER VIII

THE VERIFICATION OF CHRISTIANITY THROUGH EXPERIENCE

ALTHOUGH PRAGMATISM as a philosophy has many shortcomings, it certainly has one substantial point to make and that is this: *Whatever passes as true must have direct tangency with life and experience.* Massive intellectual structures, like the Platonic or Hegelian philosophies, do not have great multitudes of people believing them who daily walk in their guidance, for the patent reason that they do not have a relevancy to the daily routine experiences of the masses of humanity. It is to be questioned if Christianity would have had the hold it has had, and does have on hundreds of thousands of people if it lacked *direct tangency with life and experience* even though it created such an imposing theological and philosophical edifice. Because Christianity is true it must have relevancy to every significant aspect of the universe and human experience. It must not only provide us with the materials of a great philosophy—Christian trinitarian theism —and a great theology; but it must have a relevancy or tangency to human experience. Human experience is a vital and essential aspect of what is compassed by the word "universe." Part of the validation of Christianity is its ability to provide hundreds of thousands of people with *a real, genuine religious experience.* Evangelical scholarship owes much to the writ-

208

ings of E. Y. Mullins in showing the verification of Christianity from experience, especially in his *Why Is Christianity True?*

I. Preliminary Considerations of Christian Experience

In order that our argument from experience be properly understood, certain things must be said to "hang the picture."

A. *We believe that our experiences have objective reference.* No man can have a simple, uncritical attitude toward his perception of objects. Textbooks on psychology contain many illustrations to show that our sensory organs deceive us, and books on abnormal psychology reveal that people who have delusions and hallucinations consider them real and objective. Further, we know from a study of children and of primitives that the human mind can entertain many things as real which are fictional. Both scientists and philosophers have worked diligently to develop principles and rules whereby we can tell what is subjective and fictional, and what is really objective, i.e., "out there."

Although most scientists and psychologists would affirm that religion is completely subjective experience, the Christian affirms that the entities, objects, and concepts of Christian experience have objective reference. The *objectivity* of the persons (for example, God, Christ, the Holy Spirit) and of the concepts (for example, forgiveness, justification) are demonstrated by Christian apologetics and evidences. Christians believe that they have as sufficient reason for considering the objects and concepts of Christian experience objective as the scientists have for considering their objects and concepts as objective. If the opposite of "in here" for sensory percepts is "out there," then the opposite in reference to spiritual things is "up there."

B. *We believe that our consciousness has a double environment.* Scientists and philosophers admit that there are two strata to experience—the sensory and the mental. The view of the logical empiricists which asserts that the sensory and mental represent just two different languages, we consider one of the most abject examples of philosophical analysis. Modern positivistic science, psychology, and philosophy consider the sensory environment, i.e., the data we get from our senses, as the only really valid and objective environment of consciousness. The intellectual activity of the mind is admitted and recognized as necessary, *but no metaphysical deductions or claims can be made from it.* It is no wonder that our culture is so irreligious, secular, immoral, crass, and artless when the greatest source of truth, inspiration, ethics, righteousness, and spirituality is dubbed as "subjective" and *metaphysically worthless.* "We suffer from the insane delusion that we have been parachuted into the universe from outside, and are therefore clues only to what the universe is *not* like," is a correct analysis of much of contemporary thought.[1]

The Christian asserts that the consciousness of man is open to two universes—the spiritual and the sensory. The sensory world is the world conveyed to us by our senses, and we presume that our senses convey information about objects that exist "out there," even though we are aware that in certain instances we may be deceived. By reason of our spiritual nature we have access to spiritual objects, and we make the same presumption that we do about sensory objects, namely, that spiritual objects exist "up there" even though we may in some instances be deceived. The spiritual environment includes intellectual, moral, aesthetic, and spiritual *principles* and *objects.*

To a single-environment philosopher, religious experience is reprehensible. However, the Christian theists believe that the spiritual environment is just as close to human consciousness, just as real, and that its objects and principles have as

[1] D. E. Harding, "Are Angels Superfluous?" *Theology,* 55:99, March, 1952.

much validity as the objects and principles of the sensory environment. *But the case is stronger than this, for the Christian theists insist that man without the help and guidance from the spiritual environment could make no sense at all out of his sensory environment.*

In considering the argument from Christian experience, it is therefore necessary to see it in the perspective of the Christian teaching, namely, that human consciousness is "exposed" to a spiritual environment with real objects and principles.

C. *There is intentionality in Christian experience.* When we say the mind *intends* an object we mean that what we perceive is "out there." When we see an automobile, the automobile appears to be so many feet away from us and existing in three dimensions. By *intending* an object we mean then that our sensory experiences appear to be about real objects that exist outside our heads.

The Christian asserts that just as our sensory experience *intends* objects, so our religious experience *intends* objects. When we see an object we do not reason thus: I perceive certain colors, certain shadows, certain configurations, certain distance factors—presto! I merge them all together and call it a bird. No, we perceive the bird in one act of perception. This is the *intentionality* of the mind at work. The Christian asserts that this same type of intentionality is at work in Christian experience. We do not have certain imaginative, emotional, and intellectual elements we fuse into something we call "religious experience." God, Christ, salvation, forgiveness appear to the Christian consciousness as objective and real. They no more appear to be the creations of our minds than do the bird or automobile of sensory perception.

D. *The argument from Christian experience is not based solely on conversion experiences or remarkable conversions.* There is no doubt that for sheer number of instances and for degree of transformation of life, no other religion has the records of religious experience that Christianity has. However, the argument from Christian experience is not bulit solely on remarkable conversions. There are hundreds of thousands of Christians whose experiences, though not remarkable or laden with great human interest, are none the less genuine, valid Christian experiences which go a long distance toward verifying the truthfulness of the Christian religion. Nor is the case from experience built entirely on conversion experiences. Some Christians will admit that they have had experiences subsequent to their conversion experience which, for depth and transforming power, were even greater than their conversion experience; many Christians will admit that while not having experiences as great as their conversion experience, they have had real and profound experiences in their Christian life; and all Christians will admit an entire lifetime of genuine Christian experiences of guidance, blessing, inspiration, consecration, and challenge.[2]

In reviewing the evidence from Christian experience, Foster has penned some splendid lines; for example, he asks, "Are there any witnesses who have had the experience referred to? We answer unhesitatingly, yes. They are not few in number; they are not such only as have lived in some remote time or place; they are not obscure or unknown persons. They may be counted by hundreds of millions; they form an unbroken chain from the days of Christ to this day; among them is the glorious company of martyrs who sealed their testimony with their blood. Some of these witnesses are today our neighbors and kinsmen, and count by millions at the present time. There is no reader of this statement that has not personally known many of them. There is no community in the civilized world where it would be difficult to find one or many of them. . . . What are they? The best people you have ever known. If you search for them you will not find them in prisons or among

[2] Cf. J. G. Lawson, *Deeper Experiences of Famous Christians.*

the criminal classes, except it be on missions of mercy; nor among the profane in gambling dens, or brothels, or drinking saloons, or where the base and evil-minded congregate. When you look upon them you will not see the bloated cheek, and hardened countenance, and bleared eyes of dissipation and debauchery, or the averted face of conscious guilt. You will find them in the homes of purity, in pursuits of honor, at the altars of religion. They were not always so. Many of them have been redeemed from the former practices and companionships of sin. Many of them are of a long line of honorable ancestry. They comprise men, women, and youth. They are of all professions. They come from all walks of life. They are characteristically the best-informed and most reliably intelligent. The princes of intellect and high-toned morality are found in their ranks."[3] Christianity has provided religious experience of a profound and satisfying nature to every type of mentality and temperament. It calls the scholarly and intellectually minded into the sober tasks of Christian education; it sends the adventuresome and self-sacrificing to mission fields; it calls the housewife, the clerk, the salesman to ordinary but necessary tasks in the local church; it summons the artistic to church music and painting. There is an experience and a niche for every type of mentality, disposition, and training.

Further, psychological facts about conversion cannot undermine the argument from experience. Starbuck first called attention to the fact that the greater number of conversions occurred before the twenty-first year, and recent studies indicate that neurotic people are far more liable to have religious experiences than "extroverts." One must leave descriptive psychology for normative psychology, or make the judgment, "only adolescents can have a religious experience," or "only neurotic people can be religious." The mind of a child and the sensitive mind of the neurotic might be the only minds in

[3] R. S. Foster, *The Supernatural Book*, pp. 320–321.

which a spiritual message can find lodgment. The adult and extrovert may be cases of hardened or careless mentality. Furthermore, it is to be noticed that psychological explanations of conversion have no relevancy to the data of fulfilled prophecy, miracles, or the resurrection of Christ.

E. *Christians have sympathetic rapport with each other in their Christian experiences, which points toward a common source.* The writer has spent extended time in many parts of the United States which has involved visits to many towns, churches, and private homes. Besides this he has met many Christians from many parts of the world, of many nationalities, of all major racial divisions and several subdivisions. He has found that Christian experience both of conversion and Christian life is of one piece. We Christians feel that we have had the same *essential* experiences. The testimony of the man from China or India sounds so very much like that of the man from Cuba or Finland. Yet, it is not just verbal identity. There is an identity of spirit. We not only say similar things, but we feel the same way about them, and we value them the same way. It is spirit bearing witness with spirit. The underlying reason is that we have been saved by the same God, through the same Saviour, and by the same Gospel. In the true sense of the word, Christian experience is *catholic, universal,* and *ecumenical.*

II. Christianity Verifies Itself in Meeting the Deepest Needs of the Human Heart

A religion which professes to be true must not only satisfy the intellectual demands of man, but also his deep personality needs. A religion that is essentially personality frustration is usually associated with a few ascetics or priests amid a larger population possessing no essentials of vital religious experience. Christianity is supremely the religion of religious experience, and the experience it provides satisfies the deepest needs of the human heart.

A. *Christian experience satisfies the need of personal re-spect and dignity.* It is a deep need of each normal human being to feel that he is truly a person—a center of life worthy of love, respect, confidence and trust. Extreme asceticism, self-torture, senseless humiliation can never be the daily be-havior of most normal pople. These are frustrations, not self-realizations. In the evangelical doctrine that God loves each man, that Christ died for each man, that each man will re-ceive a personal reception by God, is to be found the only adequate grounds for fulfilling man's deep need of feeling like a true, worthy, human being.[4]

Christians are not proud, haughty, or Pharisaical, but they do believe that God's love and salvation is so personal that each of them may consider himself a special object of divine attention. This has put in the heart of the drunkard, the harlot, the criminal a new sense of human dignity and of personal respect.

B. *Christian experience alone provides man with an ex-perience commensurate with his nature as free spirit.* By *free spirit* we mean that man is a spiritual being with a capacity for self-realization which can only find its proper fulfillment in God. Nothing less than God can really, actually satisfy man's spirit. Anything less than God leaves the spirit of man thirsty, hungry, restless, frustrated, and incomplete. "There is a cry in the soul, even if not so articulate as to be distinctly heard by the soul itself," writes Fisher, "to which no response comes from the world."[5] It is that confused knowledge of God in the soul which Aquinas referred to, *viz.* the soul's restless thirst for happiness, yet unaware that it is a thirst to be satis-fied in God alone. It is what Augustine referred to in the open-ing paragraph of his *Confessions* in which he affirms that the

---

[4] That the liberal's doctrine of the "infinite value of human personality" is a fake doctrine in that it denies its grounds in redemption see a most telling essay by T. W. Manson, "The Failure of Liberalism to Interpret the Bible as the Word of God," Dugmore (editor), *The Interpretation of the Bible,* pp. 92–107.

[5] G. P. Fisher, *Grounds for Christian and Theistic Belief,* p. 338.

soul was made for God, and can never rest till it finds its way back to God and so rest in Him. It is what the Preacher meant when he wrote that God has set eternity in man's heart (Eccl. 3:11, A.R.V.).

He who comes to Christ never hungers and never thirsts again. He has found Life, and Light, and Bread. The deepest hunger of man's restless free spirit finds its adequate satisfaction in Christ. This is not a theological dictum. This is the testimony of thousands upon thousands of Christians.

C. *Christian experience gives man something to really live for.* Philosophers may deny purpose in the universe, but psychologists know that if purpose be taken out of human life, human personality decays. People need something to live for, or they die from melancholia. The strictest materialist who finds no meaning, value, or purpose in the universe must himself have a purpose in life or he psychologically rots. Christianity gives man the greatest purposes in life. It tells man to live for the glory of a loving, holy God; it tells man to live for man by ministering to him the gospel of the glory of God; it tells man to live for the holy, the pure, the true, the beautiful. No other religion, no other philosophy, gives a man so much to live for as Christianity. For this reason Christianity has a record of martyrology absolutely without comparison in the history of religions. Every religion has produced a Socrates here and there willing to drink poison hemlock, or a Buddha willing to forsake wealth and fortune for religious ideals. But where is the *stream* of martyrs like unto Christianity? What other devotees have been burned, tortured, torn asunder, and in many other diabolical ways have had their flesh baptized by excruciating pain, and yet have suffered it with words of forgiveness on their lips, with hymns of glory sung up to the last minute, with faces beaming and glowing amid smoke and torture, amid bleeding flesh and scorched limbs? And why do they so die? Because Christ has given them so much to live for that they choose to live for Christ and die, rather than to deny Christ and live.

D. *Christian experience gives man a sense of reality and certainty.* There are fewer needs of the human soul so cherished and so valuable as a sense of actually knowing *reality* and being *sure* that one does. Christian experience does give the Christian a wonderful conviction that in Christ he has met Reality. Christian experience introduces man to God through Christ and so the Christian knows God who is the source of all Being, the Author of all blessedness, the Sustainer of all righteousness and morality, and the Father of all who trust Him. Every person with a genuine Christian experience feels that "this is it."

Not only does the believer experience a sense of reality which he never had before, but he has with this sense of reality a great sense of assurance. The first epistle of John is filled with verses dealing with the certainty of Christian knowledge, and the assurance of Christian salvation.

Thus, Christian experience yields the wonderful and rich conviction that one not only has met reality, but one is *sure* that he has met Reality. "Thousands, millions of the most saintly Christians, living and dead," writes Foster, "have claimed to possess an absolute knowledge of Christ by inward revelation. They not only are conscious of the transforming power within them imparting to them a new life, but they profess personal communion with God. The Spirit witnesses in them. They know the things whereof they speak. No power can dissuade them of this."[6]

III. Christianity Is Verified in Christian Experience in That Christian Experience Provides Adequate Solution to Man's Spiritual Needs

Christian experience does satisfy the deep needs of human experience and will satisfy point for point Thomas' famous

[6] *Op. cit.,* pp. 324–325.

list of personality needs. Christianity penetrates beyond personality needs to mankind's deeper spiritual needs.

A. *Christian experience solves the guilt problem.* Guilt feelings exist in every normal human being. Explain them as the cumulation of the hundreds of "no's" by our parents and teachers, or the artificial inhibitions of our society, they are there in every man's breast. Further, these experiences of guilt are found wherever man is found. Call it guilt-complex, or the ought-experience, or the feeling of sin, the fundamental psychological experience is there. Naturally, atheists and materialists see no significance, metaphysical or ethical, to guilt feelings.

Guilt stands at the end of man's effort to attain to moral perfection. Men like Heim, Kierkegaard, and Brunner find it the entering wedge for religion and revelation. Be that as it may, Christian evangelical experience provides a full and wonderful release by the gospel from the guilt feelings. God's love assures us that His anger is at rest; Christ's death informs us of the adequate means of pardoning our sin and guilt *objectively;* faith is the appropriation of the death of our Saviour, and blessed, indescribable, sweet forgiveness of sins is the result. This is an experience that is a conundrum to philosophy and non-Christian religions—that the Christian has "no more conscience of sins" (Hebrews 10:2). The love of God, the death of Christ, the forgiveness of God are all objective facts to Christian consciousness.

B. *Christian experience dispenses with fear.* The constant association of fear with religion is not without good cause. The universe and its powers always appear bigger and stronger than human efforts, and the laws of the universe are mysterious until ferreted out by the critical discipline of the sciences. Eternity looms as an immense question mark to all, and the number of atheists and materialists is legion who, though bold and brazen during life, have trembled and quaked at its brim. Human consciousness seemingly has been more impressed by the possibilities of ill beyond death than benevolence. Hence, man has feared death, he has feared God, he has feared Nature, he has feared the universe, he has feared the Devil. Fear in the sense of abnormal gripping of the soul by irrational emotion is not healthy religious experience, but is bondage (Hebrews 2:15).

Christian experience casts out all fear in the human heart but fear of sin. The universe is the creation of God our Father so we fear it no longer. The Devil may be routed by the adorable name of our Lord Jesus and we need fear him no longer. God has loved us and saved us, and so our love for Him casts out all fear (I John 4:18). Christ has burst the bonds of death and loosed the cords of the grave, and has given us every promise and hope of the life to come, so our hearts are not troubled (John 14:1, 2) as we approach death's door.

C. *Christian experience gives moral energy.* Most pastors, missionaries, and Christians would be willing to rest the case for Christianity on the power of the Gospel to change life and empower it for good. From Begbie's *Twice Born Men* to Gordon's *A Book of Protestant Saints* is a small library of books dealing with remarkable conversions. There is a great tradition in Christianity from Paul through Augustine and Luther to modern times, *viz.*, the power of the gospel to win great minds and hearts to Christ and to powerfully transform them. Missionary letters, missionary news sheets, mission board magazines report one steady stream of glorious conversions to Christ among almost every people of the earth.

1. In Christian experience there is a new moral will to do the right. Men have been freed from dope, alcohol, immorality, criminality, and brutality instantly and completely by faith in Christ. Even Darwin had to confess to J. W. Fegan that through his Gospel meetings in Down, Kent, no more drunkards were to be found in the village. Darwin writes: "We have never been able to reclaim a drunkard, but through your services I do not know that there is a drunkard left in

the village."[7] The writer firmly and confidently asserts that innumerable volumes the size of the *Encyclopaedia Britannica* could be written composed entirely of the testimonies of hundreds of thousands of people—rich and poor, brilliant and mediocre, professional and humblest of laborers, of all races, of all countries, of all Christian centuries, to the intent that by faith in Christ they had a new moral power to do right which they never had before. They had power to forgive and pardon former enemies, power to resist temptation, power to love and treat tenderly, power to restrain and desist, power in moments of great solitude when temptation rages, power in moments of great and violent emotion.

2. In Christian experience there is a wonderful transformation of basic personality. Paul was not only won to Christ, but transformed in Christ. It was the same with Augustine, and with countless others. New appetites, new desires, new ambitions, new loves, new minds are characteristic of twice-born men. It is not only moral energies released or imparted, but a man's entire attitude toward life is changed. He veritably gets a new mentality. Paul the rabbinical student becomes the Christian theologian; Augustine the rhetorician becomes bishop, theologian, and apologist. Humble fishermen, coal miners, carpenters, become saintly and sober deacons and elders in our churches. The writer himself experienced this power of the gospel to change life. He was a typical high school graduate with a mind stocked with what practically all high school graduates have when they leave high school —a profound respect for the sciences, a hope for a newer and better civilization, a toleration and mild respect for religion, a delight in sports and entertainment, and a desire "to make good" in the world. Then the gospel came to him. In one three-minute period his entire life perspective and basic personality were changed. He experienced the inflowing grace

[7] This most unusual letter of Darwin's will be found in Gordon, *A Protestant Book of Saints,* p. 91.

and transforming power of the grace of God. In a few moments he received a new philosophy, a new theology, a new heart, and a new life.

3. Christian experience gives a new power to love and self-sacrifice. One of the most misunderstood groups of people on the face of the earth are missionaries. They are misrepresented constantly in fiction and literature; they are misunderstood by worldlings; they are persecuted frequently by their own family; and they are not always respected in the churches. Yet, to the mind of the writer, the purest cream of humanity are missionaries, and he counts his friendship with missionaries an invaluable privilege.

Few people really understand the deep moments of consecration to Christ that causes the heart to pledge any sacrifice or any test of obedience. To fully, completely, sacrificially yield one's entire life to God in one holy act of surrender and dedication is an experience most people are *completely* ignorant of. After the missionary has dedicated his life and chosen his mission field come the long years of preparation. He or she must find a mate of like conviction, and of ability to do such a task. The missionary must find a mission society to affiliate with; and a means of support. Although in actuality he takes no pledge of poverty, in practice he does. Many, many times in his life he must change his residence. He must make one constant series of adjustments. He faces innumerable problems with raising children in foreign countries; with sickness in his family; with times of great financial stress; with government regulations; and with the untold vexing details of any mission compound. Yet he does it all for Christ. He learns to pray and live and love and serve as other human beings never do. There is no greater trophy of the grace of God and the love of Christ than the worn-out body of an elderly missionary whose feet have walked thousands of miles for Christ; whose hands have carried countless burdens, nursed the sick, wielded the ax or the grub; whose mouth has spoken the words of grace to man, and heart-rending petitions to God; whose face has had to always be a mirror of divine love and patience; and whose mind has had to be constantly filled with divine truth. No other philosophy, no other religion, has ever produced the missionary with a heart of love, and a life of countless, heart-cutting sacrifices.

IV. Christian Experience Is Wholesome

Not only does Christian experience meet deep personality needs, and profound spiritual needs, but it is just downright practical. It is the daily fare, and millions of humble Christian believers find it adequate, sufficient, and satisfying.

A. *There is no stultification of intellect.* At times this appears to be the case, but what it amounts to is a repudiation of non-Christian modes of thinking, not of intelligence itself. Stultification of intellect? How can that be? Consider first the educational work of the Church. There are hundreds of seminaries staffed with learned men, whose halls are occupied by thousands of earnest young students. There are Christian colleges, Bible colleges, and Bible institutes. Besides, there is the Sunday school and young peoples' work of the church which is educational of nature. Consider the publication of Christian books. There are numerous publishing houses in America devoted solely to publishing Christian works. Each year numerous volumes are turned out by Christian authors and scholars.

The Christian faith calls for a surrender of the mind to Christ and He in turn sanctifies it and empowers it for His service.[8]

B. *There is no encouragement for anything harmful.* All things that contribute to human ill are forbidden by the teachings of the New Testament—murder, thieving, hate, incest, immorality, and gluttony. The Christian Church has always

---

[8] See the thrilling chapter in Gordon, *op. cit., entitled* "Certain Doctors of the Church."

censored that which is degrading or immoral or enervating or cruel or merciless. It has advocated that which is peaceful, harmless, and beneficial. Thousands of believers in America live lives free from dope, alcohol, and tobacco. They do not gamble or frequent any sort of place of amusement whose reputation plainly proves that it is detrimental to man's better interests.

On the other hand, there is no senseless asceticism. The basic appetites of the human body are recognized as of God. Christians are not followers of queer food fads, nor propounders of ascetic notions about sex, nor deniers of the right and proper place of human appetite or institution or practice.

C. *There is in Christian experience a wonderful daily walk with God.* There is the experience of comfort in hours of sorrow; of courage in times of discouragement; of spiritual vitality in times of physical sickness; of guidance in times of decision; of inspiration when surrounded by difficulties and problems. Thousands of Christians in every land, in every generation, will bear witness to the blessedness, sweetness, and delight of a daily Christian life with all the benedictions of spiritual graces given by a heavenly Father.

Conclusion: The hypothesis and the facts concur. If Christianity is the true religion of God it should be pre-eminently the religion of genuine spiritual experience. We have found it to be so. It meets the daily and practical needs of human nature; the deep and enduring thirsts of the soul; and provides comfort for the sorrowing, courage for the faltering, inspiration for the despairing, challenge for the aspiring. Christian experience is the divine *IMPRIMATUR upon human life,* and therefore a proof of the divinity of the Christian religion.

CHAPTER IX

THE VERIFICATION OF CHRISTIANITY THROUGH THE SUPERNATURAL CHARACTER OF THE BIBLE

TO THIS POINT in our argument we have discussed the Bible's specific contents, i.e., its record of the miraculous, its prophecies, its picture of Jesus Christ. It is now our purpose to discuss the Bible as a literary production, and to ask ourselves if, as a literary production, it suggests a supernatural origin. Does the Bible possess a content and a history which strongly invoke from our judgment the belief in a more than human factor in its production? How does the Bible compare with the great productions of antiquity and with the millions of volumes produced since the invention of printing?

Our logic in this case shall be rather plain. All of the various tributes paid to the Bible are in reality one tribute: *the Bible is able perennially to grip profoundly the human soul.* Wherein rests this peculiar magnetism of the Bible? Is it in its literary power or beauty? Is it in its dramatic elements? Or, perchance, it is in its human interest values? However, to keep the most significant issue to the front the real question is this: *is the power of the Bible to grip the human soul of divine or human origin?*

The Bible itself speaks to this point. In numerous passages it speaks unequivocally as the voice of God. In the many orthodox treatises on inspiration these verses have been collected and expounded. Even the most cursory reading of the prophets reveals the constant recurrence of such expressions as "the word of the Lord came," or, "thus saith the Lord," or, "the Lord spake unto me," or, "the Lord talked with Moses." We cannot countenance the rather anemic suggestion that these expressions were the pious prefixes of the prophets to their messages with the fond hope that what they uttered would be the word of Jehovah.[1] We do not argue that the *claim* to inspiration is the *proof* of inspiration as many hyperorthodox treatises on inspiration seem to reason. Our point is merely that the Bible supplies us with its own theory as to its power, namely, *that God speaks in it.* The direct deduction Paul makes from the supernatural origin of Scripture (*theopneustos,* II Tim. 3:16) is that Scripture is profitable (*ōphelimos*), i.e., it yields sacred truth (*didaskalian*) and works a spiritual result in its readers so that they become men of God completely furnished to every good work.

Such an affirmation does not deny the human origin of the Bible in that it was written by human beings using human languages, figures of speech, and making reference to human emotions, ideas, concepts, and imagery. *It is the divine through the human* just as Paul affirms that the God who is over all is also *through* all and *in* all Christians (Eph. 4:6). So the inspiration of the Bible is *in* and *through* the human by the divine. Further, at this point we propound no specific theory of inspiration save the minimal belief held by the major traditions of Christian theology—Roman Catholic, Eastern Orthodox, Protestant, Lutheran, Anglican, Reformed, Calvinistic, and Arminian—that the Bible is in a way in which no other book is, *divine,* i.e., given by supernatural inspiration. Whatever is the precise relationship between the human and the divine in Sacred Scripture, is the duty of the Christian

[1] So F. W. Farrar, *The Bible: Its Meaning and Supremacy,* p. 64. The Old Testament supplies *tests* for prophets to see if it is actually *God speaking in them* (Deut. 18:20–22, 13:1 ff., Jer. 14:14, Isaiah 41:22–33).

theologian to determine. And however it be determined it cannot be controverted that the major theological traditions of the Church have judged the vital and central doctrines of the Bible to be of divine creation even as Peter claimed that the prophecies were not of human invention (*idias epiluseōs,* and, *thelēmati anthropou*), but of divine disclosure (II Peter 1:20, 21).

If we heed the self-testimony of the Bible we shall agree that the power of the Bible to grip the human soul is from its divine inspiration, not from its literary qualities or its human interest value or its imaginative character, even though the Bible is so rich in these elements. If we deny the theory of divine inspiration we must then attribute the power of the Bible to grip human intelligence to some remarkable human trait within the Bible. As we ought to choose that alternative which brings the most harmony and unity out of the data of the literary characteristics of the Bible, we must review that data before any decision can be made.

I. The Phenomenology of the Bible[2]

By the expression "the phenomenology of the Bible" we mean all the data about the history of the Bible and the general content of it, that most people who are informed about the same accept as "the facts in the case." In order to more intelligently weigh our two alternatives (the human *or* divine origin of Scripture), we must have some of the data of the phenomenology of the Bible before us. With this data in mind we will then be able to more concretely think of our intended solution to our problem, namely, *wherein is the power of the Bible to grip the human soul?*

A. *External phenomenology.* By this expression we mean the data of the Bible as a book, for example, its circulation, its translation, its survival through persecution, its influence on

[2] Consult E. von Dobschütz, "Bible in Church," *Hastings Encyclopaedia of Religion and Ethics,* II, 579–615, for the most thorough of the encyclopaedia articles on the influence and outreach of the Bible.

human culture (literature, oratory, law, politics, ethics, philosophy, art, religion), and its popular use.

1. *Its circulation.* It cannot be questioned that the most published book in the world is the Bible, in part and as a whole. It was the first significant work translated from one language to another—the Hebrew into the Greek Septuagint. It was the first printed book—Gutenberg's Latin Vulgate. It is the most valuable book in the world. Gutenberg's Bible sells for more than $100,000 a copy, and the British paid the Russians 100,000 pounds ($510,000 at that time) for the Codex Sinaiticus. The longest telegram on record was the sending of the Revised Version New Testament from New York to Chicago.

Since the first printed Bibles were laboriously printed and set in circulation, Bibles have streamed from presses in millions of copies, climaxing with the first printing of the Revised Standard Version in one million copies for release September 30, 1952. This is the biggest edition of a book in the history of printing. The number of Bibles printed in all languages since the invention of printing mounts to a staggering total, and this is an approximation, for the exact number cannot be determined.[3] Listing the major publishing houses of England, Europe, and America and counting parts of the Bible as well as the entire Bible, one writer finds that the Bible has been published in 1,330,231,815 copies as of 1932.[4] The same writer informs us that for the British and Foreign Bible Society to keep up with the demand for Bibles it must publish "one copy every three seconds day and night; 22 copies every minute day and night; 1369 copies every hour day and night; 32,876 copies every day in the year. And it is deeply interesting to know that this amazing number of Bibles were dispatched to various parts of the world in 4583 cases weighing

[3] Details can be found in most encyclopaedias under the caption of "Bible Societies."
[4] Hy Pickering, *One Thousand Wonderful Things About the Bible,* p. 7.

490 tons."[5] Dr. North of the American Bible Society estimates that the British and Foreign Bible Society and the American Bible Society have published 84,000,000 entire Bibles; 104,000,000 New Testaments; and, 144,000,000 Gospels and single books.[6] In 1951 the American Bible Society published 952,666 Bibles, 1,913,314 Testaments, and 13,135,965 portions of the Bible. The National Bible Society of Scotland has published 88,070,068 copies (1928), the Hibernian (Dublin Bible Society), 6,978,961 (1928). The various German societies published about 900,000 for the year 1927. The Gideons in America distributed 965,000 Bibles in 1928.

These figures are approximations. Further, it is impossible to keep track of all the Bibles published as so many different movements, groups, and mission agencies publish and distribute the Bible in part and whole. Further, it must be noted that some of our figures are more than twenty years old. The Gideons, for example, were very active during the war trying to give every man in the armed forces a New Testament.

Before we pass over such mountainous figures too easily, consider the stiff competition the Bible must face. The Bible must compete with such ancient masters as Socrates, Plato, Aristotle, Demosthenes, Homer, Hesiod, Aristophanes, Thucydides, and Herodotus. It must compete with the best of Latin literature among such authors as Hortense, Cicero, Virgil, Ovid, Seneca, Lucretius, and Epictetus. As we think of the medieval period we realize that in a novel way the Bible has to compete against itself. It has to compete with the books it has inspired! It is said that in continental libraries more cards will be found on Augustine than any one man, yet the Bible outsells Augustine. The Bible must compete with Boethius, Anselm, Aquinas, Duns Scotus, Occam, St. Francis of Assissi, and Bernard of Clairvaux. Coming to the modern

[5] *Ibid.*, p. 23.
[6] Letter to the author from American Bible Society librarian, 9 October 1952.

period, the Bible must compete with all the great national literature of Russia, Germany, France, Spain, England, Scandinavia, and America. It must compete with such literary giants as Chaucer, Shakespeare, Milton, Dante, Goethe, Browning, Wordsworth, Spenser, and Poe. It must compete against the finest poetry, the most gripping of the dramas, the most fascinating of biography, and the most entertaining of mysteries. Meeting the greatest in literary genius *the Bible still wins!*

2. *Its translation.* Out of all the multitudes of books published in any language, only a small trickle finds its way into one or more foreign languages. It would not be amiss to say that the cream of human literary production could be defined as those books translated into three or more languages.

When we compare the very few books that have been translated into three or more languages, we discover that the Bible is by far the most translated Book in the world. In passing it should be noted it is also the most *retranslated* book in the world! In all major European languages there is a series of translations and revisions. The English Bible alone has a lengthy history of being translated and retranslated again and again. Besides such major efforts as the Bibles of Wycliffe, Tyndale, Coverdale, the Geneva Bible, the Bishops' Bible, King James Version, Revised Version (English and American), and the Revised Standard Version, there are the numerous translations done privately and by denominations. There are also the many translations of the New Testament by itself. No book has been translated as much as the Bible, nor has any book ever been retranslated so many times. Nor is the end in sight! There will be the Weymouths and Moffatts and Goodspeeds of the second part of the century who will endeavor to give us newer, fresher, better translations. Further, the Bible in part and in whole is being translated into new languages and dialects of the great mission fields of the world.

The number of such translations is over the thousand mark, and a few more are added to the growing list every year. The conclusion is as obvious as it is incontrovertible: *the Bible is the most translated and retranslated book in human history.*

3. *Its survival.* Being a book from antiquity, the Bible has had to undergo all the possible chances of destruction by natural and human forces of destruction. Further, because the Bible contains such strong, uncompromising language about human sin, divine holiness and judgment, the worthlessness of human goodness, the folly of human ideas about God, the sovereignty of God, and the supremacy of Christ, it is a book that has been subject to much persecution. Yet it has survived the forces of corruption and the fires of persecution.

a) *Survival through time.* Any ancient book had to run the gamut of the forces of decay and neglect. Since printing was invented most books are published by the thousands, are spread throughout a large geographical area and not infrequently cross to other countries and continents, and are kept in modern libraries with all their skills and techniques for the care and preservation of books. But in antiquity books were produced entirely by hand and so were greatly restricted in number and distribution. Through fire, sword, decay, neglect, insects, mold, storms, and all other sorts of improvidence, the toll taken on ancient manuscripts was great.

In view of all this the survival of the Bible from antiquity with such a remarkable attestation is amazing. In reference to the Old Testament we know that the Jews preserved it as no other manuscript has ever been preserved. With their *massora* (*parva, magna,* and *finalis*) they kept tabs on every letter, syllable, word, and paragraph. They had special classes of men within their culture whose sole duty was to preserve and transmit these documents with practically perfect fidelity —scribes, lawyers, massoretes. Who ever counted the letters and syllables and words of Plato or Aristotle? Cicero or Seneca?[7]

In regard to the New Testament there are about thirteen thousand manuscripts, complete and incomplete, in Greek and other languages, that have survived from antiquity. No other work from classical antiquity has such attestation. We are informed by no less an authority on ancient manuscripts than Kenyon[8] that of the plays of Aeschylus there are 50 copies; of the works of Sophocles, 100 copies; of the Greek Anthology, one copy; and of Catallus, 3 independent manuscripts. The earliest manuscript of Sophocles is 1400 years after his death; and the same holds for Aeschylus, Aristophanes, and Thucydides. For Euripedes it is 1600 years, 1300 for Plato, 1200 for Demosthenes, 900 for Horace, 700 for Terrence, 500 for Livy, 1000 for Lucretius, and 1600 for Catallus. The New Testament has an attestation of more than 4,000 Greek manuscripts, coming from the second (John Rylands fragment of John, **P.** 56) and third century (Chester Beatty Papryi) and fourth century (Codexes Vaticanus and Sinaiticus).

How many more manuscripts of either the Old or New Testament yet await discovery in some cave, mound, papyri heap or genizah, we do not know. Since the discovery of the Dead Sea Scrolls two more caves have been excavated and the world of Biblical scholarship awaits the announcement of the details. But it would be a most rash and premature judgment to say that the end of such discoveries is in sight. The Bible has survived the ravages of time in all its manifold means of destruction with a numerical and textual attestation

---

[7] There are some marks and letters in the Old Testament of great antiquity that admit of no lexical or grammatical explanation. To date the only explanation is that they represent mistakes or accidents or some other trivial thing that although meaningless to the first scribes were nonetheless transmitted as perhaps being part of the sacred Word of God. Cf. B. J. Roberts, *The Old Testament Text and Versions*, chapter II, "The Work of the Scribes," for these unexplained phenomena of great antiquity.

[8] F. G. Kenyon, *Handbook to the Textual Criticism of the New Testament*, pp. 3–5.

that is many furlongs beyond even the closest competitor.

b) *Survival through persecution.* Not only has the Bible had to run the gamut of centuries of transmission, but it has been from time to time and place to place vigorously persecuted. It has been banned, burned, and outlawed from the days of the Roman emperors to present-day Communist dominated countries. But here again, all efforts to stamp out the Bible have been unsuccessful. No other book has been so persecuted; no other book has been so victorious over its persecutions. It is the martyr among books, and always rises from the pool of its own blood to live on.

c) *Survival through criticism.* After a few rough sessions with the pagan critics such as Celsus and Porphyry, the Bible settled down for a thousand years of peaceful existence. Through the fusion of the Holy Roman Empire with the Roman Catholic Church, a definite culture was established which venerated the Holy Bible above all other writings of men. Hobbes and Spinoza started the boat gently rocking in their critical attacks upon the Bible, but the storm started with Astruc. From Astruc till today has been one series of attacks on the Bible that for vigor, intensity, and attention to microscopic detail, has been unparalleled in the known history of literature. These attacks came from scholars of many countries but mostly from Germany, Holland, France, England, and America. The attacks have been made by men of great learning and exceptional mental vigor. The attack in some instances has been made with a fantastic regard for minute details. The attacks have been publicized abroad in a never-ending stream of periodicals, journals, pamphlets, monographs, books, and encyclopaedias. The larger universities of the world and hundreds of theological seminaries have taken up the cause of radical criticism. A thousand times over, the death knell of the Bible has been sounded, the funeral procession formed, the inscription cut on the tombstone, and the committal read. But somehow the corpse **never** stays put.

No other book has been so chopped, knived, sifted, scrutinized, and villified. What book on philosophy or religion or psychology or *belles lettres* of classical or modern times has been subject to such a mass attack as the Bible? with such venom and skepticism? with such thoroughness and erudition? upon every chapter, line and tenet?

Considering the thorough learning of the critics and the ferocity and precision of the attacks, we would expect the Bible to have been permanently entombed in some Christian genizah. But such is hardly the case. The Bible is still loved by millions, read by millions, and studied by millions. No doubt a terrible amount of damage has been done by radical criticism, and millions have lost faith in the veracity and authority of the Bible, as tragically witnessed by the decay of church attendance, the spiritual enervation of our western culture, and the cancerous secularism of America, England, and continental Europe. But even so, radical criticism has not put the Bible out of circulation. It still remains the most published and most read book in the world of literature. Its survival through time, persecution, and criticism is remarkable.

4. *The influence of the Bible on culture.* "No other book has ever so completely changed the course of human destiny," writes Tiplady. "In light and power the Bible stands by itself. It borrows from none and gives to all. Where it shines, life and beauty spring to birth. It is the supreme Book of power."[9] Such has been the influence of the Bible on western culture that to form any sort of quantitative measure is an impossibility. It has profoundly influenced literature, oratory, law, politics, ethics, philosophy, art, and religion. Detailed evidence will be found in F. W. Farrar, *The Bible: Its Meaning and Supremacy.* He quotes statements regarding the supreme worth, or matchless character, or divine inspiration

[9] T. Tiplady, *The Influence of the Bible*, p. 20.

of the Holy Bible from a wide variety of witnesses as the reader may judge from the names: Newman, Heine, Theodore Parker, Renan, Huxley, Matthew Arnold, F. W. Faber, Rousseau, Lessing, Goethe, Emerson, Alfred de Musset, Kuenen, Faraday, Hooker, Milton, Spenser, Bacon, Herbert, Wither, Walton, Newton, Sir William Jones, Addison, Johnson, Pope, Young, Cowper, Collins, Wesley, Coleridge, Scott, Macaulay, Dickens, Carlyle, Ruskin, Browning, Tennyson, Froude, Charles Reade, Stevenson, Hall Caine, J. H. Green, Louis the Ninth of France, Henry the Sixth, John the Second, Alonso the Fifth of Aragon, King Edward the Sixth, Napoleon, Lord Bacon, Selden, Sir Matthew Hale, Judge Blackstone, Edmund Burke, Wilberforce, Gladstone, John Quincy Adams, Andrew Jackson, W. B. Leigh, Daniel Webster, Seward, General Grant, William Lloyd Garrison, J. Dana, Charles Dudley Warner, Walt Whitman, and George Peabody.[10] Here one finds the king and the critic, the scientist and the skeptic, and the theologian and the politician. Following this Farrar relates the unusually powerful influence of the Bible on such great personalities as Augustine, Luther, Xavier, and Livingstone. Next he notes its great powers of consolation as exhibited in the case of Paul and the martyrs, St. Perpetua, Savonarola, Huss, and others. He concludes with a narration of the unparalleled influence of the Bible on the nations (Jews, Goths, Germany, England, America, Tahiti, New Zealand, North American Indians, Japan, and Pitcairn's Island).

Consider first the influence of the Bible on *literature*. Dr. Wilbur M. Smith has compiled "A Bibliography of the Influence of the Bible on English Literature (and in part on the Fine Arts)"[11] in which he lists book after book, article after article, devoted completely to tracing out the influence of the Bible either on a body of literature or a given writer. For example entire treatises are devoted to setting forth the in-

---

[10] P. 260 ff.
[11] *Fuller Library Bulletin*, January–June, 1951, n. 9–10.

fluence of the Bible on such literary figures as Browning, Bunyan, Chaucer, Dickens, Emerson, Hardy, Longfellow, Macaulay, Milton, Poe, Ruskin, Scott, Shakespeare, Shelley, Spenser, Tennyson, Whitman, and Whittier. Without doubt the Bible has penetrated in our literature more minutely than the powers of the finest penetrating oil. As McAfee comments, men "may get away from it [the Bible] as religion; they do not get away from it as literature."[12] He continues: "Take any of the great books of literature and black out the phrases which manifestly come directly from the English Bible, and you would mark them beyond recovery."[13] No one can question Butterworth's assertion that the Bible occupies the "supreme place in English prose."[14]

Further, it must be noted that most of the evidence given by Farrar and Smith pertain to English-speaking writers. Such volumes and such bibliographies could be made of every language of Europe, and given another hundred years or so the same story may be told of the great mission fields of the Christian Church. Returning to the English language, we may comment with good support and reason that if a student of English literature does not have a good knowledge of the English Bible he is not competent to deal with English literature. This can be said of no other single book. The only possible competition is from the whole library of works, under the general caption of classical literature.

Whoever has a keen ear in listening to *oratory* will recognize countless references to the Bible. Biblical expressions

---

12 C. B. McAfee, *The Greatest English Classic*, p. 134.
13 *Loc. cit.*
14 C. C. Butterworth, *The Literary Lineage of the King James Bible*, pp. 4–6. How does the Bible compare with ancient literature of its own time? Hear this testimony: "For over thirty-five years I have specialized in the language, literature, and religion of Israel, Egypt, and Babylonia. These are exactly the disciplines required in an attempt to define and demonstrate the nature and extent of Israel's genius and legacy to mankind, that is, to show how Israel, though insignificant in material culture, towered above the greatest of her contemporaries, Egypt and Babylonia, in just those elements which have made her supreme, namely, in religion and literature." S. A. B. Mercer, *The Supremacy of Israel*, p. vii.

have become popular speech terms; Biblical characters have become personality types; Biblical stories have provided analogies, illustrations, and themes, world without end! No other book—not all books put together—has so entered into the living stream of human speech and oratory as the Bible.

In *law* the direct and indirect influence of the Bible is beyond any possible computation. As Von Dobschütz notes,[15] the Bible commenced to influence Roman law the moment some of the emperors either professed Christianity or admitted its legal status. Alfred the Great put the Decalogue in front of his *Laws of England*,[16] and the influence of the Bible upon Charlemagne's legal activity was great. Blackstone commented that "The Bible has always been regarded as part of the Common Law of England."[17] And so, the ethical, moral, and legal elements of the Bible have penetrated into the very heart and soul of Western law.

The Ten Commandments, and other ethical and legal features in the Bible, have been taken with a great seriousness, even though at times with a painful literalism and lack of appreciation of the development of revelation. The number of statutes of Biblical origin in the laws of our city, county, state, and national government is very large. So much and so long has Biblical jurisprudence filtered into Western culture that most people have long ago lost sight of its origin. The major crimes which Moses legislated against are still major crimes in Western culture. The ideals of the prophets of justice, economic equity, and legal protection of the poor are still the goals of modern jurisprudence. Moses' rules of public sanitation find their counterpart in the sanitation codes of modern

[15] *Op. cit.*, section "Bible and Law," p. 613.
[16] *Loc. cit.*
[17] Farrar, *op. cit.*, p. 285. Wilbur Smith, *op. cit.*, states that the following work is a most thorough examination of the influence of the Bible on law with a vast array of specific citations: H. B. Clark, *Biblical Law: being a Text of the Statutes, Ordinances and Judgments Established in the Holy Bible—With Many Allusions to Secular Laws: Ancient, Medieval, and Modern, Documented to the Scriptures, Judicial Decisions and Legal Literature*, p. 8.

cities. Moses' distinctions between degrees of crime, for example, manslaughter as less criminal than intentional murder, rape more criminal than fornication, are still active legal principles. His various rules about the protection of common welfare, and property owners' responsibility, for example, regulations about a goring bull, parapets on roof tops, though nowadays formulated in much more sophisticated language, are guiding principles of common law. No man would dare to write a code of laws on the simple procedure of turning the Biblical commands into negations, and the Biblical negations into affirmations. Such a procedure would foster a season of such human disgrace and infamy that even the most skeptical would pray that the fires of Hell would prematurely start their course to end such shame.

In *politics* again we see the marked influence of the Bible on Western culture. Almost every form of government has had advocates who presumed to have found Biblical grounds for their theories. The divine right of kings has been argued from the nature of the ancient Hebrew monarchy; communism from the communal sharing of the Early Church; socialism from the prophetic passages on social equity and justice; capitalism from the Biblical insistence upon the wrong of stealing and misappropriation of property; democracy on the grounds of the New Testament conception of brotherhood; nationalism from the belief that God has ordered humanity into national families with their respective boundaries. In countless political issues the Bible has been brought in correctly or incorrectly, properly or unceremoniously, to bolster up a case. Our purpose is not to decide the right and wrong of these uses of the Bible, but to present the obvious, namely, that in political theory, and around political issues, the Bible has exerted an influence varied and great.

Large sections of the history of *philosophy* are incomprehensible or enigmatic without a knowledge of the Bible and the theology it engendered. Augustine bequeathed to the

Middle Ages an exceptionally rich Christian and Biblical philosophical heritage. From Augustine to Occam are about one thousand years of philosophical activity within Christian boundaries. Although these men were not good scientific interpreters, they were Bible students as an examination of Smalley's *The Study of the Bible in the Middle Ages* (second edition) will more than verify. Aquinas' knowledge of the Bible was nothing short of encyclopaedic. Modern philosophy begins with Descartes who was steeped in scholastic thought, and the entire philosophical heritage of the time was steeped in Christian and Biblical notions. Modern philosophy continues, in part, as a rehashing of the basic problems of the Middle Ages; for example, the existence of God, the problem of universals, the origin and nature of the universe, the human soul, the highest good, and political philosophy. Certainly Descartes, Spinoza, Leibnitz, Locke and Berkeley were serious students of the Bible. Kant surely heard much of it from his pietistic parents, and who could grow up in Hume's Scotland without encountering the Bible and Biblical thought?[18]

Since the entry of Christianity upon western culture, it is very difficult to find any system of *ethics* whose basic principle cannot be found already stated in Holy Scripture. In fact, those systems which professed to skirt the Bible either are unsuccessful in the effort, or present an ethic that is the nightmare of civilization, as in the cases of nazism and communism. At the outset it is obvious that most great philosophers also made contributions to ethics, so that all philosophers in any measure in the Christian or Jewish tradition reflect in their ethical systems the influence of the Bible and Christianity upon their thought. Further, some of our keenest thinkers in ethics were either outright Christians, as Augustine, Aquinas, or Butler, or were certainly greatly influenced by Christian training or surroundings as Kant.

[18] Cf. J. V. L. Casserley, *The Christian in Philosophy* (Part I: dealing with philosophy from Paul to contemporary times), pp. 19–164.

Biblical-ethical statements have so permeated our culture in all major western countries that it is impossible for a writer on ethics to write as if the Bible had not been written. To try to write a non-Biblical ethic requires most studious effort. No other ethical treatise in the accumulated ethical literature of humanity has had the influence of the Bible.

The influence of the Bible on *art* is again beyond any quantitative estimate, it is so great.[19] The galleries of the world are resplendent witness to the Bible's unparalleled influence. In thousands of other buildings, churches, cathedrals, public buildings, private collections, and schools are the numberless objects of Christian art. In the graveyards of the world still further influences of the Bible on art will be found. Some of the greatest artists since classical times have devoted years of their lives, and the best of their efforts to paint, carve, or sculpture Biblical themes or characters. In music[20] again we have another complex labyrinth of details reflecting the direct and indirect influence of the Bible.

5. *Its surrounding literature.* Another one of the remarkable features of the phenomenology of the Bible is the literature the Bible has inspired about itself. There are complexities of bibliographical studies that are unparalleled in any other science or department of human knowledge. From the Apostolic Fathers dating from A.D. 95 to the modern times is one great literary river inspired by the Bible—Bible dictionaries, Bible encyclopaedias, Bible lexicons, Bible atlases, and Bible geographies. These may be taken as a starter. Then at random, we may mention the vast bibliographies around theology, religious education, hymnology, missions, the Biblical languages, church history, religious biography, devotional works, commentaries, philosophy of religion, evidences, apologetics, and on and on. There seems to be an endless number

---

[19] Cf. Smith, *op. cit.*, p. 8 for books on the influence of the Bible on art, and p. 10 for "Christ in Art."
[20] The Benson Collection on Christian Hymnology in the library of The Princeton Theological Seminary numbers over 8,000 volumes.

and variety of religious journals, periodicals, bulletins, weeklies, monthlies, quarterlies, and annuals. Some are very cheap pulpy affairs and others are full-fledged scholarly journals. There are in each Western country many religious publishing houses devoted entirely to the publication of Christian material, which not only turn out many books a year, but literally tons of weekly Sunday school material.

Alongside of the publishing business has grown up the religious film industry with a great array of slides and moving pictures. No other book in all human history has in turn inspired the writing of so many books as the Bible, and if such a claim is starting to sound monotonous, it is only such a testimony to the unparalleled influence of the Bible that the testimony is so great that its bare presentation becomes monotonous.

6. *Its popular use.* Perhaps the most significant influence of the Bible is its influence on common life. Certainly the two most popular books in the homes of the world are the dictionary and the Bible. The Bible is the book of the masses. In thousands upon thousands of homes throughout the world it is read and studied daily. Devotions with the Bible is stock fare with multitudes of Christians around the globe. Every Sunday in village, city, and country, thousands of Bibles are carried to church, opened, read, commented upon, and so bless and feed the souls of the faithful.

Thomas Nelson and Sons, publishers of the Revised Standard Version, employed the firm of Batten, Barton, Durstine, and Osborn to determine the extent of Bible reading in America, prior to the publishing of the full Bible in September, 30, 1952.[21] The report of the firm revealed that 90 per cent of Protestant families have Bibles, and most of them more than one; 95 per cent of Americans read the Bible at some time or other; and 41 per cent read it at least once a week.

21 Reported in *Time*, October 6, 1952, Vol. LX, pp. 52–53.

People who know little or nothing of Homer or Socrates, Dante or Milton, Browning or Emerson, know who Abraham was and what Joseph suffered, and the feats of Samson, and the miracles of Elijah and Elisha. They know the life story of Saul, David, and Solomon. They know in greater detail the life of Jesus, the characters of His disciples, and the life of Paul than they know of the founding fathers of their own country. Who has not been touched by Burns' *The Cotter's Saturday Night* in which we have a picture of a family gathered around "the priest-like father" as he reads to them from "the big ha' Bible" about Abram, Moses, Amalek, Job, etc?

The Bible is read in homes and studied at church. In addition to this are the many other evangelical and evangelistic movements and societies in which Bible reading and Bible study play a central role. In addition to these are the hundreds of Bible conferences held every summer from Washington to Florida, Maine to California, and around the world, in which the Bible is at the center of the entire program of each day.

It is the book of universal appeal. Kings and princes have studied it. It has fascinated lawyers and doctors, astronomers and housewives, farmers and physicists. A never-ending stream of humanity has been born, married, and buried under the sound of Bible-reading. It has become the Book of the Eskimo and the African, the giant Watussi and the tiny pygmies. No other book has such a universal appeal—an appeal to men of all temperaments, all races, all employments, all social standings, all economic means, and all gifts of intelligence. Canon Dyson Hague relates the touching incident of the time he was staying in some large house and discovered a nurse reading the story of Joseph to his child. The child objected to the intrusion and plead with her father: "Please don't stop her, please." At the same time, in the same house, was staying the great Canadian geologist, Sir William Dawson, who at the same moment was reading from the same Book as the nurse was reading to the child. The Bible was a delight to the infant mind and the mature scholar.[22]

Many men have spent a lifetime of devoted Bible study. Their testimony is that the more they have studied the Bible, the deeper, the richer, the more profound the truth of it becomes. Few books can stand a constant rereading and perpetual study. The Bible is not only such a book, but it is uniquely such a book.

B. *Internal phenomenology.* By this expression we mean the peculiar characteristics of the content of the Bible. Just as the Bible has an unparalleled external phenomenology, it has an unparalleled internal phenomenology.

1. *Its unparalleled treatment of certain themes.* The Bible has touched on certain themes in such a way as to have no comparable treatment in all human literature. Think of Genesis one, however you will, it is, nevertheless, the most beautiful, the most chaste, the most stately description of creation and the origin of the universe in all literature. "The account of Creation," writes the world's greatest living archaeologist, "is unique in ancient literature. It undoubtedly reflects an advanced monotheistic point of view, with a sequence of creative phases so rational that modern science cannot improve on it, given the same language and the same range of ideas in which to state its conclusions. In fact, modern scientific cosmogonies show such a disconcerting tendency to be short-lived it may be seriously doubted whether science has yet caught up with the Biblical story."[23] Like Lincoln's Gettysburg Address, it says so much so majestically in such a short space! Where is there a real competitor to Moses' Ten Commandments? How terse! How majestic! The concept of God is so exalted, and the duties for man in such conformity to the nature of God. Thousands of pages have been written in the endeavor to explore the depths of the Decalogue. We search

[22] *The Wonder of the Book* (Student Edition), p. 16.
[23] W. F. Albright, "The Old Testament and Archaeology," *Old Testament Commentary* (edited by Alleman and Flack), p. 135.

the world for a book like Job—dramatic in form, gloriously poetic, and brilliantly graphic in style. Here is a treatment on suffering that, with all our learning and literature, is still the best book to be read in dark nights and sad mornings. True, there are parallels to the Psalms, but are these parallels equals? The purest, holiest, deepest, most divine book of worship and religious piety that has ever been composed is the Hebrew Psalter. For practical religious sanity, homely yet devout guidance, where can we find the match to Proverbs? Nowhere in all literature is there the moral piety, zeal for righteousness, demand for justice and equality before law, consistency of life and profession, all set forth in majestic literary style, as in the prophets from Isaiah to Malachi? He who has never studied the prophets has missed rich treasures. Isaiah is a beautiful book filled with many choice figures of speech and lofty passages. It was written by a man who at the same time was poet and prophet, statesman and preacher, artist and diplomat. Time and space forbid painting in all the choice details and precious gems of the prophets.

When we come to the New Testament the story is the same. Where is there anywhere a discussion of happiness that compares with the Beatitudes? Who save Jesus uttered a prayer like the Lord's Prayer? Who spoke such pure religion in such beautiful simplicity as our Lord in His parabolic teaching? Line for line, thought for thought, no religious philosophy touches the works of Paul. What writer dead or alive has the profound analyses of Paul in reference to human sin, divine salvation, divine sovereignty, and human faith? Can Calvin or Augustine match Paul in Romans nine to eleven? Has Plato or Buddha, Aristotle or Gandhi, Mohammed or Joseph Smith ever written anything that can be placed within a thousand miles of I Corinthians 13? Plato's *Symposium*, a treatise on love, is marred by pederasty.

2. *The scope of its contents.* Another one of the remarkable features of the internal phenomenology of the Bible is its

complete story. It commences at the ultimate point of any possible commencement—God and the beginning of creation. It follows through with mankind's early history and then branches off into Jewish history. The record carries on into the New Testament, through the life of Christ and the early life of the Christian Church. Then in prospect in the book of Revelation, we are carried through human history to its final consummation, and are ushered into the day of eternity in the new heavens, the new earth, and the new Jerusalem. Here is a universal, comprehensive history, human and divine, cosmic and terrestrial, angelic and demonic, from Alpha-eternity to Omega-eternity which for scope, grandeur, and tangency to so much historical fact, is unparalleled in the complete annals of human history.

In Baillie's work, *The Belief in Progress*, he clearly indicates that although the Greek mind had faith, it had no *hope*. And why did it lack hope? It lacked hope because it had no philosophy of history and no eschatology. The Greek mind believed the theory of endless cycles repeating the same old story. How *hopeful* is the Christian philosophy of history! How rich! How meaningful! How laden with bright and glorious prospects! Not endless repetition, but endless joy and bliss and eternity with God!

Further, there is a surprising unity of themes in the Bible. In truth, the parallels between Genesis and Revelation are amazing. God, man, sin, Satan, paradise, and the tree of life, are themes of both Genesis and Revelation. What is introduced in Genesis is accounted for in Revelation. There is a certain secure feeling that every believer has. From the Bible he has such a clear statement of the origin of the universe and humanity, humanity's present purpose, and the final summarizing of all things in Revelation. No other work has this undesigned story of eternity through time and back to eternity. As Dyson Hague suggests, select samples of literature from 1600 years of Western culture. Take a bit here and a bit there.

Bind them together in one volume. What do you get? Nothing but a miscellaneous collection of disconnected fragments.[24] How then do we account for this amazing unity of the Bible on purely naturalistic terms?

3. *Its historical core.* The Bible is at root historical. It deals with *ideas*, but ideas that are fundamentally interpretations of historty. The sinnerhood of man is traced to a *historical* fall. The virtue of faith is exhibited in the *historical* episodes of Abraham's life. The great doctrines of redemption are also *historical* events. The incarnation is through the virgin birth; the atonement is through the death of Christ; and the new birth through the resurrection. Further, the Biblical eschatology is in terms of *concrete* event, which, when accomplished will appear as *historical* event.

As previously stated in this volume the universe is historical to the core, that is, time is central to all processes, physical, chemical, psychological, social, cultural, and historical. The historical thread of the Bible is unique in religious philosophy, and constitutes one of its most genuine watermarks of tangency with reality.

4. *Its realism.* Parallel to the Bible's historical core is its frank realism. It lacks the usual blights of the unbalanced religious life.

a) *It lacks prudishness.* It deals with sex, sin, and the facts of life realistically. It is neither delicate beyond what life is like, nor frank to the point of obscenity. It is refreshingly realistic.

b) *It lacks asceticism.* It knows that human appetites are real and God-given. The emphasis is not upon artificial abstinence but upon realistic self-control. It advocates for special persons, or for limited seasons, forms of abstinence, but not as general rules for all, at all times. Both Jesus (Mark 7:14–23) and Paul (Col. 2:18–23) condemn asceticism.

c) *It lacks fanaticism.* It advocates no strange, weird, or

24 *Op. cit.,* p. 6 fn.

fantastic practices. It asks us to practice nothing foolhardy
or ridiculous. It forbids us to tempt God, and therefore all
those that do foolhardy things (drinking poison, or letting
serpents bite them) do so contrary to the teachings of Sacred
Writ.

d) *It lacks extreme mysticism.* By extreme mysticism we
mean those unusual experiences of the mystics (unconscious-
ness, ecstasy, spiritual-eroticism). That there is a mystical
element in the Bible cannot be disputed. Prayer is not possible
save on a mystical basis. But the Bible knows that few people
are capable of extreme experiences, and so very realistically
keeps its basic religious experience free from extreme mysticism.

5. *Its constant emphasis on the holy, true, and good.* Although there might be debatable statements here and there
in the Bible about ethical propriety, nonetheless, the bulk of
the Biblical content advocates consistently that which is holy,
that which is honest, that which is true and upright. Can any
more wholesome advice be given than that of Paul who
wrote: "Finally, brethren, whatsoever things are true, whatsoever things are honest, whatsoever things are just, whatsoever things are pure, whatsoever things are lovely, whatsoever things are of good report; if there be any virtue, and if
there be any praise, think on these things" (Phil. 4:8). This
constant emphasis on the holy and true and good is even the
more remarkable when we consider the variety of writers,
and the extensive historical periods covered.

6. *Its conception of God.* The debate over controversial
items about the nature of God in the Bible, for example, the
command to slaughter *all* the Canaanites or the imprecatory
Psalms, has obscured the great wealth of expressions about
the nature of God that are incontrovertible. All of the attributes we think God ought to have, the Bible describes Him
as having. He is Spirit, so idolatry is forbidden. God is transcendent to Nature, and also immanent to Nature (Acts 17:27,

28). God is holy, just, good, righteous, and merciful. He is a God of love, pity, compassion, wisdom, and grace. He is infinite, eternal, omnipotent, omniscient. He is, as both Augustine and Anselm stated, a Being than whom no higher, nor greater, nor more perfect can be imagined.

7. *Its men.* Where else can we find such a role of men as found in Sacred Scripture? There is innocent and devout Abel; God-fearing Noah; solid, believing Abraham; trusting and quiet Isaac; clever but nonetheless God-fearing Jacob. Where is the equal to Joseph in patience, virtue, wisdom, and kindness? Look at the spiritual giants strewn through the Bible—Moses, Joshua, Gideon, David, Isaiah, Jeremiah, Zechariah, and Malachi! In the New Testament we discover ready-tongued Peter; yet, in spite of all, a spiritual giant; the devoted, devout, and tender John; the stern and moralistic James; the holy and martyred Stephen; and the "versatile" genius Paul. Can there be any other plausible explanation of a book full of God-filled men than that an actual living God called them into His holy, blessed fellowship?

8. *Its doctrines.* There are three unusual features of Biblical doctrines.

a) These doctrines are *pungent.* They are not simple, sweet, harmless assertions. They are strong and profound statements. Original sin, the incarnation, and God's sovereignty are not feathery theology. Here is no weak tea or faded colors.

b) These doctrines are in some cases *mysterious.* They have depths we cannot readily measure. The doctrines of the Trinity, the incarnation, and the atonement are not as two-foot deep wading pools. They have sudden drop-offs which leave us peering into such depths that we are dizzy. We feel confronted with the greatness, the inexhaustibility and the incomprehensibility of God.

c) Biblical doctrines *have a remarkable fitness to human need.* Although pungent and mysterious they are just what we need. There is a remarkable congruency between strong, mysterious doctrine and human need. Who is best fitted to know the virtue of the doctrine of the atonement—the calm, critical detatched speculator or the man with a distressed conscience? Who appreciates best the incarnation—the expert on formal logic or the heart of one fevered with agnosticism? To those who hunger and thirst, the Biblical doctrines alone can slake thirst and satisfy hunger.

Further, any philosophy or religion to possess real appeal and worth must be more than mundane, routine, lifeless thinking. If Christianity were a batch of inoffensive, easily entreated, logically simple doctrines, *would it be worth believing?* At the level of intellectual simplicity it might appeal, but at the deeper, richer levels of concrete human existence it would dismally fail.

II. The Divine Inspiration of the Bible

Having reviewed the remarkable external and internal phenomenology of the Bible, and having seen that it is the most unique book in all literary history, our original question is back with us. Is this uniqueness due to human genius, racial gifts, or divine inspiration? The reader will recall that the Bible itself answers that question. If Amos may speak for all the writers of the Bible, he informs us, when questioned as to his sharp sermons, that this was not his idea. He was minding his own business. He affirms that "I was no prophet, neither was I a prophet's son." Well, how is it that he is now preaching such blistering sermons to Israel? "The Lord took me as I followed the flock," he answers, "and the Lord said unto me, Go, prophesy unto my people Israel. Now therefore hear the word of the Lord" (Amos 7:14–16). His message and ministry were of God. Whatever degree of inspiration the writers possessed, and whatever measure of infallibilty may have been passed on to the penman, we must leave that to the systematic theologian. But this we may assert: it is the self-witness of the Bible that its message, its substance, came from God.

To the Christian mind, any humanistic hypothesis suggested to account for the phenomenology of the Bible must be inadequate. *The Bible uniquely possesses those categories we associate with the divine.* The witness of prophecy is a witness to divine omniscience. The witness of miracle is a witness to divine omnipotence. The witness of creation is a witness to divine wisdom and spirituality. The witness of spiritual experiences is the witness of divine disclosure. The witness of purity is a witness of divine holiness. The witness of redemption is a witness of divine love. *The sum total of the phenomenology of the Bible is a witness to the divine breath in the Bible.*

Therefore, the divine inspiration of the Bible is the only adequate hypothesis to account for the Bible. *Christianity stands verified by a supernatural Book.*

If a man remain unconvinced, certainly he cannot say that the Christian is guilty of gullibility, or of resting a huge theological edifice on a flimsy foundation. Even though, to some the evidence may not be final or conclusive, on the other hand, it is not unsubstantial in character or scanty in number. Any charge of credulity against the believer is therefore not true to the facts of the case. To the Christian the phenomenology of the Bible is substantial enough evidence to accept the Bible as a divinely inspired Book.

> We search the world for truth. We cull
> The good, the pure, the beautiful,
> From graven stone and written scroll,
> And all old flower-fields of the soul;
> And, weary seekers of the best,
> We come back laden from our quest,
> To find all the sages said
> Is in the Book our mothers read.
>
> (J. G. Whittier, *Miriam*)

DECISION

To what extent are these preceding chapters compelling? We presume that to the Christian mind they will appear as conclusive, but to the non-Christian mentality they may or may not appeal. It should be clearly understood that the type of problem determines how a solution is reached. If the problem were the proof of a given theorem in geometry or symbolic logic, all competent mathematicians and logicians could agree as to the validity of the proof. If one were to disagree he would be written off as incompetent. Problems of science are not so neatly settled, but through experimentation a very good control is exercised over proposed hypotheses. Problems in history, social sciences, and philosophy are far more difficult to settle and to call forth unanimity of opinion from all competent scholars. To sum up, problems dealing with the manipulation of symbols, or with the direct phenomena of Nature are far easier of solution than those dealing with the complexities of human history, sociology, psychology, and human mentality.

The problem of Christianity's truthfulness is not only difficult because it falls into the domain of the more complex type of problem, but because it calls into reckoning the moral and spiritual disposition of the thinker. Hence, the conviction of the truthfulness of Christianity, and faith in Christ as Saviour, is not only a matter of amassing evidence for the Christian faith, but of correctly disposing the heart to receive its spiritual message and blessing.

In many ways Blaise Pascal saw through the nature of evidences as perhaps no other apologist has. Pascal knew that Christianity demands *spiritual decision*. He knew, too, that

Christianity could not be dissolved away into pure religious feeling, nor exhaustively defined as a great intellectual and rational system. Being of the heart or spirit, Christianity calls for more than pure reason, whether of logic or of science. However, being a historical religion, Christianity cannot rest with pure religious experience. Christian evidences must find their locus in view of the very nature of the Christian religion. If one could be reasoned into faith, then Christianity would have sacrificed its moral and spiritual dimension. But if there were no evidences at all, then our faith could not be differentiated from gullibility.

Because Christianity is in part historical and in part spiritual decision, Pascal reasoned that God gave enough evidences to satisfy the mind of the man whose heart was surrendered to Christ, but not enough to tempt a man into Christianity by pure reason alone. The situation is like a skiagraph concealing the face of Christ. If one had never seen Christ one could ponder the skiagraph for hours and see no image of the Saviour. But if one has seen the face of Christ, as one gazes at the skiagraph suddenly one sees Christ looking right out at him. For those who have Christianity in their hearts as spirit, the evidence for the factuality of their faith is clear enough. For those outside the boundaries of the faith, the evidence appears equivocal.

However, Christian evidences are not to be written off the record as total loss toward unbelievers. Christian evidences possess a strong witness value. They are arrows pointing toward the Truth; they are credentials for Christian doctrines; they inform the unbeliever that although Christianity is of the heart, it does not ask for stultification of the intellect. Christian evidences inform the unbelievers that the believer has intellectual integration. They ask the unbeliever to listen to the inward promptings of his guilty conscience. They invite the thirsty or the perplexed or the discouraged or those engulfed by intellectual confusion to come to living waters.

Christian evidences can thereby be the entering wedge for the Christian message into the human heart.

He who will hear what the Spirit says through his guilty conscience, through the written Word, and through Christian evidences, will also hear what the Spirit says through Christ.